NEGLECTED SAINTS

NEGLECTED SAINTS

E. I. WATKIN

CLUNY
Providence, Rhode Island

Cluny Media edition, 2021

This Cluny edition is a republication of *Neglected Saints*,
originally published by Sheed and Ward, 1955.
Errata from that edition have been corrected.

For more information regarding this title
or any other Cluny Media publication,
please write to info@clunymedia.com, or to
Cluny Media, P.O. Box 1664, Providence, RI 02901

VISIT US ONLINE AT WWW.CLUNYMEDIA.COM

ISBN: 978-1952826641

Nihil obstat: Thomas J. McHugh, LL. D., *Censor librorum*
Imprimatur: ✠ Jerome D. Hannan, D.D., *Bishop of Scranton*
January 14, 1955

Cover design by Clarke & Clarke
Cover image: Knud Baade, *Cloud Study*,
1850, oil on paper
Courtesy of Wikimedia Commons

CONTENTS

To my dear grandchildren: Frances, Peter, Catharine

ACKNOWLEDGMENTS

I WISH TO express my grateful thanks to the Abbot, Librarian and community of Buckfast Abbey for kindly allowing me not only to make use of their library but to borrow books. But for their generosity this book could not have been written. Also to Messrs. Burns and Oates for permitting me to make use of Lady Amabel Kerr's Life of Blessed Antony Grassi, *A Saint of the Oratory*, and the Life of St. Hugh of Lincoln by a French Carthusian, translated, revised and enlarged by Father Herbert Thurston, S.J. I wish moreover to thank Father Gerald Vann, O.P., for so kindly lending me Dr. Altaner's edition of the Letters of Blessed Jordan of Saxony, and the Dominicans at Oxford for the use of their library at Blackfriars. I thank Mr. Sheed for permitting me to read and use in proof Mr. F. R. Hoare's translation and edition of Sulpicius's writings on the life of St. Martin (*The Western Fathers*).

E. I. WATKIN

INTRODUCTION

FOR CENTURIES THE gaze of the modern European, whose outlook has now spread the world over, has been increasingly directed to the breadth of human experience. In the breadth, however, the created universe with its content alone is visible. Modern man in consequence has largely lost sight of God and, because he has done so, in the midst of a brilliant intellectual day he gropes in spiritual darkness. Hitherto, for example in the centuries which preceded the Renaissance, man had looked primarily into the depth, which is also the height of experience, where he is aware of God, and where the central spirit is in contact with Him. For lack of breadth-knowledge our ancestors could seriously believe that barnacles give birth to geese. For lack of depth-knowledge many pundits today maintain that linguistic analysis, valuable no doubt in its own order, has proved metaphysics meaningless. It is no peculiar wickedness, therefore, of the modern secularist that he has lost sight of God—there is no reason to suppose modern man more wicked than his religious forebears; it is the inevitable result of an exclusive vision in the breadth of experience. The mischief can be corrected, not by moral exhortation or emotional appeal, still less by denying or depreciating the enormous growth of knowledge produced by this breadth-vision, but by restoring the depth-vision of the past and combining both. Then man will know both God and the universe—knowledge as profound as he has ever possessed and far more comprehensive.

The saint, however, is the man who looks, lives, and loves in the depth—the adept, that is to say, of depth-knowledge. For this reason the witness of his experience, his experience of God and His revelation to man, claims the attention of all whose depth-vision has been blinded or dimmed by looking exclusively or one-sidedly at the breadth experience. In His saints God is manifest as power, more powerful than created energies, complete and final Reality, more real than the partial reality of creatures. By finding Him and by his union with Him the saint has found the only satisfying explanation of the world and human life, the only satisfying purpose for which to live, act, and suffer. He has found a happiness independent of life's vicissitudes, a security no external disasters can shake, integrity and order, confidence without arrogance, peace in activity, a fixed end combined with flexibility of means, detachment from creatures combined with appreciation of them. For he has found God, who is wholly other than His world but its source and positive being.

This, to be sure, is the ideal saint of whom the real saint must inevitably fall short. For the saint does not see God clearly and his vision is therefore limited by his human limitations, individual and social. No man is so wise that he is never foolish, no body or mind so sound that it is perfectly healthy, no intellect so acute that it is infallible, no man's thought or action perfectly consistent. No saint can realise sufficiently the possibilities of human holiness.

It is not therefore enough to know one or two or even a few saints. We must have a wide acquaintance with them. Of the multitude of saints and blesseds enrolled by the Church it is but a mere handful of whom the overwhelming majority of Catholics possess any knowledge. The vast wealth of the Communion of Saints has no existence for them. Their loss, for prayer, example, and assistance must surely be enormous. *Mirabilis Deus in sanctis suis.* Since on earth we cannot see God in His own glory, we can ill afford to dispense with the sight of His glory reflected in His saints.

These studies are an attempt to enlarge a little this narrow vision. The saints whose portraits I shall sketch are either practically unknown or, if their identity is common knowledge—St. Martin of Tours, for example, or St. Bruno—knowledge is confined to one or two outstanding facts. Where the material is considerable I am not attempting full-length biography. Nor do I claim original research. My scope is but to paint, if I can, a true and lifelike picture.

SAINT MARTIN OF TOURS

[CIRCA 315–397]

THE FAMOUS GESTURE of Christian charity when the young officer cut off half his cloak to clothe a beggar "so struck the imagination," Douglas Woodruff writes,[1] "that I suppose no action of a saint has more often provided the theme of sculpture and painting. It is also the only thing that is remembered about St. Martin." This is regrettable. For not only was St. Martin's life one of outstanding achievement and importance, but it has resulted, as we shall see, in a gross misrepresentation of the saint.

Our knowledge of Martin is primarily and chiefly derived from the evidence of a contemporary, Sulpicius Severus, who was also a personal friend, had indeed sought his friendship, probably, as Boswell sought Dr. Johnson's, with the intention of recording his words and actions. Sulpicius was a nobleman of Aquitaine who practiced with success at the bar. After his wife's death, he retired from the world and would seem to have been ordained priest. It was at this time that he became Martin's friend and disciple and paid him frequent visits. He has left us a life completed while his hero was still living. Later he wrote three open letters, in one of which, addressed nominally to his mother-in-law Bassula, he described the saint's last days and death. Later still he composed two Dialogues, later divided into three. Much space is devoted to a real or imaginary voyage of a friend to the East where he visited St. Jerome and the Egyptian hermits and monks. But he also tells a number of additional stories about St. Martin.

To this day controversy rages as to the reliability of Sulpicius' evidence. For it is in fact largely the narration of miracles, many of which are not easy for a modern man to credit. Moreover, Sulpicius was a rhetorician, thoroughly trained in the idiom and devices of rhetoric. Much of his vivid detail is, we must suspect, not authentic report but rhetorical embellishment. Certainly we cannot take seriously the disclaimer of literary ornament and apology for "solecisms" with which he prefaces his life.

On the other hand, he is often at pains to give his authority for marvels he did not himself witness. Again and again he asseverates his veracity and the veracity of his informants. Nor was he writing for an audience so credulous that it would swallow the tallest stories without question. On the contrary he is well aware of a large body of sceptics, many of them in high ecclesiastical positions. Some indeed were prepared to deny the truthfulness of Martin himself. Among his detractors, his biographer tells us, there were even bishops, though but a few. "Any reader who refuses belief will be guilty of sin. My conscience bears me witness that my motives for writing were my assurance of the facts and love of Christ, that I have related what is well known and have told the truth. God, I am convinced, will reward not the man who merely reads my story, but the man who believes it."

These words on the lips of a man worthy of a saint's friendship cannot surely be dismissed as a rhetorician's lie.

Detailed certainty indeed is unattainable. For we cannot weigh the worth of the witnesses adduced, still less cross-examine them. Nor can we estimate the extent to which rhetorical convention permitted the embroidery of a substantially truthful account. But for the substance of Martin's life we may, I at least believe, trust Sulpicius. Certainly there emerges not a layfigure or legendary worker of wonders but a living man, an individual personality.

1. *The Tablet*, October 24, 1953.

The same problem arises in connection with St. Gregory's Dialogues, incidentally almost our only source for the life of St. Benedict. Here, as in Sulpicius' writings, we are faced with marvellous stories, even the tale of the nun who, picking a lettuce in the garden, swallowed a devil who happened to be taking his siesta on a leaf. St. Gregory, however, also is at pains to quote his authorities, honourable, indeed holy men who were eye-witnesses or were informed by eye-witnesses. It is certainly perplexing. The consideration, however, may help us that we can no longer believe, as it was believed in the past, that the testimony of a truthful eye-witness is a sufficient guarantee of unalloyed truth. On the contrary we are aware that a subjective element enters even into our normal perception of sensible objects and events. No two witnesses tell or can tell precisely and in every detail the same tale. The oath of our courts "to tell the whole truth and nothing but the truth" pledges us, if our witness is detailed, to the impossible.

A fortiori, if an event is remembered over years, or expectations of the miraculous predispose the witness to see a miracle, the subjective factor is enormously reinforced and reliability correspondingly diminished.[2]

When Martin died, the Roman Empire, though on the verge of collapse in the West and sorely harassed by barbarian invasions, still maintained an imposing facade of power and no one dreamed of the rapidly approaching doom. It had been Christian for the greater part of the century, though the persecution of pagan Emperors had soon been succeeded by the persecution of Arian. The monastic movement, having swept the Eastern Churches, was successfully invading the Western Church, though it incurred bitter and persistent opposition from the secular clergy, who saw in it, and not without reason, a threat to their prestige. A Preface contained in the "Leonine" sacramentary denounces in the most solemn prayer of the Mass the "hypocrisy" of the monks.

2. A contribution to the *Analecta Bollandiana* shows how the story of St. John Capistran's death on the battlefield, originally without any miraculous feature, becomes as the years pass increasingly miraculous. But the miraculous account at the end of the process is by the writer who at first gave an account devoid of marvel.

Martin was born in the first half of the fourth century about the year 315[3] at Sabaria, a town of Pannonia, in what is now Hungary. Sabaria is the present Szombathely. His father was an officer in the army who had risen from the ranks, despite Sulpicius' attempt to disguise the fact, not a gentleman. Both parents were heathen. At the age of ten the youthful Martin stole away to a church and had himself enrolled as a catechumen. But his parents' opposition prevented baptism. As the son of a soldier he was a conscript. For under the late empire imperial law sought to stabilize the social fabric by compelling a son to follow his father's profession. Even so he had to be dragged into the army, Sulpicius tells us, by force, "seized and chained." If this is not, as I suspect, an exaggeration, he must soon have resigned himself to the inevitable. For by the end of three years' service he was an officer serving in Gaul, at what is now Amiens. Here it was that the immortal deed was done and the young officer of twenty-two shared his military cloak one winter morning with a naked beggar. It is rather surprising that military discipline allowed a soldier to mutilate his uniform. The following night Martin saw our Lord wearing the halved cloak and saying, "Martin as yet but a catechumen has clothed me with this garment." The vision decided Martin to receive baptism without further delay. He stayed on, however, in the army at the persuasion of a fellow officer who shared his tent.

At the end of two years a barbarian host invaded Gaul and the army was led out to meet it. Before joining battle the general, probably the Emperor Constantius, certainly not Julian as Sulpicius calls him, distributed a present, a donative to his troops. When he came to Martin he refused to accept the donative on the ground that he could not earn it and asked permission to resign from the army. For he said, "I am a soldier of Christ, it is not lawful for me to fight." Not unnaturally his request was attributed to cowardice cloaked by a pretense of religious scruple. Martin, to disprove the charge, said he would willingly go into battle with the army and take his stand in the front ranks facing the

3. My chronology for St. Martin's Life has been taken from an article by Père Delehaye in Vol. 38 of the *Analecta Bollandiana*.

enemy. But he would go unarmed, protected, not by a shield, but the sign of the Cross. The general took him at his word and ordered him to be kept in custody until the day of battle. God, however, intervened. For the barbarians, convinced they were not a match for the Roman army, sent envoys to offer surrender. This probably happened in 339. Martin was now permitted to resign his commission and leave the forces—treatment far more lenient than would be accorded in the same circumstances today.

As I said at the outset, the cloak episode has produced a gross misrepresentation of the saint. For it has caused him to be regarded as a typical soldier saint, though he was in fact a conscientious objector to military service. This is a simple matter of historical fact, a fact which can be questioned only by those who are prepared to reject Sulpicius' life as a tissue of lies from first to last, a gratuitous slander. And it should be remembered that Martin's offer to go unarmed is among the texts chosen from Sulpicius' life for his office.[4]

Nor is Martin the only conscientious objector among the saints. A contemporary Gallic saint, Victricius, later Archbishop of Rouen, acted precisely like St. Martin, laid down his weapons on parade and asked for his discharge. The officer, not so lenient as Constantius, had him flogged and when he persisted sentenced him to death as a deserter. St. Paulinus of Nola, a contemporary, says that his life was saved by a miracle.[5] And we possess the authentic Acts of the martyr St. Maximilian, put to death solely for refusing the military service to which as a soldier's son he was liable. The judge in fact pointed out that there were Christian soldiers serving in the imperial army. But the martyr replied, "That is their business. I also am a Christian and I cannot serve." The

4. The attempt to explain away Martin's refusal to fight as the conscientious objection, not of a Christian but of a man determined to become a monk, is unconvincing. No man is bound in conscience by an obligation attaching to a state he merely intends to embrace—unless of course, like celibacy for a prospective priest, it is involved by the simple possibility of that state. Moreover, had Martin considered himself as somehow a monk already, he would not have remained in the army.

5. For St. Victricius, see Butler's *Lives of the Saints*, eds. Thurston and Attwater, August 7.

judge then informed him he would condemn him to death, *not* for his Christian faith, but for "contempt of the army."[6] Nor was it a question of unjustifiable war. For no war surely could be more justifiable than the defense of the Roman Empire and its peace against barbarian invaders. The Church has enrolled among her saints both conscientious objectors and soldiers—a proof surely that a Catholic may adopt either position, and, whether he follows St. Martin or St. Maurice, St. Maximilian or St. Louis, is not entitled to stigmatize the other choice as un-Christian.

Nor are Catholic pacifists extinct today. In Austria there is Father Uhde, author of *Du Sollst nicbt Toten,* in the United States the group whose organ is the *Catholic Worker.*

Martin now made his way to St. Hilary at Poitiers, who ordained him an exorcist. It was about this time that his intrepid faith overawed and converted a brigand who had taken him captive. We next hear of him at Milan where he founded a hermitage. From Milan he paid a visit to his parents at Patavium (Padua) or possibly Pannonia. Doubt as to the readings leaves it uncertain whether they had migrated to northern Italy. He converted his mother. But his father was obdurate. Martin visited Illyricum to combat Arianism, which under imperial patronage was making great headway. For this he was publicly flogged and expelled. Once more persecuted and expelled from Milan by an Arian bishop, he spent some time as a recluse in the company of a priest in Gallinaria, Gallinare, an uninhabited island off the coast of the Italian Riviera. He then attached himself to St. Hilary on his return from exile for his Catholic faith and seems to have accompanied him to Gaul, where he spent the remainder of his life. Outside Poitiers at Ligugé he founded a hermitage which shortly expanded into a community of hermits, a monastery of the primitive and oriental type.

He was elected Bishop of Tours solely for the repute of his sanctity. But the enthusiastic welcome he received from the majority of his flock was diminished by the opposition of a minority, even of some

6. For a translation of the *Acta* see Donald Attwater, First Supplementary Volume to the *Lives of the Saints*, pp. 45–47.

of the bishops who came to Tours for his consecration. "His person," they complained, "was contemptible." "A man so despicable, with dirty clothes and unkempt hair, was unworthy to be a bishop." Many, probably most of the Gallic episcopate, were cultured noblemen who had no welcome for a colleague whose sole recommendation was holiness and who, as we have seen, was not of gentle birth. And their feelings were shared by a section of his own clergy, those no doubt of good birth and worldly views. He was consecrated on July 4, 370 or 371.

Though, as the episodes related by Sulpicius show, Martin would remain a thaumaturge to the end, his power as a worker of miracles decreased after his promotion to the episcopate. He said so himself and Sulpicius has recorded his admission, a guarantee surely of honesty. Martin had no intention of abandoning his monastic life because he was now a bishop. He built a monastery outside the city, Marmoutier, and made it his headquarters. When Sulpicius visited it many years later, the community numbered eighty, practicing a life partly cenobitic, partly eremitical, under obedience to Martin.

We cannot expect a chronology of his episcopate. But his relations with the usurping Emperor Maximus must be placed between the years 383 and 385.

It will be best therefore to speak of his episcopate under three headings: his prayer, his miracles, and his relations with the civil power. Elis missionary activities for their range and success would deserve special treatment. Since, however, we know of these only the miracles or supposed miracles which assisted his missionary work, they cannot easily be separated from the latter.

In those early days the psychology and theology of prayer had not yet been developed. We can have no information as to the saint's essential prayer, his union with God and consciousness of it. But his holiness shows that it must have been intimate and at a very high level, a conviction borne out by the incidental phenomena of which we are informed.

When Martin repeated his charity of clothing the naked, divine approval was shown by an apparition visible to others. He was preparing to sing Mass when a shivering beggar asked for clothes. He took off the tunic (tunicle) he wore under his chasuble and gave it to the beggar. In the fourth century these garments, now a bishop's pontifical vestments, were still the civilian clothing of everyday life. The late Dom Fabian Dix compared them to the frock coat in which dissenting ministers continue to take their Sunday services. In the sacristy he asked his archdeacon for a tunic for a beggar, meaning himself. The latter in a temper put his hands on a tunic, "a *bigerrica*,"[7] short and rough, and flung it at his Bishop's feet. He must have belonged to the clergy who disliked and despised their uncouth and plebeian Bishop. Martin put it on and proceeded to the altar. When he imparted his solemn blessing a ball of flame was seen to encompass his head. But of the entire congregation it was seen only by one nun, one priest, and three monks. This precision encourages our confidence in Sulpicius. It would have been so easy to say it was seen by all or most of the congregation.

We are told of colloquies with angels—an angel cured wounds received by a fall—and visible encounters with devils, sometimes on the occasion of exorcisms. Sixteen demons expelled from their victim confessed to spreading the false rumor of a barbarian incursion—a warning to alarmist journalists. A demon appeared flourishing the bloodstained horn of an ox and it was found that a woodman in the service of the monastery had been gored to death by the oxen dragging his wagon. A devil was expelled from a mad cow. And a devil was seen seated on the back of a bloodthirsty imperial official, Count Avitianus. The devil once appeared in the guise of our Lord and demanded worship. But his royal clothing and gems betrayed his identity. "Unless I see Him in the fashion and form wherein He suffered and displaying the wounds of His crucifixion, I shall not believe Christ is present." The reasoning perhaps is not altogether conclusive. For our Lord is in glory. But it was sufficient to banish Satan, who for proof of his diabolic presence left behind him a foul stink. On another occasion Satan taunted Martin for admitting as monks men guilty of serious sin after baptism, and denied that such sinners could be pardoned. To which he retorted, "If you yourself,

7. *Bigerrica*, a rough garment called after the inhabitants of Bigorre.

wretched being, would even now repent of your misdeeds, I have such trust in the Lord Jesus Christ, that I would promise you mercy."

Such stories perplex the modern reader. They are not peculiar to these remote ages, though they were certainly far commoner. The attacks made upon the Curé d'Ars by le Grappin are quite as perplexing and quite as grotesque as Martin's encounters with devils. And it would be obviously illogical to reject these stories *en bloc* while accepting the Gospel exorcisms. It is a reasonable conclusion that spiritual forces of evil were perceived by Martin in an external garb woven from the images in his subconscious, and therefore determined by the beliefs and imaginations of his environment.

It was no doubt for this reason that devils were often seen under the guise of pagan deities, Jupiter, Mercury, Venus, and Minerva. Of these Mercury was his worst tormentor, Jupiter, he used to say, was "brutish and stupid"—a far cry from the majestic Zeus at Olympia, chiseled by Pheidias and the subject of an encomium by Dio Chrysostom.

On one occasion Sulpicius and his friend Posthumian called on the saint very early in the morning. For two hours they waited outside his cell listening to the indistinct sounds of voices in conversation. Finally he came out to them. Pressed by their questions he admitted that "Agnes, Thecla, and Mary had been with" him—that in fact they paid him frequent visits, as also did the Apostles Peter and Paul.

Agnes is the child martyr of Rome, put to death probably in Diocletian's persecution at the beginning of the century. Thecla is the heroine of episodes in the *Acts of Patil and Thecla,* a romance concocted to his undoing—for he was punished by degradation—by a priest in Asia Minor in the second century. Though incredible as it stands with its stories of impossible escapes from death, there are indications that the story contains a nucleus of fact,[8] and we are justified in believing that Thecla was an historical personage and St. Paul's convert.

8. "He saw Paul coming, a man little of stature, thin-haired upon the head, bandy-legged, of good state of body, with eyebrows joining, and nose somewhat hooked, full of grace, for sometimes he appeared like a man and sometimes he had the face of an angel." Surely an authentic tradition. *The Apocryphal New Testament,* trans. M. R. James, p. 273.

Mary is our Lady and in this lies the special interest of the story. For it marks the dawning upon the Western Church of devotion to Mary and appreciation of her place in the economy of redemption—already far advanced in Eastern Christianity. We watch the birth of a movement that in this very Gaul will culminate in the apparitions and pilgrimages of Lourdes. But it is only the dawn. For Mary is but one of three virgin saints, and of the three Agnes and Thecla take precedence, in the saint's mind, of our Lord's mother.

Martin's prophecies of the approaching end of the world, so great a stumbling block to many readers that the most detailed account of them has been omitted from many manuscripts of Sulpicius, were, of course, as he understood them literally, as untrue as similar expectations have proved throughout Christian history. But they may perhaps have been the distorted expression of an authentic intuition, an awareness that the world, as he knew it, the Western Roman Empire with its civilisation, order,z and comparative security, was in truth on the verge of collapse, rapidly approaching its end.[9]

Among the many miracles attributed to him Martin, we are told, raised three dead men to life, one of them being, like the widow's son at Naim, the only son of his mother. In view of the fact that the determination of life or death was then a rough and ready affair and it is but recently that we have learned that life lingers long after apparent death, we may be excused for thinking that these three were not in fact dead but merely in a state of deathlike coma. For the history of the Church in recent times does not know of any resuscitations of the dead. He also cured a woman with an issue of blood. A girl was cured of fever when her father placed a letter from Martin in her clothing. He cured a leper with a kiss. A girl almost wholly paralyzed he cured by pouring oil into her mouth. Such cures are altogether credible, though it must be doubtful whether they are in the strict sense miracles rather than the natural effects of a faith supernaturally infused by God.

9. The same perhaps may be said of St. Vincent Ferrer's assurance that the end of the world was at hand, when in fact it was to be the end of the undivided mediaeval Christendom of Western Europe.

Martin one day was travelling along the highway when he met a wagon full of soldiers. The apparition of this unkempt and haggard figure clad "in a rough and black cloak[10] which trailed on the ground" made the mules shy and a scene of confusion followed. The soldiers jumped out of the wagon and beat Martin up with straps and cudgels. His patience only exasperated them the more. When his companions reached him, they found him bleeding from wounds in every part of his body, and unconscious. They placed him on his donkey and hurried from the scene. A Celtic saint would have cursed his assailants and the consequences would have been unpleasant. Not being a Celtic saint Martin did not curse them. But the consequences were unpleasant, nevertheless. When the soldiers attempted to drive on, the mules would not budge. No amount of blows could move them. Finally the soldiers recognized something preternatural at work and, when they learned that their victim was the holy Bishop of Tours, they understood. They hastened after Martin and when they found him humbly begged his pardon. When he forgave them and they went back to their mules, they had no more difficulty with them. Martin recalls a more sympathetic aspect Celtic sanctity, its love of animals, when he saves a hare from its hunters.

Supported no doubt by his knowledge that the government was Christian, Martin adopted a missionary method more violent than would commend itself today—the destruction of pagan shrines without regard to their worshippers' beliefs. On one occasion having demolished a temple he proceeded to cut down a sacred pine tree adjoining it. This was too much for the rustics and their priest, who formed a threatening crowd and prepared to defend the tree. One of them at last exclaimed, "If you really have confidence in this God of yours, we will cut down the tree ourselves. But you must stand in the path of its fall and, if your God is really helping you, no doubt you will escape." Martin agreed to the test and took up his stand where the tree must fall. The rustics now were all eagerness to cut the tree down that it might slay the enemy of their god. Just as it was toppling to its fall Martin made the

10. Black clothes must have been unusual at that time.

sign of the cross. Straightway the trunk bent in the opposite direction and away from the saint. Wholesale conversion followed. This divine intervention need not have been miraculous. A misdirected stroke of the axe or a sudden gust of wind, natural agents of God's purpose, might well have accounted for the unexpected direction in which the tree fell.

On the other hand a multiplication of oil witnessed by a priest named Harpagus known to Sulpicius cannot be explained without supernatural agency. It is, however, paralleled by modern instances which passed even the severe censorship of Father Thurston.[11]

During a riot caused by his destruction of another temple a heathen drew his sword to kill Martin. When the saint meekly offered his neck the uplifted arm fell down powerless and the assailant must crave pardon. In another locality the opposition was so powerful that the saint was obliged to withdraw. He betook himself to three days' prayer. He saw in a vision two angels armed, who told him they had been commissioned to protect him. He thereupon returned to the village and the crowd looked on without an attempt to interfere while he demolished the temple, its altars, and its image.[12]

Martin was the Apostle, no less, of rural Gaul. For his missionary campaigns were by no means confined to his diocese. As the very name pagan—villager—reminds us, the countryman with his ingrained conservatism adopted Christianity later than the townsman, as he has been slower to abandon it. To overcome his resistance Martin might well need the awe produced by the action of God, whether or no strictly miraculous.

Of particular interest are the relations between Martin and the civil power. Valentinian, influenced by an Arian wife, refused him audience. After seven days' prayer and fasting an angel bade him boldly approach the Emperor. No one at the palace attempted to stop him, as he made his

11. For other multiplications of food, see the lives of Blessed Osanna of Mantua, Blessed Jordan of Saxony, St. Thomas of Villanueva and Blessed Antony Grassi.

12. At this very time in Britain a pagan temple was being erected on the site of a prehistoric camp, Maiden Castle near Dorchester.

way into the imperial presence. Valentinian, furious at the intrusion, sat fixed in his chair, glowering upon the saint. But a fire surrounded the chair and burned "that part of his body with which he sat." He leapt up and promised Martin all he wanted, before he had time even to ask for it.

Later Gaul came under the rule of Maximus, a general in Britain raised by his troops to the purple, who had defeated and slain the Emperor Gratian. At first Martin refused to have any dealings with a man guilty of usurpation and murder. But he gave way when Maximus pointed out that once he had been proclaimed Emperor by his army his only safety lay in accepting the offer, and that he had killed no one except in open battle. Gratian, it is true, captured after his defeat, had been put to death. But Maximus denied that it was by his orders, and Martin accepted his assurance. The Emperor was delighted by the recognition of an accepted St.. Martin, however, foretold the doom that would befall him later in Italy.

When dining with Maximus, Martin handed the wine cup first to his chaplain to show that the sacerdotal dignity is higher than the imperial. Maximus' wife in particular paid recognition to Martin's sanctity. She pressed upon him an invitation to dine at the palace, where she waited upon him in person, brought him water to wash his hands and food she had cooked herself, and mixed his wine.[13] While he was at table she sat on the ground in the humble posture of a slave and, when the meal was over, ate the crumbs he had left. The Empress was Welsh, Helen by name. Later legend confused her with the mother of Constantine the Great, St. Helena, whence the unfounded belief that the daughter of a Balkan innkeeper was of British extraction—the fact that this Helen also was the mother of a Constantine would have helped the confusion of the two empresses. She seems to have been equally deserving of the honours of sanctity which she received in her native Wales.

About this time a heresy had arisen in Spain called Priscillianism from the name of its founder, Priscillian, Bishop of Ávila. What

13. In antiquity wine was a thick syrup and was drunk mixed with water.

precisely Priscillian's doctrines were it seems impossible to determine. But the heresy, which long survived, soon crystallized into a blend of Gnosticism, Docetism, Origenism, and above all Manichaeanism.[14] For it taught that the body is a creation of evil angels and marriage therefore sinful. It bore in fact a family resemblance to the later Catharism, was indeed so closely akin to Albigensianism that one wonders whether, when the latter was introduced from the Balkans, lingering memories of Priscillianism had not prepared the ground for it. Priscillian, when hard pressed by Bishop Ithacius and other champions of orthodoxy, imprudently appealed to Maximus. On a charge of magic the Emperor condemned him to death and along with him two clerics, a deacon, and a woman. This scarcely veiled death sentence for heresy inflicted by the secular power aroused vehement protests from Catholic bishops who could not be suspected of favouring Priscillianism—among them the Pope and St. Ambrose, who, visiting the court, refused to communicate with Ithacius and his colleagues.

No one was more indignant than Martin. Before the execution he had protested so strongly to Maximus that he promised not to execute Priscillian. When the Emperor broke his word, Martin returned to his court at Trèves (Trier) and denounced his action. Like St. Ambrose, he refused to communicate with the bishops, Ithacius and his supporters, who had advised or encouraged it.

Maximus, partly persuaded by the bishops, partly attracted by the prospect of profit from confiscations, had sent officers to Spain with orders to liquidate the Priscillianists. He was, however, anxious to win over a bishop generally regarded as a saint. He therefore promised that, if Martin would communicate with the bishops, he would recall the tribune he had dispatched to Spain. To prevent further slaughter Martin yielded. But his conscience reproached him. These events can be dated with certainty to the year 385. Thenceforward Martin ceased to attend synods. One cannot, however, be sure that his motive for abstention was, as Sulpicius represents it, regret for his compliance, and not rather

14. See Tixeront, *Histoire des Dogmes*, Vol. 2, pp. 231–43.

the knowledge that he was now a *persona ingrata* with so many of his fellow bishops, and his attendance might cause strife.[15]

One so bold with an Emperor could stand up to a government official, however redoubtable. Count Avitianus, on whose back, as we have heard, Martin saw the demon seated, was feared everywhere for his cruelty: "that beast," Sulpicius calls him, "who fed on human blood and the death of the unfortunate." He arrived at Tours with a gang of prisoners in chains whom it was his intention to put to death with hideous tortures. That night Martin lay prostrate in prayer before the closed door of the pretorium. An angel woke Avitianus and told him that the servant of God was lying outside his door. Slaves sent out to look for him reported after a cursory glance that nobody was to be seen. Avitianus went off to sleep. But the angel again awoke him with the same admonition. This time he went out himself and found Martin. Smitten with the awe which, in those ages of faith, manifest sanctity aroused even in hardened sinners, without waiting to be asked (for he knew Martin's errand) he promised to release his prospective victims. Martin would not have been so successful at Belsen or Buchenwald. The modern sadist knows no God to fear.

We who have witnessed the tyranny and atrocities of totalitarian states should appreciate the achievement of Martin and other saintly prelates in upholding the supremacy of the spiritual order and curbing, though they could not abolish, the cruelty and oppression exercised by kings, officers of state or powerful nobles. There was, however, a class with whom Martin was not successful. The laity even of the highest rank—even "the bloodthirsty beast" Avitanius—were overawed by his holiness—the divine presence of which they were sensible in him.[16]

15. Because one motive for preventing the imperial commission to Spain was fear lest Catholics might be killed along with the heretics—for asceticism was held suspect as a sign of Manichaean hatred for the flesh—the marginal note of Surius in the sixteenth century suggests that this was Martin's sole reason for objecting to the persecution of heretics. This, however, was by no means the case, in the fourth century the Church was still opposed to persecution.

16. We shall notice the same awe produced by St. Hugh of Lincoln.

The clergy, the bishops in particular, were not equally overawed. I have indeed the impression, though it cannot be more, that in later days the episcopal opposition increased, presumably after Martin's reluctance to communicate with the bishops at Maximus' court. This in fact, as I have just suggested, may have been the reason why Martin no longer attended synods.

The leader of the opposition at Tours was a priest named Brictius, Brice. Immaculately dressed, wealthy and worldly, he owned a large household of slaves and a stable of horses. He had nothing but hatred and contempt for his bishop, whom no doubt he regarded as quite impossible, a rank outsider. On one occasion at least he abused him violently in public, scoffing at "his empty superstitions, imagined visions and ridiculous ravings." We are told, it is true, that on recovering his temper he begged Martin's pardon. If he did, it was insincere, his motive fear of popular indignation. For he continued to be, as before, Martin's adversary and a worldly priest. If we can trust St. Gregory of Tours, writing some two centuries later the life of his illustrious predecessor, when a sick man desiring a miraculous cure asked Brice where Martin was to be found and how he was engaged, Brice replied: "If you are in search of that maniac, look over there. As usual he's gazing up at the sky like a loony." Martin, however, could not be persuaded to take disciplinary action against him. "Since Christ," he would often say, "put up with Judas, why should not I put up with Brice?"[17]

Martin is said to have foretold that Brice would succeed him as bishop. If he did, it was not, perhaps, an instance of the gift of prophecy, but a shrewd deduction from his knowledge of his unpopularity with his fellow bishops, who would therefore be likely to choose his enemy

17. The most recent translator of Sulpicius denies the authenticity of this remark, which he attributes to Sulpicius' malice against Brice. His judgment however, necessarily a personal impression, seems to be based on the conviction that *Saint* Martin could not have used this language of *Saint* Brice. Couldn't he? St. Bernard is quite as uncomplimentary when he writes about St. William of York. And Brice at any rate was still very far from being a saint.

for his successor. It was the normal practice for a bishop to be elected by the bishops of the province.

When Martin, visiting his diocese, had arrived at a village named Candes, where his services as a peacemaker were required, he fell mortally ill. Refusing to go to bed, he lay on ashes spread on the ground, absorbed in prayer. His followers gathered round him lamenting his approaching decease. "Why are you deserting us, Father? To whose tender mercies are you leaving us in our desolation? Ravening wolves will attack your flock, and when the shepherd is no more, who will defend us from them?" The wolves were Brice and his party. Martin's reply to their entreaties was an immortal prayer: "Lord, if Thy people still need me I do not shirk the toil. Thy will be done." "Surely I have already fought long enough. But if thou biddest me still stand in the line of battle to defend Thy camp"—the language of the dying old man is reminiscent of his youth in the army—"I will not plead the excuse of failing strength. I will conscientiously perform the tasks Thou layest upon me and as long as Thou commandest fight under Thy standard.... But if Thou sparest my age, Thy good pleasure will be welcome." The sacrifice was not asked, and the saint died, trusting his flock to God's care. It was November 8, 397. His body was taken back to Tours, where he was buried on November 11. His feast therefore is kept on the day not of his death but his burial.

The number of monks said to have attended his funeral, no less than two thousand, is no doubt grossly exaggerated. Sulpicius in fact gives the figure as a hearsay estimate. But it was certainly thronged by monks and consecrated virgins, that is to say virgins living under vows but in their own homes—the earliest, as it may perhaps be the latest, form of religious life for women. The Archbishop of Cologne, St. Severinus, is said to have heard the angels carrying Martin's soul up to heaven with hymns of joy. Such tales, not from Sulpicius' pen, are later legend. According to the story told by St. Gregory of Tours, St. Ambrose while singing Mass at Milan was wrapped in spirit to Tours to assist at Martin's funeral, while, sunk in apparent sleep at the altar, he kept an amazingly patient congregation waiting "some two or three hours" between the Old Testament Lesson and the Epistle.[18] Unfortunately for the truth of this tale St. Ambrose died a few months before St. Martin.[19]

Martin, whose holiness and miracles had been spread throughout the Christian world by Sulpicius' writings, seems to have been the first saint other than a martyr to receive the cultus of a saint—was in fact the first Confessor.[20]

As Martin expected and his supporters feared, Brice was elected his successor. According to St. Gregory of Tours he was falsely accused of being the father of his washerwoman's child, but in answer to his prayer the infant spoke and vindicated his innocence. In addition he successfully underwent the ordeal of walking on burning coals. However that may be, his flock was not convinced and he was expelled from his see. One suspects that, innocent or guilty, he was unable to clear himself satisfactorily. For some years he lived in exile in Rome while his see was occupied by two successors. He was certainly able to convince Pope Zozimus of his innocence. For the Pope condemned his accuser Lazarus as the calumniator of an innocent bishop. After seven years he returned to Tours to find the second bishop just dead and was accepted as bishop. His latter years at any rate must have been edifying. For he was accorded the honours of sanctity and took his place in the calendar as St. Brice, his feast following St. Martin's by two days.[21] It is to be found on November 13 in most, perhaps all, local mediaeval calendars and was in the Roman Calendar until the reform of Pope Pius V in the sixteenth century. For more than a millennium, that is to say, Martin had to put up with the company of his Judas. Nor has he shaken him off

18. The Milanese rite has three lessons at Mass, from the Old Testament, the Epistle, the Gospel. The Roman rite, originally, I am convinced, no more than another use of the same rite, had also these three lessons. The Gradual separated the prophetic lesson from the Epistle, the Alleluia or Tract, the Epistle from the Gospel.

19. Gregory is also our authority for the story about St. Severinus.

20. But once introduced the cult of confessors became almost immediately general.

21. From the *Magna Vita* of St. Hugh of Lincoln it appears that in the Middle Ages the seven legendary Sleepers of Ephesus were believed to have been Martin's kinsmen, "cousins of St. Martin, our Hugh's patron." And their final decease was believed to be the answer to his prayer. *Magna Vita*, bk. V, ch. 19.

entirely even now. For a memorial of St. Brice survives in the Dominican calendar.[22] But Brice is no longer his Judas, but his penitent Peter.

22. Since the feast of St. Thomas, patron of Catholic schools, is kept on November 13, the memorial of St. Brice has been transferred to the following day.

SAINT BRUNO

[circa 1030–1101]

THE PERIOD OF William the Conqueror, "1066 and all that," has often seemed to the imagination unreal, an historical pageant enacted by queer-looking figures wearing armor, a stage decor of jousts and the single combat of knights, baronial halls and dungeons, the players bold bad barons and distressed damsels.

It was in this age that there lived a man far more real than the vast majority of our contemporaries, utterly real, because he found reality and lived in it, in fact lived it. He was the founder of an order still with us and once more in its original home—the Carthusian. He was St. Bruno. Unlike many founders of religious orders Bruno did not receive almost from his death the honours of sanctity. Spiritual sons, St. Hugh of Avalon and Lincoln, St. Anthelmus of Belley, were soon enrolled among the saints. For their father there was no cultus. Centuries passed, until in 1514 Leo X formally permitted the Carthusians to celebrate his feast, and it was not until 1623 that Gregory XV extended it to the universal Church. In consequence there is no early life of St. Bruno. The oldest, the *Vita Antiqua*, is no older than the fourteenth century and already unreliable.

Our materials for his life are scanty. Mentions by contemporary historians, charters, information contained in Prior Guigo's Life of St. Hugh of Grenoble, and in accounts of the early days of the order—these are not much. Happily there are two other sources. When a bishop, abbot, or other religious superior died, it was the custom to send round to chapters and monastic houses a mortuary roll announcing the death. Each recipient in turn wrote on the roll a tribute to the deceased in prose or elegiac verse, often with a pledge of prayers and Masses for his soul. We still possess the roll sent out at St. Bruno's death with the tributes attached to it.[1] These memorial tributes—*tituli funebres,* the Bollandists term them—exceptionally numerous on St. Bruno's roll, are an invaluable source of information, whatever discount must be made for a conventional and hyperbolical fashion of speech.

Most valuable of all, however, are two letters written by the saint himself. We possess, it is true, commentaries on the Psalms and St. Paul's Epistles. These, however, tell us little more than the extent of his theological knowledge. The letters reveal his personality. The Bollandist who in 1768 published a life in which every available scrap of evidence is carefully weighed—he calls himself C. B. and as such I shall refer to him—devotes pages to establishing the authenticity of a charter or determining a date, and his conclusion is often a probability. He includes the letters and by way of appendix gives us the complete funerary roll. My account of the saint has been taken from his work.

Bruno was a German, born about 1030 at Cologne, and of no mean parentage. A memorial tribute from St. Mary's, Rouen, calls him "*vir nobilis.*" He started his life therefore with the advantage of noble birth. There is some evidence that his family was Von der Hartenfaust—"the hard-fisted." This, however, is uncertain.

As a young man he left Cologne for the cathedral school of Rheims. These schools were the precursors of the later universities. Here he studied first the humanities, *litterae humaniores.* It was the beginning of a brilliant career. And from first to last Bruno is a humanist, a Christian humanist. The surviving letters written near his death are written in

1. For these mortuary rolls see Rock, *Church of Our Fathers*, eds. Hart and Frere (1905), Vol. 2, pp. 308ff.

the rhetorical idiom which was a legacy of the rhetorical education and literature of the Roman Empire.

He seems to have studied philosophy at Tours under Berengarius, shortly to become notorious for his denial, finally retracted, of Transubstantiation.[2] It may well have been the memory of his teacher's heresy that made him insist on the Real Presence in his dying profession of faith. He probably went to Tours in 1047 about the age of seventeen. Whether he studied theology at Rheims or at Cologne is uncertain.

In any case he became a master at Rheims. He first taught grammar and poetry. So we gather from a tribute by the Chapter of Ghent.

Poetry, it is true, was little more than an academic exercise, verses manufactured according to a traditional recipe and stuffed with conventional clichés, much like the verses turned off by schoolboys with the help of their *Gradus ad Parnassum*. But it kept alive the tradition of classical poetry—Bruno will have lectured on Virgil and Ovid. And the fact that he lectured on poetry suggests an attraction to it. C. B. accepts as authentic some verses attributed to him. If genuine they show already the preoccupation with the eternal issues confronting man which would later drive him far from the schools. For he complains that men live as though hell were "an empty fable." "Would that all men might so live that they would not need to fear the pool below."

From literature Bruno went on to philosophy and theology. Though evidence is lacking, it seems most likely that it was as a professor of theology that he composed his Biblical commentaries.[3] They display knowledge of Greek and Hebrew, an accomplishment uncommon in the mediaeval West. Before 1060—that is before he was thirty—Bruno

2. In view of the somewhat crude formula of retraction forced upon him it is, I think, possible that Berengarius would not have rejected transubstantiation, had it been presented to him in the carefully qualified statement of St. Thomas or as Newman explains the doctrine in a well-known passage, that the presence of our Lord's Body in the consecrated species is not local but after the manner of a spirit.

3. The writer, however, of an article on Carthusian spirituality in the *Dictionnaire de Spiritualité* thinks this is true only of the Commentary on the Psalms, and that the Commentary on St. Paul's Epistles was written towards the close of Bruno's life in his Calabrian hermitage.

succeeded Herimann—another German—as head of the Rheims school—"*scholarcha.*" This rapid success and, when every allowance is made for rhetoric, the memorial tributes, prove that Bruno was recognized as a man of outstanding ability and learning. Those who leave the world for God are not the incompetent for whom the world has no use.

"The whole world waits on you, Bruno, as the moon on the sun." He is "a gem of wisdom, a luminary of the Churches." "His outstanding wisdom is the subject of universal praise—his command of language excels Virgil's, Plato's renown pales beside Bruno's." So the good canons of Ghent! But had he not been in the front rank of contemporary culture and philosophy—St. Anselm, the solitary original genius of the century, was still in the future—such things could not have been said of him. "He excelled all other teachers," the Canons continue; "his teaching produced clerks of highest standing, a teacher of teachers he." "The flower and fruit was he"—another tribute runs—"of all philosophers... Those who drank of his spring became philosophers."

No, not all rhetoric. The most promising young men flocked to Rheims to be Bruno's pupils. Among them were several future Abbots, Robert, who will be Bishop of Langres, and Odo of Chatillon, to be first Prior of Cluny, then Cardinal Bishop, finally Pope Urban II. And Urban will be a Beatus as well as a Pope. For it was not only Bruno's learning but his life that drew these pupils to his chair. He was not, I think, the saint he was to be. He led a life of devotion, of strict, even austere, morality. But he was not yet the man to sacrifice all for the love of God. He was still, I believe, very much the college don savoring the intellectual delights of teaching and disputing in the schools—and not insensible of his popularity and renown. To the end of his life he sought and valued friends—and his pupils' respect and affection must have meant much to him.

Moreover his activities enlarged. A canon of the cathedral chapter, in 1070 at earliest he became chancellor. This meant considerable responsibility and authority in the administration of the diocese—attractive also to a man by nature a leader as well as a teacher.

Hitherto Bruno had basked in the sunshine. Outstanding gifts of intellect, wide popularity, friends, successful and congenial work, renown, responsible and honourable posts—all these had been lavished upon him. Had the sun continued to shine so brightly, he might well have continued to the end the life he had led so successfully, so happily. He would most certainly have become a bishop, and inevitably one of the leading prelates of the French Church. He might very well have become a cardinal, even Pope. He would have come down to us as an outstanding figure of Church history, her teacher and defender in dark days. But he would not have endowed the Church with something far more valuable, more permanent and more powerful than any product of erudition or administrative ability, an order devoted to contemplative prayer. And since this was God's purpose for him, God's call to his heart, one thing would have been lacking to him, as to the young man in the Gospel. Irreproachable conduct and devotion, yes: all these he had kept from his youth—but not the one thing necessary for himself and for the Church.

So the sun was overclouded. Days are coming of darkness and distress when he will lose his dignities and possessions, will be banished from the chair where he taught, from the diocese in whose administration he played so prominent a part.

The trouble began, though it did not as yet come to the surface, when in 1068 Archbishop Gervase died and was succeeded by Manasses. Manasses obtained the see by simony, and I find it hard to believe, with C. B., that Bruno was unaware of it. Yet for some time he was in favour with Manasses, even became his chancellor. Simony was then so rife on the verge of Hildebrand's campaign against it, that, since Manasses gave promise that he would at least govern well the see he had wrongfully obtained, Bruno may well have thought it more prudent not to engage in a struggle probably fruitless but to make the best of the situation. Nevertheless his acquiescence suggests wishful thinking, the rationalization of a desire for the easier and more pleasant course, the reluctance of the successful and the popular to make a dangerous enemy and jeopardize his career and his work. When, however, after a time Manasses showed his true colours, sold benefices and misappropriated church property,

Bruno was too conscientious to stand aside, opposed his Archbishop, resigned his dignities and left Rheims. It was in 1076 or 1077.

In 1077 at the Council of Clermont or of Autun or at both Bruno denounced Manasses. His conduct won a most favourable report from the Papal Legate, Hugh of Die. Where he lived during this period of exile is uncertain. The Archbishop had confiscated his property at Rheims together with the property of two other Canons who opposed him. He may even have engineered an attack on Bruno when on a journey.

Bruno spent some of his exile at a place in France called "Roccius"—Le Rocher. Here occurred what was to be the turning point of his life. He was staying at the house of a man called Adam with two friends, Canons of Rheims, Radulphus Viridis (Ralph Green) and Fulcius Monoculus (Fulk One-Eye).[4] They talked together in the garden of the world's deceitful pleasures, heaven's everlasting joys, and vowed to leave the world and embrace the monastic life at the first opportunity.

We may conjecture that Adam's garden suggested the garden of Paradise, and this in turn, heaven and the contemplative life which is its early foretaste. Of this conversation we are informed by Bruno himself in a letter to Ralph. Fulk, however, must go to Rome to denounce Manasses to the Pope. They would wait till his return. "During the delay divine love became enfeebled, the spirit grew cold, fervour melted away." The humanist, the student, the don, the administrator were not so easily vanquished by the contemplative.

Manasses contrived to hoodwink Pope Gregory VII for a time, obtaining a suspension, even an annulment of the Council's decree against him (1078). On his return, however, he broke his undertaking to purge himself of the charges against him at another Council held at Lyons under the Papal Legate. He was too well aware of his guilt. The Council therefore deprived him of his see (1080), and Gregory confirmed its sentence. Meanwhile, Bruno may have returned to Cologne, may have become a Canon of St. Cunebert's in that city. We cannot be sure.

---

4. Presumably he was blind in one eye.

Manasses on his condemnation fled from Rheims to the Pope's arch-enemy, the excommunicated Emperor Henry IV. Bruno returned to Rheims and his former offices. He seemed in fact likely to be Manasses' successor. The following year however, 1081, Helinand was chosen Archbishop, and Bruno turned his back forever on Rheims and the world. He was at last on the road to his goal, had chosen the life of experienced union with God in prayer which is called contemplation.[5]

A later tradition ascribed Bruno's decision to a scene he is supposed to have witnessed. The Office of the Dead was being sung round the bier of a master in the Paris schools. The corpse rose up and cried out, "Before God's just judgment I have been accused." A second time the dead man exclaimed, "By God's just judgment I am judged." A third time: "by God's just judgment I have been condemned." C. B. devotes no less than sixty pages to the question whether this macabre story is true and reaches no certain conclusion. No early writer, however, mentions it, and today it is universally rejected. Bruno was not driven to the desert by sheer terrorism, though, as his letter to Ralph proves, he believed that refusal to fulfil a solemn pledge to God would endanger his soul. His motive was obedience to God's will, because it was His will, obedience to a divine call heard clearly, also to satisfy the deepest need and strongest desire of his spirit, intimate converse with God in a secluded and contemplative life.

With a few companions Bruno settled as a hermit at Sèche-Fontaine. It is close to Molesmes where St. Robert, who would found Cîteaux and thus be the father of the Cistercians, was then Abbot. The mortuary tribute from Molesmes speaks of Bruno as *familiarisimus*, "very well known." C. B. may therefore be right in his conjecture that Bruno was for a short time actually a member of St. Robert's community. In any case there was a close tie between the Carthusians and the Cistercians at these first beginnings of both.

Bruno, however, did not stay very long at Sèche-Fontaine. In 1084 he set out with six companions for Grenoble, where the Bishop was St.

5. Misleadingly. For its substance is not contemplation or any kind of experience but union with God through the radical will.

Hugh. He had accepted the see with great reluctance. For like the Curé d'Ars he longed for a life of contemplation. The Cure twice attempted to fly from his parish. The young Bishop—he was only twenty-five—almost immediately after consecration fled from his diocese, and took the habit at the Cluniac Abbey of Chaise Dieu. Pope Gregory obliged him to return to his see. Bruno must have known that he would find in him the sympathy and support he required for the half-cenobitic, half-eremitical life he proposed to lead.

His six companions were Master Landuin, Stephen of Bourges, Stephen of Die, both Canons Regular, Hugh called the Chaplain, for at that time he was the only priest among them, and two lay brothers Andrew and Guarin. Before their arrival—some say on the night before—St. Hugh dreamed he saw seven stars standing over a remote valley in his diocese where, he understood, it was God's will that a sanctuary should be erected. Though the details are uncertain, there seems no good reason to reject the story.

It was Midsummer, the feast of St. John the Baptist, when the seven reached Grenoble and told their purpose.

The newcomers stayed a little while with St. Hugh at Grenoble. Then they set out for the Chartreuse. The Bishop accompanied them. They took with them everything necessary to make their foundation.

The Grande Chartreuse lies high up among the mountains. Its beauty is austere, awe-inspiring. And it must have seemed even sterner to men accustomed by a tradition reaching back to antiquity to dislike mountains and find their ideal scenery in soft and well-cultivated landscape. Such is the cold of winter that, as I was informed by a friend who had tried his vocation there, one of the duties most urgently impressed on a novice is never to let the stove in his cell bum out. A torrent rushes down from the wooded slopes beneath a bridge built by the monks. Beyond is the monastery of the lay brethren, built somewhat later than the monks' first arrival, and higher up the mountainside the monastery of the choir monks. Here Bruno built a church near the spring which bears his name, said by later legend to have been brought miraculously into being at his prayer. The cells were grouped around it, each inhabited at first by two monks. The life was a blend of community life and the life of hermits. The night office, Vespers and the conventual Mass were sung in common, the lesser hours recited privately. On feast days alone the monks took a common meal.

As William of St. Thierry said truly in the letter on prayer he addressed to the Carthusians of Mont Dieu, it was a revival of primitive Egyptian monasticism. But it was also the monasticism of St. Martin of Tours, as it had been lived at Marmoutier. It is significant that in both cases the monks' occupation was copying manuscripts. I feel little doubt that Bruno was inspired by his knowledge of St. Martin's life and that Martin, as reported by Sulpicius, was a link between the monasticism of the eastern deserts and its Carthusian revival. Bruno probably was also acquainted with the Camaldolese blend of monk and hermit. The primitive fasts were more severe even than those now practiced and were still kept when Peter the Venerable described the Carthusian life in the following century. Meat was never permitted—as is the rule to this day. Fish might be eaten, if it were a gift. On Sunday and Thursday the fare was cheese and eggs, on Tuesday and Saturday vegetables, on Monday, Wednesday and Friday nothing but bread and water. Except on the great feasts and during the octaves there was only one meal a day—an austere diet indeed. Originally private masses were not said daily—a peculiarity dropped at the close of the following century.

We do not know when Bruno himself was ordained. It must have been before he solemnly baptised a benefactor's child. St. Hugh may have ordained him before he reluctantly left the Chartreuse to return to his episcopal duties.[6]

6. The author of a metrical life of St. Bruno published in 1510, Zacharias Benedictus, gave rein to his imagination, when he described the dedication of the church at the Grande Chartreuse, the elaborate ceremonial, the music, even instrumental—all this *décor* totally incompatible with Carthusian austerity, and the building adorned, regardless of season and altitude, with the conventional flowers and shrubs of classical verse. Nor was this all. Although, as C. B. points out, the monks had long since taken the habit, he describes a supposed clothing by the Bishop. He even expatiates on the handsome bodies of the young monks when stripped of their former clothing: "*apparent juvenum generosa et lactea membra*"—"the young men's limbs come into view, refined and

Bruno would not long enjoy his solitude at the Grande Chartreuse. In 1088 his former pupil Odo of Chatillon became Pope Urban II and two years later, 1090, he summoned Bruno to Rome to assist him with his advice. Obedience tore the saint from his home and monastic family, which he left in charge of Master Landuin. He had hardly departed when the monks, finding life intolerable without their father, deserted the Chartreuse and hurried after him to Rome. At the first news of this Bruno, to prevent usurpations by lay nobles, handed the Chartreuse over to Siguier, Abbot of Chaise Dieu.

When, however, the brethren reached Rome, probably in the winter of 1090, Bruno persuaded them to return and Urban sent with them a charter requiring Abbot Siguier to restore the property, which by a formal instrument he did. Thus the Chartreuse was saved and the Carthusians would be Carthusian. Some of the monks however, among them Lanuin and Lambert, stayed with Bruno.

Bruno did not remain long with the Papal Curia. The call to contemplation was too insistent. He was successful in persuading the Pope of this and was permitted to retire with a band of disciples into the desert. He could not, however, return to France. Urban no doubt wished to keep him within call.

Robert Guiscard, the Norman adventurer who had carved out for himself a kingdom in Southern Italy and Sicily, had left a brother, at least his equal for prowess and ability, Count Roger. Roger ruled half of Norman Italy—the other half being the portion of his nephew—enlarged and firmly established the Norman kingdom of Sicily in which Norman French culture met and in many respects blended with the culture of the Muslims who had hitherto ruled the island. These Norman rulers were closely allied with the Holy See in its warfare against the Emperor, and it was presumably in Rome that Count Roger met Bruno, became his close friend and gave him the hermitage of La Torre in Calabria in

white," though some at least were in fact middle-aged. This instance of the Renaissance admiration for the naked human form obtruding itself into the most unlikely context is worth notice for its historical interest.

the diocese of Squillace—the toe of Italy. The later story that he met the saint accidentally in a cave when hunting is apocryphal.

Here the saint built another laura on the Chartreuse pattern, where he passed the remainder of his life—though he may have attended Italian councils summoned by Pope Urban. He built first a chapel in honour of St. Stephen, to be followed by a monastery and church dedicated to our Lady and St. John the Baptist. The latter was not finished before 1094, when it was solemnly consecrated by the Archbishop of Palermo assisted by five bishops. But it is not easy to believe that it was richly furnished by Count Roger. Carthusian churches in those early days were austere.

In 1095 Bruno baptised Count Roger's son Roger, later King of Sicily, and the following year was among those who advised the Count to appoint a Latin bishop of Squillace to succeed the Greek bishop deceased. It was a step towards the Latinization of the Church in South Italy which must have prevented the danger that a Greek Church would follow the Church of Byzantium into the schism recently consummated in 1054. The community of La Torre meanwhile increased so rapidly that it became necessary to found a second monastery, the monastery of St. Stephen in the wood, "*de bosco*" or "*de nemore.*"

When Count Roger was besieging Capua, probably in 1099, he was in great danger from the treachery of a Greek cavalry general in his service, named Sergius. Sergius and his accomplices had plotted with the besieged Capuans against him. The very night when the treacherous assault would have been delivered, Roger was aroused from sleep by an apparition of Bruno warning him of his peril. He was able to take timely action, frustrated the plot, and shortly afterwards captured the city.[7] The story (far from incredible, for telepathic communication is excellently attested) is related in a charter granted by the grateful Count to his

7. St. Anselm, banished from England by William Rufus, visited Count Roger during the siege and remarked on his host of Arab and Muslim mercenaries. The anti-clerical and probably unbelieving Emperor Frederick II was therefore not the first Christian ruler to employ Saracens. They had already assisted the campaigns of the Pope's Norman ally.

friend. He had intended to put the traitors to death. But at Bruno's intercession their lives were spared and themselves and their descendants made serfs of the Charterhouse. The mercy is admirable. The culprits could have expected nothing better than death and probably a painful one. Nevertheless this is surely one of those blind spots which prove the limitations even of a saint's moral vision. Though the offenders richly deserved their fate, it was unjust to punish their children and even their remote descendants for a crime of which they were innocent.

In 1099, or at latest 1100, Prior Landuin from the Grande Chartreuse arrived at La Torre—this time alone. He hoped to persuade Bruno to return. He was unsuccessful. Whether there was a Papal prohibition, whether Bruno, now a man of seventy or thereabouts, felt himself unequal to the journey, or whether he could not bring himself to leave his community at La Torre, we do not know. Possibly his motives were mixed. But he tried to keep Landuin with him. For the Prior was a sick man and Bruno wished to spare him the long journey home and take care of his health. Landuin, however, could not bring himself to desert his brethren at the Chartreuse and pleaded to be allowed to return. Bruno yielded to his desire but, when he left, gave him a letter, one of the only two which have come down to us, to the community at the Grande Chartreuse.

> Brother Bruno greets in the Lord those who in Christ are dearest to him. Since I have heard Brother Landuin's assurance, often repeated, that you are living as reason bids, keeping your praiseworthy observance with an unbending strictness, also his report of your holy love and unremitting pursuit of all that is honourable and perfect, my spirit is glad in the Lord. I rejoice and am carried away in praise and thanksgiving to God. Yet I also sigh from bitterness of heart. As is fitting, I rejoice for your progress in every virtue. But I grieve and am ashamed that I lie sluggishly in the filth of my sins. Therefore, my dear brothers, rejoice for your blessed lot and the grace God has bestowed with lavish hand. Rejoice that you have

> escaped the many perils and shipwrecks of an unstable world. Rejoice that you have reached the peaceful and secluded haven many desire and strive in vain to reach. Many even have been driven out later, because it has not been given to them by God.

He then turns to the lay brothers.

> My soul doth magnify the Lord for the abundant mercy He has shown you which I know from the report of your loving Prior and father who boasts of you and rejoices over you. I rejoice that, although you know nothing of letters, God's mighty finger writes in your hearts not only love but knowledge of His holy law. For their extent is shown by your conduct. The performance of God's commands is the key and seal of all spiritual discipline. For it is impossible without great humility and the utmost patience, cannot exist without chaste love of God and true charity. Your scrupulous obedience therefore proves that you gather[8] the delicious and profitable fruit of holy Scripture… I wanted to keep Landuin here with me. For he is afflicted with many serious infirmities. But without you he can find no health, no pleasure, no life worth living. He therefore refused my desire, protesting with tears and sighs his love for you and the store he sets on your society. I would not constrain him against his will. For I would not hurt him or you whom your virtues have so greatly endeared to me.

Bruno then asks the brethren to provide Landuin with everything his ill health requires and gives them authority to insist on his taking and doing whatever they think necessary for his health. "As for me, brethren, be assured that my one desire after my desire for God is to return to you and see you once more. When I can do so, God helping, I will."

8. There is here a play upon the meaning of *legere*, "to gather" but also "to read."

The rhetorical manner of this letter and the second, the convention of Latin humanism, does not conceal the genuine and deep feeling, the human love raised to charity by love of God.

The Prior was not destined to see the Chartreuse again. On his way through Italy he fell into the hands of partisans of the imperialist anti-pope Guibert. Because he stoutly refused to acknowledge his usurpation, he was thrown into a dungeon, where very shortly he died. He lived to hear of the anti-pope's death, and his charitable sorrow for the unfortunate rebel amazed those incapable of understanding it. He is said to have been starved to death. But the effect of his imprisonment on a health already so feeble was surely a sufficient cause of death, the death of a martyr. Bruno's letter presumably got through safely. Otherwise it would hardly have survived.

More valuable, however, is the second surviving letter. For it is even more revealing, reveals as nothing else Bruno's personality. We may remember how, years before in Adam's French garden, the three friends Bruno, Ralph Green, and Fulk One-Eye had pledged themselves to a monastic life. Bruno after a few years' delay fulfilled his vow. Of Fulk One-Eye after his journey to Rome we know nothing. Ralph Green remained in the world and became *praepositus*, provost,[9] of the chapter of Rheims. Bruno writes from La Torre, therefore in the last decade of his life, to urge his old friend to keep his pledge. The occasion of the letter would seem to have been a communication from Ralph, certainly a service done by him to the saint.

> Your faithful friendship is the more valuable, because friendship is so rare. Neither distance nor long absence can part our souls. This is proved by your letter and by all the kindness you have shown me and for my sake to Brother Bernard. My thanks, though inadequate, are heartfelt. A letter I wrote has not, it seems, reached you. I am now sending this letter by one of our brethren whose words will supply what I cannot set

9. The English equivalent is "dean."

> down in writing. You will be glad to hear that my body enjoys good health, would my soul were as healthy, and my circumstances are on the whole satisfactory. For the future I look with confidence to God's merciful hand to "heal all my infirmities and fulfil my desire with good things." Here in Calabria I and my religious brethren, some of whom are learned, are on the watch for the Lord's coming, to hear His knock and open to Him.
>
> I am living in a hermitage in every direction remote from human habitations. I could not sufficiently convey to you the amenities of the place, the temperate and healthy climate, could not adequately describe the wide plain with its pleasing view, which penetrates far into the hills, its green meadows and pastures, bright with flowers. Nor could I describe the landscape of hills rising on all sides with a gentle slope and shady valleys watered by streams, brooks and springs. There are well-watered gardens and an abundance of trees of various kinds.

"It was only," wrote Ruskin in his study of mediaeval landscape,[10] "for their punishment or in their despair that men consented to tread the crocused slopes of the Chartreuse." And his judgment seemed to be confirmed by the monk, who, when he spoke of the scenery at the Grande Chartreuse, replied: "We do not come here to look at the mountains."[11] That monk was hardly faithful to the spirit of his founder. Nor would Bruno have endorsed Ruskin's verdict on the Carthusian attitude to landscape. For there speaks here the lover of natural beauty who, like St. John of the Cross who led his friars into the hills to pray and lingered late into the night contemplating the stars, found it an aid to prayer, an incentive to raise the spirit to God. Nor has the monk extinguished the humanist.

10. *Modern Painters*, Part IV, ch. 14.
11. *Modern Painters*, Part IV, ch. 11.

But first things first. So Bruno continues:

> Enough of this. The wise man knows delights far more attractive and profitable, because they are divine. Nevertheless, when human weakness has been fatigued by a strict discipline and spiritual exercise, the spirit often finds rest and refreshment in the prospect of these natural beauties. A bow cannot be always bent. But the profit and delight which the solitude and silence of a hermitage bestow on those who love it can be known only from personal experience. Here toilers can retire into themselves, as often as they please, enjoy their own company, cultivate the seeds of virtue, pluck the fruits of Paradise. Here that eye is opened whose calm gaze wounds the Bridegroom with love, whose purity beholds God. Here leisure is busy, activity repose. Here God rewards His athletes' exertions with a peace unknown to the world, the joy which is the gift of the Holy Spirit. This contemplative life is the beautiful Rachel dearer to Jacob, though less fertile, than the more fruitful but blear-eyed Leah. The children of contemplation to be sure are fewer than the children of action. But Joseph and Benjamin are loved by their father more than their brothers. This life is that best part Mary chose which shall not be taken from her. It is the lovely Shulamite who alone in Israel was found worthy to cherish and warm the aged David. Would that you, dear brother, might love her alone and in her embraces be warmed with love of God.
>
> If once that love took possession of your soul, the deceptive renown of the world would become cheap in your eyes. You would lightheartedly cast off the burden of riches. You would feel disgust for the pleasures which harm spirit and body. You are well acquainted with the text "If a man love the world and the things of the world"—pleasures of the flesh, lust of the eyes, worldly ambitions—"the charity of the Father is not in him." "The world's friend is God's foe." What could be more wicked,

more insane, more foolhardy, more harmful, more productive of unhappiness than deliberately to oppose His will whose power is irresistible, from whose justice there is no escape? Are we stronger than He? Because His patient compassion still urges us to repent, will He not therefore avenge our contempt? For what can be more perverse, more contrary to reason, justice, nature itself, than to love the creature more than the Creator? What then, dear friend, should you do? Surrender to God's designs upon you, to a truth which cannot delude. He invites us all: "Come to me all you that labour and are heavy burdened and I will refresh you." What grievous and unprofitable toil, then, to be swollen with desires, to be tormented with cares and worries, with fear and sorrow for the objects of your desire. No burden could be heavier than that which thrusts the spirit down from its sublime dignity to the lowest depths. That burden is unrighteousness of any kind. Fly then, brother, from these afflictions and miseries: take refuge from the tempests of the world in a safe and peaceful haven. You well know the words of Wisdom: "Unless a man renounce all he possesses, he cannot be my disciple." No one surely can fail to see how charming, profitable, and pleasant it is to attend His school, where the Holy Spirit is our master, and acquire the divine philosophy which alone bestows true happiness. These are considerations you should weigh most carefully and, if the love of God is no inducement, if you are not attracted by these great prizes, at least fear of penalties should compel you to do so.

For you are well aware of the obligation you contracted and that He is omnipotent and awful to whom you vowed yourself as a pleasing and acceptable offering, One to whom you may not and cannot lie. He does not permit us to mock Him with impunity. You remember that day when you and I and Fulk the One-Eyed were together in the garden of Adam with whom I was staying at that time, how we talked, for a long while I think, of the world's deceitful and fleeting pleasures, the joys of everlasting glory. Inflamed by divine love we pledged and vowed ourselves to the Holy Spirit, promising to forsake without delay the perishable goods of this world, take hold of things eternal and don the monastic habit. This we would have done immediately, if Fulk had not left just then for Rome. We put it off until his return. During the delay caused by his journey and other circumstances which cropped up, divine love became enfeebled, the spirit grew cold, fervour melted away. Now, dear friend, your only course is as quickly as possible to pay so heavy a debt, lest a breach of promise in so weighty a matter and in which you have persisted so long, incur the wrath of the Almighty and thereby fearful pains. For no ruler would suffer a subject to defraud him with impunity of what he had promised, particularly if it were something to which he attached great value. Believe not me but the prophet or rather the Holy Spirit when He says: "To the Lord your God let your vows be made and paid…to God that is feared by awestricken princes, feared among all the kings of the earth."[12] What are those words but a divine admonition to perform what you have vowed? Why are you so reluctant to pay a debt when its payment does not deprive you of anything of worth, does not diminish your wealth, is your gain rather than your Creditor's? Do not then allow yourself to be held back by deceitful riches which cannot free you from poverty, nor by your ecclesiastical dignity which you cannot exercise without peril to your soul. To convert to your own use the property you administer but do not own is, forgive my saying so, as immoral as it is unjust. If in your love of pomp and display you keep a staff of servants which the revenue that is truly your own cannot support, are you not giving to one man what you rob from another? This is neither beneficence nor liberality. For without justice there is

12. Psalm 75. Mgr. Knox's translation.

> no genuine liberality. I hope, however, you are assured that not even to serve the Archbishop who depends very much on your advice, which after all is not likely to be always just or wise, are you entitled to break so solemn a pledge or depart from a love of God whose justice is the measure of its profit. For what is so just, so profitable, so deep-rooted in human nature and in such conformity with it as to love what is good? And what else is so good as God? Nay, rather what is good save God alone? A holy soul therefore which has experienced in some measure the incomparable comeliness, splendour, and beauty of this divine Good is set on fire with love and exclaims "My soul hath thirsted for God, the spring of living water. When shall I appear before the face of God?"

If the motive of fear is not absent from this plea, it soon gives place to the attraction of love, love of God, the perfect Good and the perfect Beauty.

> Do not, I pray you, despise a friend's warning. Do not turn a deaf ear to the plea of the Spirit. Satisfy, my dear friend, my desire and long expectation, that my heart may no longer be harassed by anxiety and fear on your account. For if, which God forbid, you die with your debt unpaid, you will leave me a prey to unremitting sorrow unconsoled by hope. Therefore I entreat you at least to make a pilgrimage to St. Nicholas [his body had just been translated to Bari] and then come on to us here, to see a man who is your devoted friend, the conditions of our life and the rule under which we live that together we may discuss what is profitable to us both. I am confident in the Lord that you will not regret the toil of so long a journey. I have exceeded the limits of a letter. For, since I must miss your bodily presence, I will at least prolong this written conversation. I wish you long-continued health. Bear my advice in mind and do not forget your vow. Be so kind as to send us a life

of St. Remi. For it is not to be had in these parts.

The poignant note of deep and warm affection is almost painfully sensible. Ralph became a monk.[13] But it was at Rheims where he was later Archbishop. He never satisfied the desire of his friend to see him after so many years.

In the autumn of 1101 Bruno was seized by the illness which proved fatal. Assembling the community, he made his solemn profession of faith, particularly in our Lord's Real Presence in the Host, and the Blessed Trinity.[14] On October 6, when his feast is now kept, he died.

Bruno's mortuary roll went on its journey accompanied by an encyclical letter from the monks of La Torre announcing his death and speaking of his dying profession of faith. It was filled with elegiacs, prose tributes, and pledges of prayer, chiefly from France. Among those however who subscribed their tributes were Malmesbury Abbey, the Chapter of Lincoln Cathedral, St. Mary's Abbey, York, the Chapter of York Minster, and the Canons of Beverley Minster.

In the church of Sancta Maria degli Angeli in Rome, formerly Carthusian, is a statue by Houdon. It is a lifelike portrait, not indeed of St. Bruno whose name it bears, but of his contemplation.

Bruno's successor at La Torre was Lanuin who had accompanied him when he founded the hermitage. He has received the honours of a Beatus. For the cultus paid to him at La Torre on April 11 was officially confirmed in 1893.

13. C. B. The Carthusian author, however, of St. Hugh's life, says that he became Archbishop of Rheims.

14. Somewhat strangely, Bruno spoke only of the Spirit's procession from the Father: "*Ex quo*" the Father "*Spiritus Sanctus processionem accepit*." For St. Anselm had just been defending at Bari against the Greeks His double procession.

SAINT HUGH OF LINCOLN

[1140–1200]

OF ALL THE mediaeval saints there is no one of whom we possess a more living portrait than St. Hugh. For he has been fortunate in his biographer. The author of the *Magna Vita* of St. Hugh[1] was his chaplain Adam, a Benedictine monk of the monastery of Eynsham near Oxford, who would later become its Abbot. He entered Hugh's service three years and five days before the saint's death, and during that time spent only one night away from his master. His veracity is unquestioned, proved wherever it can be tested. He possessed an exceptional eye for detail which renders his story often as vivid and as actual as the account of a practiced reporter. Its only fault indeed is an irritating habit of excusing what the writer relates or omits.

There is moreover a life by another contemporary, Giraldus Cambrensis, which provided the material for a life in verse, the *Metrica Vita*. Though far less full, Giraldus' account not only supplies many episodes omitted in the *Magna Vita* but provides another angle on Hugh's personality. The substance of all these sources was used for a life of St. Hugh by a French Carthusian published in 1890. In 1898 an English translation by the late Father Thurston[2] was published. He revised and adapted his original, and enriched it with most valuable appendices and notes. Were this book in print—though one could wish, however, that it had been entirely written by Thurston, instead of the prudish and somewhat unctuous Carthusian—this sketch would be superfluous. Since, however, it cannot now be readily accessible I have, not without hesitation, decided to select what seems to me most illuminating and of most general interest. I have also employed the original text of the *Magna Vita.*[3]

St. Hugh was born in 1140 at Avalon in Burgundy of a noble family, Lords of Avalon. At the age of eight he lost his mother, and his father then quitted the world. Leaving his estates to his eldest son, he became a religious in the neighbouring priory of Villard-Benoît, a small community consisting of seven Augustinian Canons Regular, affiliated to the Canons serving the Cathedral of Grenoble. With him he took his little son Hugh, and the child was solemnly offered to God as a religious. The ceremony took place at Mass when the boy was clothed with the habit. This offering of children to the religious life was a parallel to the betrothal or even marriage of children, not uncommon in royal or noble families. But whereas the latter could be rescinded by the subject's free choice on reaching puberty, until the thirteenth century—and therefore when St. Hugh lived—the child oblate was not permitted by ecclesiastical law to ratify or refuse at puberty the religious state, with its celibacy, to which he had been committed by a parent.[4] Such at least was the law at this period. Objections, however, had already been raised in many quarters, and the fact that Hugh did not take his vows until seven years later proves that it was the custom at Villard-Benoît, as no doubt elsewhere, to permit, even require, free ratification. In principle this dedication of children to the religious life was an indefensible abuse and would finally be abolished. In practice, however, it often worked well, protecting the childhood of studious and devout children from the uncongenial surroundings and

1. Edited for the Rolls Series in 1864 by the Rev. Dimock—a learned and careful editor.
2. Burns and Oates, 1898.
3. In two or three instances I have noticed omissions or interpretations by the Carthusian or Father Thurston with which I am unable to agree. Dom Hugh Farmer of Quart Abbey is, I am informed, preparing a critical edition of the *Magna Vita* with translation, notes, and introduction. I greatly regret that it is not yet available.
4. In the Eastern Church free choice was always required.

education of children brought up to a life of sport and warfare. This was certainly the case with Hugh. Though we hear, it is true, of a master who administered to Hugh the floggings then regarded as an indispensable part of education, he seems to have soon passed into the care of a Canon who truly loved the boy, treated him as a son and moreover recognized his possibilities of exceptional holiness. He would not allow him to take part in the games of other boys educated at Villard-Benoît, but for life in the world. "My dear little Hugh," he would say, "it is for Jesus Christ that I am bringing you up—these sports are not for you."

In this congenial environment Hugh's bent for study and his religious devotion found full satisfaction. At fifteen he took his religious vows and henceforward lived among his fellow Canons. Already he was remarkable for the devotion to liturgical worship which marked his entire life. When later on he had occasion to rebuke slovenliness, carelessness in the celebration of an Office, he could appeal to his own example—could say that he could not remember being guilty of holding up an Office by any blunder that must be corrected.

His father became a chronic invalid incapable of looking after himself. The Prior, probably Hugh's fatherly teacher, entrusted him to the care of his son. It was a devoted service. He guides, when necessary even carries, the old man, washes and dries him, puts on his clothes, makes his bed, prepares and serves his food. So the father ended his days in his son's loving care. As he entered his nineteenth year Hugh was ordained deacon. This however was not, as always today, an immediate step to the priesthood. Many remained deacons for years—even, like St. Francis, for life. Celestine III, when elected Pope in 1191, was still the deacon he had been for sixty-five years.

Not long after, the Prior, now certainly his teacher, sent Hugh, as we should put it today, on the mission. That is to say, he put him in charge of a parish belonging to the Priory of St. Maximin. He insisted on taking with him an older Canon in priest's orders. St. Maximin shortly became a model parish and attracted visitors especially from neighbouring parishes. Offerings flowed in, but not to be spent on the clergy, content with daily necessaries.

It might well have seemed that Hugh was destined to be a mediaeval Curé d'Ars. But like the Curé he was drawn to the contemplative and solitary life, and unlike the Curé would be able for many years to satisfy his attrait. His Prior took him on a visit to the Grande Chartreuse. As the desire of his heart was to keep Hugh in his community, it was from his point of view an imprudence. For Hugh fell instantly and irrevocably in love with the Carthusian life and the Chartreuse. He loved its "situation loftier almost than the clouds, near heaven and remote from the turmoil of human life. Here you could be occupied with God alone. There was undisturbed leisure for prayer." Also there was a fine library. For the humanism of St. Bruno, the university professor, had not deserted his spiritual sons. Books, alone of worldly goods, were prized. Hugh would retain his love of books to the end. During his last visit to France less than three months before his death, he expressed his admiration for the fine library at the Charterhouse of Mont Dieu at Rheims and "inveighed against the lazy neglect of the moderns who not only refuse to imitate the zeal of their fathers in composing and copying books, but will not read or even handle reverently the manuscripts of holy books handed down to them."[5]

Then and there Hugh told the Prior of the Chartreuse his eager desire to be a Carthusian. As in duty bound, the Prior put before him in the strongest terms the austerities of the Carthusian life, unendurable surely by a young man so delicate as Hugh appeared to be. Could he live the life of men "harder than the rocks among which they dwelt, merciless in their treatment of themselves and their fellows? The place was fearful to behold" (our modern love of Alpine scenery, as I have already noted, was rare in the Middle Ages),[6] "the rule extremely hard, the disciplines severe and the hairshirt" perpetually worn "would cut his flesh to the bones." Other monks, however, were more encouraging. Hugh's companion, the Prior, guessed his secret—it must have been easy to

5. I doubt, however, whether the complaint was justified. The twelfth century surely showed more love of literature than the darker ages which preceded it.

6. St. Bruno appreciated mountains, at any rate from a distance. See above, p. 39.

guess—and, when they returned, implored Hugh not to desert his old age. He must swear by our Lord never to become a Carthusian so long as the Prior lived. Affection and gratitude for the moment prevailed and Hugh took the oath asked of him. But having done so he had no peace of mind. His conscience pressed upon him that he was being false to a divine call. Finally he broke an unlawful oath to disobey God's will for him and secretly left for the Grande Chartreuse. It was in 1163 when he was twenty-three years old. Adam asked him if he ever felt any scruple about the broken oath. He assured him emphatically of the contrary. "I have never felt any scruple, but on the contrary intense joy whenever I recall my choice and the blessings I have derived from it."

This time we hear of no opposition to the eager postulant. No sooner, however, had Hugh entered the cell where he hoped to find the peace of God, than he was assailed by a temptation of the flesh[7] so violent it seemed of diabolic origin. Earnest prayer brought our Lord's help, an interior consolation, it would seem, not a vision; and the tempest was followed by calm. It would not, however, be permanent. During these years in the desert war and peace would alternate. But the reward did not disappoint expectation. A hint was given by Hugh to Adam. "Thou, O God," he would say, "gavest me, weary and fainting, to taste from time to time that hidden manna. But that little which by my struggle I merited to savour was such and so great that to obtain it I could lightly despise whatever the world knows of sweet or bitter, smooth or rough. These delights, however, came but seldom and brief the space they endured. I was flung back into the fray." "These secrets of his interior life, which, he lamented, had been changed since he became a bishop, what his human nature endured and the favours God granted, he was wont to relate not only for our consolation but to feed his devotion and increase his humility. For he had, he said, not corresponded as he ought with these graces in the years of youthful strength, and now with age he lacked the strength." The change Hugh deplored cannot, however, have been any diminution of his union with God; it must have been simply

7. *Stimulus carnis*—a goad in the flesh—an exegesis which misunderstood St. Paul's words.

a weaker and less frequent consciousness of it, the result of the episcopal duties which hindered his contemplation. As he travelled about his diocese Hugh's prayer made him oblivious of his surroundings. Possibly passive contemplation—contemplation by infused images—became less frequent. Hugh's normal contemplation was, we may suppose, the imageless and often arid contemplation Baker regards as active and infused, a contemplation, however, which may reach the summits of mystical union. Saints of these earlier times have told us nothing or very little of their life of prayer. The more welcome then such a glimpse as this. The Prior at this time was Basil (1151–1173, died 1179).

Hugh's days were divided between reading, contemplation, and formal prayer—a life austere indeed but with an austerity tempered by discretion. He was entrusted with the care of an aged and infirm monk, as before at Villard-Benoît with the care of his father. An ordination was approaching and the monk told Hugh that, if he wished to be ordained priest, he could. "So far as I am concerned, Father," was his reply, "there is nothing in the world I would like better." "What have you said?" replied the old man. "Oh, what *have* you said? Who would have expected such presumption? How often you have read that he who does not receive the priesthood unwillingly, receives it unworthily. You however, far from being reluctant, as you have yourself admitted, are eager for it." Hugh fell down and begged pardon, weeping. The monk, however, had but tested him and now said, "Be not troubled, you who are no longer my son but my lord, be not troubled, I say. I know with what sentiments you spoke as you did. And I tell you and you will find it true, you will very soon be a priest and later in God's good time a bishop."

Ordained he was, and said Mass with the utmost devotion. At this period Carthusian priests did not, save by special permission, say Mass daily. Hugh celebrated as often as he was permitted and later on when, as bishop, he could do as he pleased, never omitted his daily Mass when it was possible to say it.

Not content with the austerities of the rule Hugh multiplied additional genuflections and prayers. Evidently he was far from sharing the belief that vocal prayer excludes contemplative. In Lent he fasted three times a week on bread and water. His fasts indeed injured his stomach and, in Adam's opinion, were paradoxically the cause of corpulence in later life.

St. Peter, a Cistercian, Bishop of Tarentaise from 1174 to 1191, was a frequent visitor at the Chartreuse, sometimes spending months on end in his cell "raised to the third heaven of contemplation." Once more Hugh performed the congenial office of a personal attendant. Among other services he looked up references for St. Peter in the library, "that vast sea of books." For he was thoroughly acquainted with the Bible, lives of saints, theological treatises. He should be the patron saint of librarians. He washed Peter's feet. And while he was washing his feet and the lower part of his legs the saint would say to him, "My son, the parts above also need washing, wash them without hesitation and wash them well." Since he was too old to climb the steep path without resting on the way, a rough seat had been made for Peter, a plank whose ends were inserted in the trunks of two firs. When he visited the Chartreuse just before his death Hugh showed it to Adam.

In 1173 Dom Basil resigned his office and was succeeded by Dom Guigo, the second Prior of that name. Hugh was chosen to succeed Guigo as Procurator, the monk responsible for the temporal administration of the monastery. As such he left the upper monastery and went to live in the lower house, the monastery of the lay brethren.

Already temporal occupations were beginning to beset his life of prayer. But he could recollect himself at will. As he entered choir for Office, as he took off his outer cloak, he would say to his cares, "Stay here with my cloak: when Office is over, I will take you all up again."

While he was Procurator, an incident occurred which illustrates the harsher aspect of Carthusian life. There was an aged lay brother named Aynard, renowned for his holiness, who had taken part in the foundation of several daughter houses. While in Spain for the foundation of Scala Dei, he made his way to Africa to ransom two hermits captured by Moorish pirates and was successful in discovering them and obtaining their release without ransom. Somewhere about the year 1173 or 1174 he was ordered to go to Denmark to take part in a new foundation. He is said to have been already a hundred years old—hardly a credible age for such a journey. I am disposed to think he must have been many years younger. But he was certainly a very old man, and it is not surprising that he shrank from travelling into a strange land among men he imagined to be as barbarous as the earlier Norsemen. For once he was disobedient and flatly refused to go. He was expelled from the monastery, thrust out of doors. In the depth of winter the old man, scantily clad, made his way on foot from one Charterhouse to another to obtain letters of intercession. When he had obtained them and presented himself once more at the Grande Chartreuse, he was compelled to pass an entire winter's night out of doors, his teeth chattering with cold. Only after this terrific penance was he re-admitted. It is not, I confess, an attractive story, and I am not surprised that the French Carthusian has glossed over the detailed account in the *Magna Vita*. On the other hand Aynard must have been amazingly tough. For he was none the worse for his sufferings and survived thirty years longer.

Hugh's years at the Grande Chartreuse, however, were now drawing to a close. Henry II had decided to found a Charterhouse at Witham in Somerset. In 1178, at his request, monks were sent from the Grande Chartreuse. They were under the charge of Dom Norbert, and among them was Brother Aynard, obedient this time to his Prior's order. The foundation, however, did not prosper. No preparations had been made, no buildings were ready. And the site was inhabited by serfs and tenants of the crown, bitterly hostile to these foreigners whose arrival threatened their homes. The monks were obliged to live in temporary shacks, wooden huts in the forest. Dom Norbert, discouraged, returned to the Chartreuse to find, not altogether justly, treatment more lenient than that meted out to Brother Aynard, and a new Prior was sent in his place, only to die shortly afterwards. King Henry was displeased by the failure of his royal foundation, though it was largely due to his own negligence, and consulted a French nobleman visiting his court. The Count of Maurienne told him that the priory could be saved on one condition, if he could obtain, for Prior, Hugh of Avalon, "a man adorned with every virtue. Everyone who knows him likes him, is charmed indeed by the very sight of him. His words are received as divine oracles." "He will not find foreigners difficult to get on with. For he will love all men and be dear to all. His brethren, however, will be most reluctant to part with him." Henry thereupon dispatched an embassy to the Grande Chartreuse to ask for Hugh. It was headed by Bishop Reginald of Bath. To strengthen their hand the envoys persuaded the Carthusian Bishop of Grenoble to accompany them to the Chartreuse.

Meanwhile Hugh had been assailed by the temptation of the flesh with greater force than ever before. Throughout the night he fought, calling on our Lord for aid, until exhausted by the struggle he fell into a light slumber. In a dream Prior Basil, recently dead, appeared to him and asked what ailed him. "The law of sin and death in my members torments me to death, and unless you come to my aid your servant must die." "Help you I will," replied Basil. With that he took a razor and "cut out a tumour" from Hugh's body. The symbolic cure was effective. From that day, Hugh confided to Adam, he never felt any rebellious motion not easily overcome.

What strikes one particularly in Hugh's later life is the power of God working through his obedient confidence and proving itself more than a match for the power and violence of men. It was no doubt to make the surrender perfect that Hugh was thus permitted to experience the utmost of human weakness, "that the power of God might be displayed in man's infirmity."

When the King's envoys reached the Chartreuse, the Prior, Dom Guigo,[8] at first opposed the request for Hugh. The community was

8. Unfortunately the Carthusian tradition is inconsistent. On the one hand it informs us that it was Prior Guigo who dispatched Hugh to Witham, an event which, as Father Thurston conclusively proves, cannot be dated earlier than 1180. On the other hand it informs us that when his successor Dom Jancelin died in 1233 he had been Prior fifty-eight years, and that he succeeded Dom Guigo, who had resigned his office, in 1176. This contradiction passes unnoticed in the Carthusian-Thurston life. On p. 86 we are told that Guigo sent Hugh to England, and on p. 65 that he resigned in 1180; but on p. 473 that Dom Jancelin became Prior in 1176 and was Prior for fifty-eight years, until 1233. And the same contradiction is found in *La Grande Chartreuse* by an

divided. One monk in particular, Bovo, later to be Prior of Witham, urged the impossibility of keeping such a man as Hugh permanently in seclusion. When his own opinion was asked, Hugh of course declared himself totally unfit and asked the Prior to send Henry a more suitable monk. The entire community was now won over to Hugh's departure. The Prior alone stood out. Like the Augustinian Prior before him he refused to dispense with Hugh's support in his old age. Finally, however, he agreed to abide by the decision of the Bishop of Grenoble. Without hesitation the bishop decided that Hugh must go. Did not St. Benedict, he said, part with St. Maurus? Did not the Heavenly Father send His own Son into the world for our sakes?

Hugh therefore was despatched to England. For the present he would not be completely separated from the Grande Chartreuse. So long as he would be Prior of Witham he would return yearly[9] to attend the General Chapter. But the time would come when his Bishopric would make these visits impossible. Once only, on the verge of death, would he see the beloved monastery where he had found God in prayer.

It was the year 1180 and Hugh was forty years old. The first thing to be done at Witham was to build the community a home. This involved clearing out the inhabitants of the site. It had been the King's intention to give them the option of being transferred to another royal manor or, if serfs, to be freed from serfdom and left to find a living where they

anonymous Carthusian, quite possibly the author of St. Hugh's Life. In the body of the text he tells us that Dom Jancelin was Prior fifty-eight years; in his list of Priors, that he succeeded Guigo in 1180 and was Prior fifty-three years. It is my personal belief that Guigo was still Prior in 1180 and sent Hugh to Witham. The persistent refusal to part with Hugh is more intelligible in an old man oppressed by the burden of office than in Dom Jancelin, who must have been comparatively young, since he would be Prior for over fifty years. We may indeed conjecture that it was the loss of Hugh which decided Guigo to resign the same year. I agree with a suggestion that an erroneous reckoning of Dom Jancelin's Priorate may have arisen from a scribe's error, LVIII instead of LIII, or in Arabic numerals 58 instead of 53. In any case, fifty-eight fits badly. For it takes us back not to 1176 but to 1175—which would leave only two years for Guigo's Priorate.

9. I find it difficult to believe that the Prior of a Somerset Charterhouse must so often make the long and toilsome journey to the Grande Chartreuse. Such however seems to have been the rule.

could. Hugh in the King's name offered them this alternative and they made their choice. For not all the inhabitants of Witham were villains. There were also two private owners, sub-tenants of an overlord, and one of these had no fewer than twenty-seven subtenants. All these were provided with holdings elsewhere on the same terms as before—in effect compulsory purchase, on terms, however, more equitable than are often granted today. Hugh insisted that Henry should pay full compensation for buildings and improvements. Otherwise the monks would return to France. He yielded and paid good money for "huts insecure from age, rotten timber, and crumbling walls." Hugh, however, was not yet satisfied. He returned to Henry. "See, my Lord King," he said, "though a foreigner and a pauper I have enriched you with many houses in your own land." The King with a smile: "I had no wish to be enriched in this fashion. I've no notion to what use this wealth of mine can be put." Hugh: "If you value these things so little, give them to me." Henry: "Whatever can you want with them? Do you not believe I can build you new dwellings?" Hugh: "It is beneath your royal dignity to enquire into such trifles." Henry: "What a man—almost violent on foreign soil! What might he do, if he were to use force, when he presses so hard in words? But before he puts further pressure on me, let him have his will." Hugh restored the materials to their former owners to make what use or profit they could of them.

The King, however, failed to send the funds for building he had promised. The builders pressed for payment and threatened to cease work. Two deputations from the monastery waited on Henry, only to be put off with promises. Finally building operations were suspended. The community urged Hugh to go himself to the King. A monk named Gerard was particularly insistent. Hugh, he said, must tell Henry roundly that, unless the money were forthcoming, the monks would leave. If Hugh shrank from telling the King this, he would. It was decided that Hugh, the fiery-tempered Gerard and old Brother Aynard should go to Henry. Despite Hugh's warnings Gerard burst out in an abusive tirade. The majority of the monks at the Grande Chartreuse were probably, Gerard certainly, like Hugh himself, of noble birth. The feudal baron, prepared to give his overlord a piece of his mind, had banished the humble monk. "Complete the buildings," Gerard exclaimed "or not, as you please. I at any rate am returning to France. Do you suppose you are doing us a favour by providing food we can obtain elsewhere? Keep the money you prize so highly, to leave it to an unworthy heir. Neither Christ nor any good Christian would condescend to touch it." Hugh stood silent, blushing with confusion. When Gerard had finished his outburst, Henry turned to Hugh: "What are you turning over in your mind, my good man? Do you too intend to depart?" In mild tones he replied: "I do not despair of you, my Lord. On the contrary you have my sympathy, hindered as you are by so many anxieties and occupations from caring for your salvation. At the moment you are taken up with business. But when God gives you time you will perform what you have undertaken." Henry embraced him and swore, "As I hope for salvation, so long as I live you shall never leave my kingdom. You shall be my spiritual adviser." He dispatched the funds without further delay and the building proceeded.[10] From this time, despite subsequent quarrels, Henry's affection and regard for Hugh were unshaken. In danger of shipwreck he invoked the aid of his prayers and the storm fell. Such was the favour he showed him that ill-informed gossip declared that Hugh was the King's son, was even prepared to detect a physical resemblance between them. Though Hugh could and would be as uncompromising as St. Thomas had been in the defense of the Church's rights, he possessed a quality wanting to that counterpart of Gerard, the sensitive tact that knows how to say just the right word. Had he, rather than Thomas, confronted Henry at Northampton, victory might have been won without a struggle to the death.

Hugh made use of his influence with the King to equip Witham with a library. He asked Henry for money to buy parchment for copying. He asked for a silver mark. "You grasping fellow," said the King;

10. Of the Witham Charterhouse there remains only the chapel of the lay brothers, used as the parish church of the village. And this chapel, though strengthened and probably roofed by Hugh, was not built by him. Its walls are of earlier date. It must have been a chapel serving the inhabitants of Witham.

"and gave him ten." Hugh also asked for a Bible. Soon after a copy, magnificently written, reached Witham. Later, however, the visit of a monk from Winchester revealed the fact that Henry had put pressure on the monastery to surrender to him a Bible they had just completed. Hugh insisted on returning it, secretly, however, lest the King should be displeased with the Winchester monks. At Witham Hugh continued his Carthusian life of prayer. Even asleep he could be heard repeating "Amen." But it was in his sleep. For he fell asleep as soon as he lay down. As the fame of the newly founded Charterhouse spread, visitors arrived with recruits for the Order, among them monks and Canons. Hugh, however, was cautious about receiving novices. For some left, among them a former Canon of Lewes, named Alexander, who bitterly attacked the Order he had abandoned. Too late he repented and sought in vain to be re-admitted.

But the old monk's prophecy was now to be fulfilled. In May 1186 the Archbishop of Canterbury, Baldwin, and his suffragans held a Council at the Abbey where Adam was a monk, Eynsham. To attend it, the King rode over every day from his palace at Woodstock. Except for a brief interval the see of Lincoln, the most extensive in England, had been without a bishop for nineteen years. For Henry often kept sees vacant, while he enjoyed their revenues. Hugh had taken him to task for this. And it was perhaps as a result of his remonstrances that the Council now decided to fill the Lincoln vacancy. The King was bent on the choice of Hugh. And it was so obviously an excellent choice, that it was not only royal influence which led to its adoption by the Canons who attended the Council for the election. Hugh, however, declined to recognize as valid an election conducted as it had been under the King's eye. Let the Canons, he said, return to Lincoln and there hold a free and canonical election. They did so, but only to re-elect the man who had championed their liberty. Even now Hugh would not accept. As a Carthusian, he said, he was under obedience to the Prior of the Grande Chartreuse, now Dom Jancelin, just as the Archbishop of Canterbury, though primate and leader of the English Church, was subject to the Sovereign Pontiff. Once more a deputation of Canons was sent to the Chartreuse, and this time the reply was not in doubt. Hugh was commanded to accept the see. He bewailed the threat to his contemplative life. "He was afraid intimate contemplation might give place to repulsive phantasms." No doubt he remembered St. Gregory's lament for contemplation, destroyed by his Papal duties. But he bowed to God's will.

It was already September when Hugh left Witham for his consecration in London. To the annoyance of his entourage, he insisted on carrying on his horse a bundle of sheepskins for his bedding. As they were approaching Marlborough, where Hugh was to attend a Council of magnates,[11] an attendant surreptitiously cut the cord and thus got rid of the offensive bundle.

Hugh was consecrated by Archbishop Baldwin at Westminster Abbey on St. Matthew's Day, September 21, and proceeded to Lincoln for his enthronement. When asked by his bailiff how many deer in his park should be slaughtered for the customary banquet, with nonchalant generosity he replied, "Three hundred or more, if there is need." As the story circulated, "the Bishop of Lincoln's deer" became a standing joke. But he refused to pay the Archdeacon the customary fee for his enthronement, which he regarded as simoniacal.

At the Grande Chartreuse Hugh used to feed from his hand the wild birds and squirrels, until the Prior mistakenly forbade it as a distraction. At Witham a barnacle goose frequented his cell and ate from his hand. Nor did she leave him except to hatch her eggs, after which she would present her little family to Hugh. We have now to speak of his famous swan. The *Magna Vita* inserts a detailed account of it written by Giraldus Cambrensis, which Adam completed from his personal knowledge. The day of the enthronement or the day following a swan appeared on the lake at the episcopal manor of Stow, about eight miles from the city. From Giraldus' description of its yellow beak without protuberance, the

11. The *Magna Vita* says Winchester. But I agree with Dimock that it must have been Marlborough. For unlike Marlborough, Winchester is not on the route from Witham to London. Hugh's attendant would find his plebeian bundle particularly offensive when he was to meet the King and a concourse of nobles and prelates.

bird was a species of wild swan known as the "whooper."[12] It killed all the swans on the lake except one female.[13] When shortly afterwards Hugh arrived at Stow, it was decided to make him a present of the bird. To the universal surprise the swan made no resistance to capture and was taken to the Bishop's room. It ate the bread he offered it and became his inseparable companion. Regardless of the company, it showed delight in his caresses. It would bury its head and neck in his sleeves, uttering cries of joy. He would feed it with long strips of bread. When Hugh left Stow the swan returned to the lake. But three or four days before his return it knew he was coming shortly, flew excitedly over the lake, beating the water and flying round with cries of joy. It even left the lake and, as though to meet Hugh, stalked around the inner court or went to the gate. "When the swan was present," Adam writes, "it was impossible for anyone to approach the Bishop without being attacked by it. While he slept it kept guard over the bed. If we had occasion to pass anywhere near, the swan would raise its head threateningly and come forward to bar the way. If we tried to frighten it or use force, it would utter the most hideous cries, so that we were obliged to withdraw for fear of awakening the Bishop."

In Hugh's absence the swan would take food from the bailiff's hand. But on his return it repulsed the bailiff, if he came near it. But Hugh was never forgotten. Once after two years' absence the swan met him with such demonstrations of joy, that it was obvious how impatiently it had been longing for his return. Sometimes its behavior made known that Hugh was coming when nobody was expecting him. "As soon as it heard his voice, it uttered a cry of joy and advanced with extended

12. It is strange that though Giraldus noticed the beak so carefully he must have been wildly astray about the bird's size. He says it was "as much bigger than other swans as a swan is bigger than a goose." In fact, neither the whooper nor the other species of wild swan visiting Britain is larger than the domesticated swan. The length of the whooper and the mute swan is in fact identical, sixty inches. See *The Birds of the British Isles*, T. E. Coward, 6th ed., Vol. 2, pp. 1559. This particular swan may of course have been exceptionally large, but not to the degree Giraldus asserts.

13. Giraldus notes that no family was raised, which he seems to attribute to the chastity of a saint's swan. No doubt mating between the two species was infertile.

wings, followed him into the inner court, walked upstairs after him, and entered his bed chamber."[14]

The year before Hugh's episcopate began, an earthquake had seriously damaged Lincoln Cathedral. Hugh undertook a complete reconstruction. Begun in 1192, it was still in progress when he died. The architect was Geoffrey de Noyers, who however does not seem to have been a Frenchman. For the style of the work is distinctively English. Hugh completed the choir, its aisles, the two eastern transepts and the east side of the west transept—all still existing as then built. He also built an apse to the east of the choir, which was soon demolished, to be replaced by the magnificent Angel Choir or rather retro-choir built over his shrine. Hugh was not content to order and finance the work. When in Lincoln he became a workman himself, a Bishop worker in fact. He hewed stones or carried bricks and mortar. A cripple who asked to be allowed to use his hod was cured of his lameness.[15] The new style of architecture won the admiration of contemporaries. And well it might. It was one of the earliest examples of the style we call "Early English."[16]

14. With this friendship between Hugh and the swan we may compare St. Gregory's story of the hermit Florentius, who shared his cell with a bear which led his flock every morning out to pasture and brought it home at night; or the lion which gave loving service to the Palestinian Abbot, St. Gerasimus. It fetched water from the Jordan and guarded the monastic donkey. When after five years Gerasimus died the lion was inconsolable. It refused to eat, and when taken to the grave refused to leave it, dying there a few days later. This lion has no doubt been erroneously transferred to St. Jerome (Geronimus). (See Thurston's *Butler*, Vol. 1, March, p. 60.) St. Colette, reformer of the Poor Clares in the fifteenth century, had a tame lark and a lamb as faithful as Mary's. For it followed her to chapel, where it was said (by her confessor) to show reverence at the Elevation. It would also precede her to choir and lie down in her stall.

15. The cure, however, is not mentioned in the *Magna Vita*.

16. "English Gothic," writes Bond (*Gothic Architecture in England*, p. 205), "is usually assumed to commence with the building of St. Hugh's choir at Lincoln in 1192. Really, however, the first complete Gothic of England commences with the choir at Wells, as begun by Reginald Fitz Bohun, who was Bishop from 1174 to 1191." Presumably St. Hugh, when Prior of Witham, saw Wells' choir in course of erection, or at least the plans.

And Hugh was equally concerned to provide for the lighting of his cathedral. So many were the candles, Adam tells us, that the brilliance at night vied with daylight.

Hugh indeed never lost sight of the fact that a bishop is first and foremost the chief liturgical minister. He would never permit the least slovenliness in singing the Office. Once he was assisting at Mass with another Bishop, Hugh de Nonant of Coventry. They were then to dine with the King. Not to delay the royal dinner, the Bishop of Coventry wanted a Low Mass and began to read the Introit of a Confessor, *Os justi,* in his speaking voice. Hugh would have none of it and began to chant the Introit with all the notes of the Proper. Like St. Dominic who sang his daily Mass, Hugh seems to have followed an excellent principle, the reverse unfortunately of that obtaining today: do not say Mass if you can sing it. One can imagine his judgment of the numerous parishes where the Mass is not sung, even on Sundays and great feasts. Many bishops, as they rode about their diocese, were content to administer Confirmation perfunctorily on horseback. Hugh would make his way to the nearest church and confer the sacrament with the reverence due to it. An obstinate rustic once refused to accompany him to the church and demanded to be confirmed on the spot. Hugh so far humored him as to dismount and confirm him. But he made the ritual slap, the "alapa," so much of a reality as to make the yokel sensible of his misdemeanor. Another rustic asked Hugh to change his son's luck by changing his Christian name. Hearing the boy's name was John, Hugh turned on the superstitious father. "What more beautiful name could you wish for your son? 'John' signifies the grace of God. Would you have him called fork or rake? You see what a dreadful state of mind your request has thrown me into. I shall give you cause to remember it." And he imposed a severe penance.

Hugh's special devotion was to the dead. He attended any funeral he might meet with on a journey, would, if possible, conduct it. In large towns he would often make a round of funerals—all he could hear of. First Henry II, then Richard, had to wait for his appearance at dinner till he had performed these offices of charity. The King can begin his dinner without me, was his reply to a remonstrance. One St. Stephen's day at Lincoln, when he had finished Mass, he buried the brother of one of his masons, spent the rest of the day at funerals, and once again was late for dinner—a clerical banquet at which the Archdeacon of Bedford was host. When in London to attend an important meeting of nobles and prelates at Westminster he heard that an Abbot, probably Abbot Simon of Pershore, had just died and would be buried at Bermondsey. On account of the meeting, however, his colleagues would be unable to attend the funeral. Hugh thought it his duty to be present at the funeral rather than at the opening of the meeting. He duly performed the last rites. Owing no doubt to the disease which had killed him, and the weather, the Abbot's corpse stank most offensively. All who came near it stuffed their noses with incense or other sweet-scented substances, or carried scent to sniff. Hugh alone took no precaution and seemed quite unconcerned. Though sensitive to smells he had smelt nothing unpleasant. Travelling in France, Hugh noticed by the roadside what appeared to be the mound of a new tomb. On inquiry he learned that a pauper had been buried there, to save the expense and trouble of burying him in the churchyard. Hugh read the funeral office over the body and denounced the negligent priest to his Bishop. Near Buckingham the relatives and neighbours of a man lately dead were tormented by the apparition of the deceased. Hugh, when consulted, refused to countenance the procedure commonly employed in England in such cases, to exhume and burn the corpse. He ordered his Archdeacon to have the grave opened and lay on the breast of the corpse a form of absolution he had written. His instructions were carried out and the ghost effectively laid.

Like many other saints Hugh had a special devotion to lepers, outcast as well as diseased. He would wash, dry, and kiss their feet, embrace the male lepers and speak to all of the heavenly bliss that would more than compensate their earthly sufferings. When his chancellor reminded him that St. Martin's kisses, so it was believed, healed lepers, Hugh replied, "With me it is the other way, the lepers' kisses heal my sick soul."

Hugh loved children, children loved him, little children, even babies. "He would treat them with a playful and tender affection and when they were too little to speak articulate language he drew from them most attractive babbling." He loved to baptize or confirm them. For at this period infants were often confirmed. Woe to any attendant who treated a child roughly. Hugh would not only rebuke but sometimes even cuff the offender. Even shy children came to him readily. Adam saw a child of six months old crowing with delight and stretching out his arms. He clasped Hugh's hands tightly and kissed them. At the same time he pushed his nurse away. Hugh then told the company how, when he stayed at the castle of his brother William on his way from Witham to the Grande Chartreuse, his little nephew, left beside him on his bed, beamed with delight and showed every sign of joy. As Adam observes, Hugh saw God in these children, they were aware of God in him.

Hugh moreover brought up several children in his household, almost all of whom became clerics and received benefices from their patron. We are told in particular of Robert, whom Archbishop Baldwin found at Senlis, a child of five or six. The Archbishop bought him for a trifling sum—a disquieting possibility—and brought him back to Lambeth. When Hugh visited the Archbishop, the child ran at once into his arms. Hugh took him away and later sent him to be educated at Elstow. We hear of little Benedict who riding behind the Archdeacon of Leicester fell into a stream. At Hugh's intercession he was taken out unharmed. We are also told of children cured by the saint—one in particular at Alconbury, who had swallowed a broken knife-blade. When Hugh blessed his throat, the blade came away.

Unfortunately Hugh's contacts could not always be so gracious as these. A mediaeval bishop was fitted tightly into the social and economic structure. He had temporal rights to defend, feudal obligations to fulfil. He must judge many suits, in particular those concerned with wills, which are now decided by the secular courts. Hugh, it is true, did all he could to reduce these secular activities. He would not, like other bishops, supply for the illiteracy of most lay barons by undertaking duties today performed by cabinet ministers, civil servants, and diplomats. Entrapped for a moment to sit down at the Exchequer, he jumped up as soon as his attention was drawn to the fact. He showed his disapproval plainly when Baldwin's successor Hubert combined the functions of Archbishop and Justiciar, roughly speaking, a Prime Minister. He would not even concern himself with accounts, but left the financial business of the diocese to an official, as St. Ambrose had left it to his brother, the layman St. Saturus.

Judge, however, he must, and maintain the rights and liberties of his see. Moreover he must enforce discipline on clerics and laymen alike. A wealthy knight, for example, under his wife's thumb had conspired with her to defraud his brother of his inheritance by palming off a supposititious child as his own, and, more afraid of his wife than his Bishop, had refused to confess the crime. He died a sudden death the night after excommunication and, though she finally confessed, his wife's last days were unhappy, her death painful. An excommunicated forester was shortly afterwards murdered and mutilated. The wife of an Oxford tradesman[17] who had attempted a bigamous marriage and, in the Bishop's presence, spat in her husband's face when he came forward to receive her back, also found Hugh's sentence of excommunication a sentence of death. So dreaded indeed was his excommunication that when King Richard had decided to send the captain of his guards, the savage Marchadaeus, to Lincoln to enforce his will on the Bishop, he was advised not to expose to such danger a man whose services he valued so highly. Prudence prevailed.

In this age of violence, when spiritual power was at grips with material force, penances were often severe. At Brackley servants of the Earl of Leicester had dragged a thief from the sanctuary of a church and hanged him. The penance imposed by Hugh was grim. In the cold of winter, naked save for a pair of drawers, they must dig up the rotting corpse of their victim and bury it in the churchyard, receiving moreover a flogging from the local clergy. In the same state of semi-nudity—barefoot in the

17. Until the reign of Henry VIII Oxford belonged to the diocese of Lincoln.

slush or snow of the streets—they must visit every church in Lincoln—and in mediaeval Lincoln there were at least forty-nine churches—and be flogged at each. All submitted except the steward, who fled to France. But his master disowned him and he sank into such complete wretchedness that, when Hugh was in Normandy, he begged for pardon on any terms and was thankful to accept a seven years' penance.

The forester mentioned above was not the only forester to come into conflict with Hugh. In feudal days a forest, not necessarily wooded, "was a territory declared such by the king" set apart for the royal chase "within which the code of forest law superseded the common law of the land."[18] It was a ruthless code, ruthlessly administered by ruthless functionaries, the foresters. They were generally and deservedly detested. In the royal antechamber, in grim jest Hugh had told some foresters that just as their jurisdiction was outside—"foris"[19]—the legal system of the realm, they would be outside—"foris"—the kingdom of heaven. The chief forester, Galfrid, presuming on his power and the royal favour, encroached upon the rights of the Church of Lincoln. Hugh promptly excommunicated him and by doing so gave great offence to Henry. The King's indignation, fanned by courtiers jealous of Hugh's influence, was not lessened when the Bishop refused his request to bestow a vacant prebend on a courtier at Henry's request. "See how ungrateful he is," said the courtiers, "for all you have done for him."

Henry summoned Hugh to meet him at Woodstock. He was then at Dorchester, the village on the Thames from which Remigius had removed his see to Lincoln. The King prepared to overawe him by a theatrical display of his displeasure. He gathered his courtiers, magnates of the realm, round him in a glade near the palace, and they sat down in a circle. No one, were the King's orders, was to make room for the Bishop or return his greeting. Hugh arrived, greeted the King and his lords. No one took any notice. Stony silence. He came closer and shouldered his

18. I have made use of the definition in the *Encyclopaedia Britannica*, 11th edition, Article "Forest Laws."

19. Hence the name "forest," territory outside.

way into the circle, thrusting himself between the King and the nearest baron. The silence continued. To relieve the tension the King asked for a needle and thread and began to sew a rag[20] round a finger he had cut. Hugh broke the silence. Turning to Henry, he said: "You remind me now of your ancestress at Falaise." Those who understood the point of the remark were astounded at his audacity, the others were puzzled. But the King burst into fits of laughter, rolling on the ground in his mirth. His anger was extinguished. "You seem not to understand," he said, "the impertinence of this foreigner. I will explain it myself. The mother of my great-grandfather William the Conqueror was of humble origin. She was born at Falaise, a place famed for its tanneries. When he saw me sewing this cloth round my finger, he said I was like my relations in that city." In this melting mood he accepted Hugh's defense of his action in excommunicating the forester and refusing the benefice. Galfrid must obtain his reconciliation with the Church by a public flogging. It is surprising, though edifying, to hear that the humiliation, instead of making him Hugh's mortal enemy, was the beginning of a warm friendship. The mediaeval man, good or bad, was a child and like a child liable to sudden and violent emotional changes. Hence also his need of stern discipline, whether the self-discipline of the ascetic or the discipline imposed by the Church.

On three occasions, Adam tells us, Hugh faced an angry mob and overawed it. It was in Lincoln Cathedral, in Holland, a district of Lincolnshire, and at Northampton. Though he refuses to tell us the occasion of these riots, other information and our knowledge of contemporary events enable us to answer the question with certainty or very great probability.

The riot in Lincoln Cathedral was no doubt connected with the anti-semitic pogroms which, beginning at his coronation, disfigured the opening of Coeur de Lion's reign. We are informed that a mob burst into York Minster, seized the bonds of Jewish creditors deposited there for safety, and burned them on the spot. The mob no doubt was

20. "Panniculus." Possibly, in this instance, a piece of leather.

attempting to do the same in Lincoln Cathedral. For the Jewish colony in Lincoln was second in size to the London Jewry and perhaps richer. A Lincoln Jew, Aaron, had St. Alban's Abbey deeply in his debt. The clergy attending on Hugh cowered in terror beneath the altar stones. Hugh stood firm and in the literal sense put the fear of God into the rioters.

The Northampton riot was also connected indirectly with the antisemitic outbreaks. A rascal named John who had taken part in a pogrom at Stamford carried off to Northampton the booty he had plundered from the Jews. He entrusted part of it to a man no better than himself who, to get possession of the entire loot, murdered John. His body was discovered and the townsfolk proceeded to the popular canonisation of a martyr to Jewish hatred of Christ. A shrine was erected and adorned and offerings began to flow in. It came to the Bishop's knowledge and he was not slow to put a stop to this cultus of a scoundrel. But he had to face the wrath of the townsfolk thus deprived of their shrine, its prestige, and its offerings.

Just as he had demolished this shrine at Northampton, Hugh ordered the nuns of Godstow near Oxford to remove from their choir, where it lay in a prominent tomb decked with silk and surrounded by burning tapers and lamps, the body of King Henry's mistress, the celebrated "fair Rosamund," and bury it in the cemetery among the undistinguished dead.

The riot in Holland was, it would seem, an episode in a violent dispute between the monasteries of Croyland and Spalding. On this occasion Hugh was supported by his brother, William of Avalon, on a visit to England. William snatched his sword from a rioter who threatened his brother's life, and would have dispatched him on the spot. Hugh forbade physical violence. The censure of the Church was, he said, a weapon more powerful than any a soldier could wield. In his hands it undoubtedly was.

This spiritual power, however, so evident in the field of external conflict, was the effect and expression of Hugh's profound life of contemplative prayer. He did not suppose a life of exterior service could supply for a lack of interior spiritual life, could ever be fruitful without it. So absorbed was he in prayer that on his many journeys he was oblivious of the scenes through which he rode. It cannot be said that he shared St. Bruno's appreciation of beautiful scenery. An attendant on horseback rode just ahead of his horse, which followed automatically. The Bishop therefore had no more need to find his own way than a man today who travels by omnibus or train.[21]

We have already remarked upon Hugh's devotion to the Mass. It would seem to have been recompensed by a symbolic vision of our Lord's Eucharistic Presence.

One day Hugh was consecrating a chalice at his Buckden manor and taking occasion to contrast the offering with the neglect shown by too many priests to provide decent ornaments of worship.[22] A monk arrived from Adam's monastery of Eynsham. As he was saying psalms for the repose of the dead, an interior voice had urged him to go to the Bishop of Lincoln and inform him of the divine indignation against clerical abuses. As he waited till Hugh had finished his Mass, the monk saw at the Consecration the apparition of a Child. After Mass he gave him his message and for proof of its divine origin told him what he had seen. Hugh presumably had also seen the Child. The same monk somewhat later, in a long cataleptic trance during the last days of Holy Week, had a detailed vision of Purgatory which has come down to us. Among its inmates he saw the late King Henry and Archbishop Baldwin in grievous torment. That the vision was woven by subconscious artistry does not disprove a genuine intuition of truth translated into these images by the subconscious. Nor should we be surprised that the spiritual suffering of Purgatory should be represented by images of physical torment. Simple minds—and even the greatest mediaeval

21. This absorption in prayer is difficult to reconcile with Hugh's statement to Adam that his experience of God's presence had diminished since he became Bishop.

22. For all the splendid furniture of cathedrals and collegiate or monastic churches, parish churches were often ill-equipped with ornaments required for the liturgical services. They became progressively better furnished and at the sixteenth-century spoliation were richly supplied. This was not the case in contemporary Spain (see below, p. 172).

intellects were in many respects naïve—required this pictorial language to convey spiritual truth through the imagination. In this connection we should do well to bear in mind the wise words of the Cambridge Platonist, John Smith: "Divine truth hath its humiliation and exinanition as well as its exaltation. If God should speak in the language of eternity who could understand Him or interpret His meaning… Truth is content when it comes into the world to wear our mantles, to learn our language… It speaks with the most idiotical [simple, naïve] sort of men in the most idiotical way and becomes all things to all men for their good." Here lies the explanation not only of the monk of Eynsham's vision but of the imaginative visions so common in the lives of many saints.[23]

Whatever Eucharistic visions Hugh may have enjoyed, he refused when in France the invitation of a priest to visit what he claimed to be a miraculous Host with appearances of flesh and blood. Let those go who had no faith in the teaching of the Church. His faith sufficed for him.[24]

To maintain this contemplative life Hugh retired yearly, usually in autumn, to Witham for a long retreat, a month or even two months. As he drew near his face lit up with joy. Here he lived like a simple monk, enjoying no special privilege. With the rest of the community he queued at the refectory door after supper on Sunday to receive the loaf which must serve for the following week. Sometimes he even collected crusts. He washed up with such care "that you might suppose he was handling a chalice."

On one of these visits Brother Aynard all but repeated his disobedient refusal to go to Denmark. For he left the Priory and set out to return to the Grande Chartreuse. Hugh won him back by a stratagem. Overtaking the fugitive he said he would resign his see and accompany him. Aynard implored him not to desert his post of duty. "Very well," Hugh replied, "let us make a compact. I will remain at Lincoln, if you

23. Blessed Osanna, for example, or St. Teresa.

24. In any case the beautiful image of a living child was very different from the crude and repulsive appearances of the French "miracle."

remain at Witham." His tact saved Aynard from a second and irretrievable disaster.

Giraldus Cambrensis, well acquainted with both, depicts an instructive contrast between a good man, the well-intentioned and conscientious Archbishop Baldwin, and a saint: "The Archbishop was slow and sparing of speech, Bishop Hugh a pleasant companion full of talk and fun; the one was gloomy and timid, the other bright and cheerful of heart as if his mind were free from cares… The one [Baldwin] was slow and self-restrained in his anger as in all other things, the other [Hugh] could easily be roused even upon a small occasion"—Hugh spoke of himself as "peppery": "The Archbishop was smooth-spoken, lukewarm, and easy-going, Hugh on the other hand brusque, full of enthusiasm, and a strict disciplinarian."

To finance his Crusade and later his warfare against the French King Philip Augustus, Richard Coeur de Lion was in chronic want of funds. He therefore lent a ready ear to any suggestion for mulcting the possessions of the Church, a practice which led inevitably to collisions with a champion of the Church's rights so intrepid as Hugh.

On the first occasion, however, the Bishop was obliged to accept a costly compromise. In the earlier part of the century a custom had been permitted to grow up by which the Church of Lincoln made the King the yearly present of a mantle trimmed with sable. It had lapsed for many years until Richard suddenly demanded the payment of arrears. All Hugh could do was to purchase for his church future immunity from the annual charge by payment of a large lump sum. To raise it he decided to retire to Witham until the consequent reduction in expenditure had recouped the cost. His clergy, however, determined not to be deprived of their beloved Bishop, raised the money by subscriptions among themselves which, however, Hugh insisted must be voluntary. This happened in the year 1194.

The following year Hugh successfully challenged the claim of the crown to appoint the Abbot of Eynsham—Adam's monastery. For the right of the see of Lincoln had been officially recognised by the Conqueror.

In December 1197 a Council of barons was held at Oxford. The King, through the Justiciar Archbishop Hubert, demanded from them all bishops as well as lay barons—a supply of troops for his war in France. The bishops were for consenting. "*Episcopi semper pavidi*"—"bishops are always timid"—was a mediaeval adage. Hugh, however, was a bishop of different caliber. He took a firm stand on the principle that his church was bound to provide military service only in England. The Bishop of Salisbury took courage and supported him. Baffled and irate, the Archbishop dissolved the Council and informed Richard who was responsible for his failure. The King was even more angry and ordered the possessions of the two offending prelates to be confiscated. This was carried out in the case of the Bishopric of Salisbury, and the Bishop was obliged to redeem the property of his see by payment of a heavy fine. But no one dared face Hugh's dreaded anathema.

The impasse continuing, Hugh decided to approach Richard in person, and the following August (1198) he crossed to France. He found Richard at the castle he had just built, the Chateau Gaillard, in the chapel, surrounded by prelates, hearing the solemn Mass of St. Augustine (August 28). As he entered the chapel the choir was singing the sequence: *Ave inclyte presul Christi*—"Hail noble Pontiff of Christ"—a suitable welcome to Hugh himself. Hugh went straight up to Richard and asked for his kiss—the more effusive mediaeval equivalent of our handshake. Richard turned his face away and looked in the opposite direction. Hugh then took hold of the King's mantle and shook it violently. "Give me your kiss," he said. "For I have travelled a long way to see you." "You have not deserved a kiss" was his reply. Hugh shook the mantle even more violently and held it fast in his hand. "I *have* deserved it," he said. "Now, kiss me." As with Henry at Woodstock, his bold tactics were successful. Richard, admiring his courage, smiled and kissed him. After Mass he expostulated with the King, who threw the blame on Archbishop Hubert. At Richard's invitation Hugh accepted hospitality at his castle of Porte Joie. The following day in a private interview he enquired as to the state of Richard's soul. "You, my lord King," he said, "belong to our diocese"—in virtue no doubt of his palace at Woodstock—"and therefore as your pastor I am responsible for the health of your soul, redeemed by God's blood and accountable to His judgment. Tell me then how it stands with your soul." Richard replied that except for hating his enemies he had a good conscience. On his deathbed, possibly remembering this conversation with Hugh, he did forgive the archer who had inflicted a mortal wound.[25]

Hugh's departure, however, was less amicable. For he declined to take back with him letters asking for financial assistance. It was the last time he would see Richard alive.

Shortly afterwards Coeur de Lion defeated his enemy King Philip at Gisors. He attributed his victory to Hugh's prayer. It was not, however, as complete as it might have been. He did not, as at one moment seemed certain, capture Philip. For he was rescued by the timely intervention of a French baron as valiant as himself, the man who would become Blessed John of Montmirail.[26]

Toward the close of the year, however, trouble recurred. Through the obsequious Hubert, Richard sent Hugh twelve letters to be given to twelve Canons of Lincoln requiring them to proceed to Normandy and place themselves at the King's service, in other words to act as unpaid diplomats. Hugh flatly refused to detach his clergy from their ecclesiastical duties. Once more Richard lost his temper and once more ordered confiscation of Hugh's possessions. And this time he compelled a knight, Stephen of Turnham, on pain of death to execute his order. Stephen, though he dared not come in person to Lincoln, sent a body of officers to attach the property of the see. Once more Hugh set out for France to confront Richard in person, hoping to repeat his victory of the previous autumn. On his way to London, pressing the right of sanctuary as belonging to a bishop's person—a proposition, it seems, legally dubious—he rescued a condemned man from the gallows. And at Buckden he converted or cured a woman who was regarded and

25. Unbeknown, however, to the King, or after his death, Marchadaeus had him flayed alive.

26. See below, p. 87.

regarded herself as a witch. Not long before, at Cheshunt, he had cured a lunatic tied hand and foot to a post.

As Hugh passed through Rochester a man came to meet him and through an interpreter told his unhappy story. Despairing of pardon for grievous sin, he was on the verge of suicide. That very morning only the presence of a crowd had prevented him from throwing himself off the bridge into the Medway. Hugh dispelled the temptation, took him with him to the coast, reconciled him and left him penitent and comforted, to make a pilgrimage to Rome from which he would return to embrace the monastic life.

In February 1199 Hugh was once more in Normandy. At Angers, at the beginning of Lent, in the Bishop's absence he performed an ordination at St. Nicholas' Abbey of the Order of Grandmont. But he refused the request of his Oxford Archdeacon, Walter Map, to ordain one of his servants a subdeacon. He gave no reason—probably could not do so. It was what we should call a hunch. When pressed he showed that peppery temper which was with him to the end. It was not long before the man became a leper, "in punishment of his faults," Adam says.

At Angers he met some Canons of Hereford on their way to the King to arrange the election of a new Bishop. The candidate they favoured was Walter Map. They were afraid, however, that Richard in his present mood would not accept a Lincoln ecclesiastic. They therefore joined with some Lincoln Canons in imploring Hugh to offer the King financial aid. He could then return to his diocese, before the state of Normandy in the throes of war made return impossible. Badgered persistently, Hugh weakened so far as to say he would give his final answer next day. That night as he lay asleep he heard a voice utter a text from Psalm 67: "God is wonderful in His saints, even the God of Israel. He shall give His people might and strength. Blessed be God." It was Saturday, the day of Hugh's weekly confession. He confessed his hesitation the previous day and stood firm.

The same day the Abbess of Fontevrault sent him a secret message that Richard had been wounded and his condition was critical. She knew this, because Queen Eleanor had been her guest when Richard summoned her to his deathbed. Hugh had agreed to pontificate at the Palm Sunday ceremonies at Angers cathedral. For the recently elected Bishop had not returned from Rome. On his way, however, to the city on the Saturday (April 10) he was met by Gilbert de Laci who informed him that Richard had died and would be buried (near his father) at Fontevrault the following day. He insisted on attending the funeral, though warned that brigands had made the roads unsafe. "For," Adam comments, "he was the righteous man who in every danger was confident and undaunted *as a lion.*" He must surely intend to contrast his master as the Coeur de Lion of spiritual warfare with the royal Coeur de Lion of valor in the field. When his followers expostulated he replied that the wrongs Richard did him were the work of bad advisers. He himself was always courteous. Therefore he must not fail him in death. On his way to Fontevrault he turned aside to visit and console the widowed Queen Berengaria.[27] He said Mass for her and gave her his blessing. He reached Fontevrault on Palm Sunday just as the funeral cortege was entering the Abbey church.

The following Wednesday, April 14, John was accepted as King at Chinon, to the exclusion of his elder brother's young son Arthur, with whom, however, he had just been staying in Brittany. He sent for Hugh, received him with every mark of honour and asked him to stay with him till he went to England. Hugh refused but accompanied the King to Saumur and Fontevrault. Only with reluctance did he consent to inform the nuns of John's promised gifts. For he did not trust him to keep his word. John showed Hugh an amulet, a stone set in gold, an heirloom which he wore round his neck. It had, he said, been promised that its royal wearer could not lose any of his ancestral domains. Hugh bade him rather trust in God. On the porch at Fontevrault a representation was carved of the Last Judgment. Hugh meaningfully pointed out the kings among the lost and warned him not to lose sight of possible damnation. For the moment John was all meekness, returning the

27. We may notice that the dying King had sent not for his wife but for his mother. It suggests, pathetically, something of the child in Richard.

salute of everyone he met on the road. Next Sunday (Easter Sunday, April 18), however, he showed his true colours. For when he should have made the celebrant, Hugh, an offering of gold pieces, he stood irresolute, turning them over in his hand. When Hugh asked for an explanation he said, "I am thinking that had I had these gold pieces a few days ago, I should not have offered them to you but kept them for myself." Hugh's reply to this irreverent insolence was to bid the King throw the coins into a basin. He would not touch them. He preached a long sermon on good and bad rulers. The congregation applauded but John sent messages to bid him leave off. He was hungry for his dinner. No notice was taken.

Soon after, at his investiture as Duke of Normandy, when in the same irresponsible spirit he turned round to grimace at his boon companions, John let fall the banner of the duchy just placed in his hand—an omen of the future. Hugh had already left on his return to England. On the journey, at La Flèche, his horses and baggage were stolen. He duly proceeded to celebrate a Pontifical Mass, and when he left the church the stolen property was returned. What bishop today would pontificate under such circumstances? Nor at Le Mans would he curtail Matins for a surprise attack upon the town by a Breton army sent by Arthur's mother. He made his way out of the town in safety. On his return to Lincoln, by moral pressure he compelled a powerful citizen of London, Jordan de Turri, to restore the inheritance of two orphans. Admitting that Jordan would be able to defeat his clients at law by the influence he could bring to bear, he warned him that he would inform the Pope, who had committed the case to him, that alone in England Jordan defied his authority. Jordan yielded and the orphans had justice.

The autumn after his return Hugh made what would be his last visit to Witham. While staying in the monastery, by his prayer he prevented a fire which had broken out from doing more damage than the destruction of a wooden kitchen already condemned as unsafe and in any case to be replaced by a building of stone. The following spring Hugh visited Stow. This time the swan did not come to meet him. It remained aloof and melancholy in the center of the lake. At the end of three days it allowed itself to be caught, but gave no sign of joy at the sight of the Bishop. It stood with head hanging down, a picture of sorrow. When Hugh died six months later it seemed evident that the swan had known it was his last visit. It survived Hugh several years.

John had asked Hugh to be present at the treaty of peace with the French King, to be signed at Les Andelys on May 22, 1200. He accepted the invitation and was witness to a peace, destined however to be no more than a truce.

On May 31, Hugh set out for a last visit to the home of his soul, the Grande Chartreuse. At Paris he stayed with a master of the university named Raymund, later to be a Canon of Lincoln and Archdeacon of Leicester. Such close links between the Churches in England and in France were later destroyed by the growth of nationalism, and unhappily exist no longer.

In Paris Hugh was visited by the son of King Philip, later Louis VIII, and by Arthur. Louis received his words with respect, but Arthur scornfully rejected his advice to be at peace with his uncle. Louis invited him to visit his child bride, Blanche of Castile, in riper years to bear him St. Louis. She was unhappy. The reason we are not told. It may well have been that at the age of twelve she had left her parents' home to go to a foreign husband in a foreign land.[28]

On his way to the Chartreuse Hugh visited the hospice where, near the supposed relics of the Egyptian father of monasticism, sufferers from the strange disease known as St. Antony's fire were received and nursed. At Grenoble, still ruled by the same Carthusian Bishop whose decision had sent Hugh to England, he was received with public rejoicing. In the Cathedral he sang Mass and preached and baptised his nephew, the son of Count William.[29] It was St. John the Baptist's Day.

---

28. In later years when she will be Queen of France, Blanche will be a friend of Blessed Jordan of Saxony, and ask his advice. See below, p. 115.

29. Though it is certainly surprising that the baptism was deferred till the age of seven, it is not easy, with the French Carthusian and Father Thurston, to understand Adam's *baptizavit* as meaning no more than "supply ceremonies omitted at a private baptism." Adam, we must not forget, was present.

Next day Hugh set out for the Chartreuse. The Prior was Dom Jancelin, who had taken office in 1180 shortly after Hugh's departure from England.[30] There he spent three weeks, sharing fully, as at Witham, the monks' life. Visitors, however, he could not avoid. He spent three days with the lay brothers in their lower monastery. He also received the poor of the neighbourhood, giving lavish alms. Before his departure he gave the community a collection of relics. He would also have given a ring he wore at ordinations, containing the relics he prized most highly, had he not been reminded that it had been promised to Our Lady of Lincoln.[31]

On his return journey Hugh spent two days at the Castle of Avalon with his brothers William and Peter. He also visited the Canons of Villard-Benoît where he had made his apprenticeship of the religious life. He gave them a fine copy of the Bible. He also visited the parochial cell of St. Maximin where he was greeted affectionately by former parishioners, now aged men and women. At Belley he saw in the cathedral the shrine of his old friend St. Anthelmus and venerated what was believed to be a portion of the Baptist's hand. He visited the Charterhouse of Arvières to see a future saint, Arthaud, who also had been Bishop of Belley but had resigned his see, and was now a very old man. He had sent to beg Hugh to visit him. They met on July 25 and spoke at length of the heavenly bliss they both desired so ardently. Hugh, however, refused Arthaud's request that he would inform the community of the terms of the peace concluded at Andely. It was not for monks to concern themselves with politics. The older man lived the longer—until 1206, when he was said to be a hundred and five years old.

Hugh then visited Cluny and was edified where St. Bernard had taken scandal; and Cîteaux, where he said Mass on the Assumption. At the request of Jean de Bellesmes who had retired from his see of

30. See above, pp. 53–54, note 8.

31. Hugh, it must be confessed, carried his devotion to relics to extravagant lengths, when he bit off two fragments of a supposed bone of St. Mary Magdalen presented to his veneration and defended his action by a view of our Lord's Sacramental Presence not easy to reconcile with the theology of St. Thomas as expressed, for example, in the Lauda Sion: "*Signi tantum* fit fractura."

Lyons, he went on to Clairvaux. He asked the Archbishop, well known for his devotion to Scripture, which was his favourite book. "The Book of Psalms," he replied. "I make it my constant subject of meditation. In it I find a charm that is ever new, which captivates my understanding, and an unfailing food which nourishes and strengthens my soul." Hugh spent two days at the Charterhouse of Mont Dieu at Rheims, where he expressed his appreciation of its well-furnished library. He then visited another Charterhouse near Laon and from there made his way towards the coast. His health was beginning to fail. He stopped at St. Omer, where he was bled, but could eat hardly anything for three days. Nevertheless on the eve of our Lady's birthday (September 7) he dragged himself to the neighbouring Cistercian Abbey of Clairmarais,[32] where he passed the night in the infirmary. Next day he said Mass and returned, still fasting, to St. Omer. He felt somewhat better. On Saturday September 9 he reached Wissant, where he embarked for England on September 10. In this connection Adam speaks of a special devotion of the sailors to St. Anne, not to be placed in the calendar for nearly two centuries. They prayed to her for a fair wind, a devotion shared by Hugh.[33] A favourable breeze soon sprang up and in a few hours Hugh reached Dover where his first act was to say Mass in honour of our Lady. It was the last Mass he would celebrate.

Hugh had hoped to attend a Council of Bishops summoned by the Archbishop to meet at Westminster. When, however, he reached London on September 18 he was so ill that he was compelled to take to his bed at the town house of the Lincoln diocese in Holborn. Here he lingered for two months on his deathbed. His sentiments were those of the dying St. Martin. If it were the divine will he was ready to return to his see; if not, he would be glad to go to God.

On September 19 he spoke at length to Adam of the evil times he foresaw for England. He gave him to understand that the offspring of

32. He could not say Mass in a parish church. For France was then under an interdict.

33. Presumably the special devotion of the Bretons to St. Anne is derived from this devotion of seamen. So many Bretons are fisher folk.

the marriage between Henry II and Eleanor, which he stigmatised as adulterous, would be rooted out, destroyed by Philip Augustus. Writing under the impact of the loss of Normandy and the interdict, Adam regarded this forecast as prophetic. We must, however, rather see in it an instructive instance of the human limitations even of a saint. For a descendant of Henry and Eleanor sits on the British throne today, whereas no descendant of Louis VII and his son rules in France. Moreover, since the Church had annulled the marriage between Louis VII and Eleanor on the ground of undispensed consanguinity—they were first cousins—it is not easy to understand how St. Hugh could denounce Eleanor's subsequent marriage to Henry as adulterous, the less so that he had no condemnation for the subsequent marriages of Louis, from the latter of which Philip had been born. Sanctity is not infallible nor even perfectly consistent.

On September 21, the anniversary of his consecration, Hugh received Viaticum and Unction after a semi-public confession. Urged to make his will, he declared his reluctance to do so. Bishops, he said, have nothing to leave. Everything they possess belongs of right not to themselves but to the Church. Nevertheless, to make certain his possessions would not be seized and improperly applied, were he to die intestate, he bequeathed them to the Dean of Lincoln and the Archdeacons to distribute to the poor.

King John visited him and was lavish in words of respect and sympathy. Nor was he, I believe, insincere. For he consistently displayed his regard, even reverence, for Hugh. And he showed the same respect for the saintly hermit, Robert of Knaresborough, though Robert spoke to him rudely. After all, he had Catholic faith and with it an awe, were it even somewhat superstitious, for those generally recognised as God's friends. Hugh, however, received his advances with marked coldness, though he did commend his will to the royal protection. Throughout, his attitude to John contrasts strikingly with his attitude to Henry and Richard. It is difficult to resist the conclusion that whereas he believed Henry and Richard had saved their souls, he was convinced John would be damned.

Another visitor was Archbishop Hubert, who hinted that the dying man might well express sorrow for his frequent opposition to himself. Hugh's reply was blunt. "I am well aware that I have often annoyed you. But my sole regret is that I did not oppose you more often and, if God should spare my life, I am resolved to take a firmer line towards you. I have too often offended God, because I shrank from offending you."

During these two bedridden months Hugh continued to display his love of the liturgy. He had the Offices chanted in his room, insisting as always on punctilious observance of ceremonies, careful and reverent pronunciation of the words. He received Communion frequently but does not seem to have had Mass said in his room, a scruple doubtless of reverence.

Obedient to the command of the Archbishop, supported by the Prior of Witham, Hugh consented to break his Carthusian abstinence and ate a little meat. But he would not dispense with his hairshirt, though it cut into the flesh and produced deep sores. Nor would he, though in burning fever, take off his thick and rough habit.

His last days were saddened by the insolence and ingratitude of his steward Pontius whom he had raised from beggary to this position of trust. "I am more necessary to the Bishop," he said, "than he is to me." So badly did Pontius behave that Hugh cursed him on his deathbed. Though he repented afterwards of the anger he felt when he did it, he believed the curse itself to have been uttered under an impulse from God and would not withdraw it. Retribution overtook Pontius. After falling three times into the hands of brigands he died, at Angers, a most painful death.

A meeting of barons and bishops was to open at Lincoln in November at which William King of Scots would do homage to his overlord King John. Hugh sent for his architect and bade him complete the chapel of St. John the Baptist, probably the chapel in the apse. For it was his wish to be buried there. He must be buried in the simple vestments he wore at his consecration and with the same ring, a sapphire of inferior value, lest more valuable ornaments might tempt a thief to rob his corpse. And his tomb must be against a wall, that no one could stumble over it.

As his suffering increased, Hugh often cried out in prayer, "Merciful Saviour, give me rest." "Blessed," he exclaimed, "are those whom the Day of Judgment will introduce into endless rest." To which Adam replied, "The Day of Judgment is coming for you. God will soon deliver you from the burden of the flesh." "No," said Hugh, "the day of my death will not be a day of judgment, but a day of grace and mercy." In this confidence he agrees rather with St. Thérèse of Lisieux, certain of heaven and sanctity, than with her namesake of Ávila, afraid that her nuns believing her to be in heaven might fail to aid her in purgatory.

The day before he died Hugh had a Gospel read, ending where the Gospel read at a funeral Mass begins. And in reply to a question he solemnly testified that never had he knowingly pronounced an unjust judgment for fear or favour. He had made arrangements for monks from Westminster and clerks from St. Paul's to be present when he died, that a liturgical life might be crowned by a liturgical death.

Adam, who draws an elaborate comparison between Hugh and St. Martin, a saint for whom Hugh had a particular devotion, seems to have hoped that his master would go to heaven on St. Martin's feast. It was not to be. Death, however, came within the octave. Hugh died on Thursday, November 16, shortly after sunset, lying, as he had commanded, on the floor on a cross of ashes, while the assembled clergy were singing Compline and had begun the *Nunc dimittis*: "Now lettest Thou Thy servant depart in peace."

The previous night Adam had dreamed that a large and beautiful pear tree lay uprooted in the garden. It represented Hugh. He lifted it up easily, held it in his arms and detached some branches. The gesture signified the life of Hugh he was to write. After Hugh's death he dreamed a second dream. He was in a large church where he heard singing more beautiful than any he had heard on earth. The Bishop was lying on a couch richly adorned. He signed to Adam to approach. A crowd present melted into the background and Adam drew near. Hugh rose to his feet, took Adam's hand and led him to a remote altar. He bade him ask what he desired to know. How has his master fared since death? "I have never ceased to hear this sweet music." Adam then asked if it were true that

Hugh had seen the Child Jesus at Mass. "If," replied Hugh, "God did show me what you mention and other things at other times, what concern is it of yours?" Adam then spoke of his fear of death, a fear which had troubled him from boyhood, fear of leaving every familiar person and scene and going out into the unknown. "Take care to lead a good life before you die and leave in God's hands what will follow death." Never again did Adam fear the prospect of death.

Hugh's body was embalmed, and on Saturday, November 18, the funeral cortege set out for Lincoln. It was a triumphal and crowded procession. Storms of wind and rain failed to extinguish lighted torches carried by horsemen beside the bier. The following Thursday, November 23, the procession reached Lincoln. On the way, at Stamford, a devout shoemaker prayed so fervently to be allowed to touch the coffin that the crowd made way for him. Thanking God that his prayer had been heard, in the spirit of Simeon's *Nunc dimittis* he prayed that his soul that very night might be united with Hugh's in heaven.[34] He had hardly returned home, when he was taken ill, received the last sacraments, and died.

The presence of the royal assembly lent exceptional honour to Hugh's funeral. In the procession which came to meet the corpse three Archbishops were present, the Archbishops of Canterbury and Dublin and the exiled Archbishop of Ragusa, a city of what is now Yugoslavia. There were fourteen bishops, more than a hundred abbots. There was a Welsh prince and two kings, John and William of Scotland. John was among those who bore the coffin up to the cathedral. The procession made its way through streets which rain had made so muddy that the mire came up to the mourners' calves, sometimes even their knees. In the cathedral a solemn dirge was sung. The burial took place the following day. King John was so moved that in a passing access of penitence he prostrated himself before some Cistercian Abbots, begged their pardon

34. In his prayer the cobbler quoted with full understanding a phrase from the Little Chapter of the First Vespers of Sunday (Sarum use), of Second Vespers (present Roman use).

with tears, and promised to build a monastery. Indeed he kept his promise and founded Beaulieu Abbey. A more impressive tribute, however, to the departed saint than even these royal honours was paid by the Lincoln Jews who, coming from their houses in the Dernestall, some of which still remain, as they watched the funeral pass, wept for the loss of the Christian Bishop who had so bravely defended the human rights of their persecuted race.

Cures well attested and accepted as such were worked at Hugh's tomb. Whether or no they were strictly miraculous, they were undoubtedly works of God declaring the holiness of His servant.

Hugh was canonised by Honorius III in 1220 and sixty years later his body was translated to a worthier shrine in the Angel retrochoir. On this occasion the head, which fell apart from the trunk, exuded oil, as also, we are told, did the body of a later Bishop of Lincoln, Robert Grosseteste. When the leaden coffin in which his body had hitherto lain was discovered in 1887, traces of a liquid substance were found. There the body remained till the Reformation. Today nothing is left but this empty coffin which once contained his body, found beneath a marble memorial erected by Bishop Fuller in the seventeenth century.

Since Hugh died after sunset on November 16 and in the Middle Ages the ecclesiastical day was reckoned, like the Jewish, from sunset to sunset,[35] his festival is November 17.

35. A relic of this reckoning is the First Vespers of a Sunday or feast recited the previous evening.

BLESSED JOHN OF MONTMIRAIL

[before 1170–1217]

IF BLESSED JOHN of Montmirail ever heard of St. Francis and his followers, it must have been in the closing years of his life when he was already a professed monk. Otherwise he might well have been attracted to them. For this older contemporary of St. Francis was an *anima naturaliter Franciscana* whose behavior and spirit were closely akin to his. If on this account alone, he deserves to be rescued from oblivion and made known to the many who will appreciate a Franciscan, whether in his own or in Cistercian garb.

Our authority for John's life is good—a short but illuminating life written by an anonymous monk of his monastery, Longpont in the diocese of Soissons. He neither claims nor disclaims personal knowledge of his hero. But, as the Bollandist who edited his work[1] points out, even if he did not know the Beatus himself, he was sufficiently close to him to know those who did. For he speaks of an anchoress who had been the friend of Blessed John, Marie de Goignelieu, as being still alive, and tells us that he had been informed of certain matters by his former servants. Moreover he wrote before the translation of John's body in 1252 to a tomb within the choir. The French Benedictines date the life about 1230, some thirteen years after John's death.[2]

John was of noble birth, a wealthy and powerful Baron of France. His castle of Montmirail was in Brie on the border of Champagne. His great-great-grandfather Dalmace (Dalmatius) served King Philip I—contemporary and foe of William the Conqueror. His great-grandfather was named Walter. Walter's elder son was John's grandfather Elie (Elias), a younger Walter. Walter became a monk at Clairvaux under St. Bernard. There was therefore already a family connection with the Cistercians.

John's grandmother, Elie's wife, and her son, his uncle, yet another Walter, are praised by William of St. Thierry in his life of St. Bernard. The saint himself blessed the baby Walter, who was observed to heap kisses on his hand.

The saint's father Andrew was an elder brother. His mother Hildiarde d'Oisy was also of illustrious lineage. One of her two brothers was killed in battle in 1160, the other despite two marriages died childless. Hildiarde therefore was sole heiress and her d'Oisy estates swelled those of Montmirail.

John was probably born before 1170. He lost his mother when still very young, before 1177 at latest, and his father remarried. Not later than 1194 John himself married. It was another of the brilliant matches usual in his family. For his wife was Helvide de Dampierre, sister of Guy Lord of Dampierre and Bourbon, whose daughter married King Theobald II of Navarre. King Theobald therefore would acknowledge John's son Matthew as a near relative. Guy's wife, John's sister-in-law, was a daughter of Baldwin VIII, Earl of Flanders and Latin Emperor of Constantinople. By his marriage John had six children, three sons, William of Montmirail who died before his father, John, and Matthew, and three daughters, Elizabeth, Félice, and Mary. All died without issue except Mary, who married Ingelram of Coucy and became through this marriage an ancestress, the Bollandist claims, of "the leading royal houses of Europe."[3]

1. *Acta Sanctorum*. September, Vol. 8, pp. 186–235.
2. *Vies des Saints et Bienheureux* by the Pères Benedictins. Septembre, p. 615.
3. The Bollandist also says that she was an ancestress of the Hapsburg Emperors through the marriage of Catherine to Albert I. Albert's wife, however, was Elizabeth not Catherine.

These genealogical facts, not to be found in the life, but labouriously collected by the Bollandist, prove that John was in the front rank of the French nobility—and as wealthy as noble—fortune's favourite indeed.

The writer of the life—I shall call him the biographer—deliberately refuses to speak of the saint's military achievements in his unconverted youth. He does, however, relate one exploit. When King Philip Augustus was fighting the Plantagenet king Richard Coeur de Lion at Gisors, he rashly penetrated too deeply into the enemy's lines at the head of a small body of knights, leaving the main body of his troops behind. Surrounded by the enemy, John's timely assistance enabled him to make his way back to safety. And on a later occasion in the same struggle John came to his assistance with a large body of reinforcements he had collected. No wonder his King prized him highly and counted him among his close friends.

John was also renowned for the lavish display of his tournaments and his own prowess at the jousts. As he confessed himself later, his most grievous sins at this time were vainglory in his renown as a valiant knight and his extravagant expenditure. He had spent, he said, no less than a thousand livres on a single tournament. The youthful St. Francis was equally enamoured of lavish display and craved for the life of a knight. But whereas he was but the son of a merchant aping the manners of knights and seeking admittance into their ranks, John with the same tastes was a noble, able therefore to gratify them to the full.

A warning voice called him to higher things. A Canon Regular famed for his personal holiness persisted in accosting him, as he rode home proud and exultant from a triumph in the lists. "He would rebuke and annoy him with words to this effect: 'What good, I ask, have you gained from this tournament of yours? What a wise merchant you are to purchase at the cost of so much money, fruitless exertions and, I take it, blows received in the contest, nothing but wind for all your pains.'" Though they might irritate, the Canon's words gradually sank in. For John after all was an unquestioning and devout Catholic believer—he had already restored to a monastery tithes to which it had been proved he was not entitled—and as such well aware of the comparative values of the temporal and the eternal.

Finally he became, like St. Francis, a wholehearted convert, ready, indeed eager, to renounce all the world had bestowed so lavishly upon him. "So deep he sank by humility as to deserve to contemplate the God of gods in Sion."

But the first fruits of his new zeal for God's service were unfortunate—another proof that the moral insight, even of personal holiness, is limited by the moral and religious convictions of the social environment. For he decided to expel the Jews on his domain. "The soldier of Christ, resolved that the example of his religious living should bear fruit among his subjects, determined first of all to eradicate like a good farmer brambles and thorns, unprofitable and injurious thistles, namely the synagogue of Jews dwelling in his fief." The voice surely of Hitler! For such language reminds us of the Nazis and the Jews herded into gas chambers. Its significance, however, was not so sinister. The anti-Semitism of the mediaeval Catholic, lamentable as it was, cruel and stupid as it was, did not equal the atrocity of contemporary anti-Semitism. Nor was it based on the blasphemy that the race to which Jesus Christ and His mother belonged is despicable and evil.[4] John did not kill the Jews, though he banished them. Moreover, personal charity being at war with wrong-headed conviction, he gave each of the unfortunates three coins and, since harvest was approaching, a sickle, that the Jews might be employed as harvesters on the domain of other lords. On the other

4. Until Pius V reformed the Missal in the sixteenth century, the hymn sung at the Palm Sunday procession contained the verse:

Fecerat Hebraeos hos gloria sanguinis almi,
Nos facit Hebraeos transitus ecce pius.

(The glory of noble blood had made them Hebrews,
This devout passage makes us Hebrews.)

There is a play on an etymology deriving "Hebrew" from a word meaning "to pass by." Mediaeval anti-Semitism was due not to racial antipathy but in part to the general belief that men are morally guilty of religious error, in part to the further belief that the obdurate rejection of Christ continued the guilt of the Jews who brought Him to the Cross. Moreover, as a money-lender at high interest the Jew was hated by his debtors.

hand he proclaimed the release of his Christian subjects from any debts they had incurred to Jewish money-lenders.[5] At this very time England was disgraced by pogroms, though honoured by St. Hugh's defense of the Jews.

Henceforward John was devoted without reserve to charity and humility. Impetuous and wholehearted, as when he staked his life so lightheartedly on the battle field, wrecked nothing of the tournaments' blows and perils, he gave all he had and himself to the service of the poor. No longer did he wear the costly armor of his knighthood, the robes of a lord. When once he so far yielded to a wistful longing for the old days, as to have his armor brought to him for the pleasure of a look, he repented bitterly.[6] He wore, at least at times, the ragged clothing of the vagabond, the down-and-out.

At his castle of Montmirail he built and endowed a hospice for paupers, especially sick paupers, strangers and travelers.

When an inmate died he bore him to burial, if possible unassisted, on his own shoulders. A poor woman in the hospice suffered from "a running sore in her breast." The sight of the sufferer stirred his impulsive compassion. "On bended knee he began to kiss a wound so loathsome, that no one else could behold it without disgust, so that his lips bore the traces of the purulent matter." Another patient suffered from a sore in her side which gave out a stench so intolerable that she was secluded from the rest. This time the odour proved too much for John. No sooner had he entered the room where she lay, than he rushed out again, exclaiming, "It makes me faint [lit., "It has taken my heart from me"]—the unendurable stink." The matron in charge of the sick scolded him unmercifully. "What a fine soldier, how honourable, how courageous, defeated in a moment by a stench! It is the stink of your own sins that you smell."

5. According to mediaeval law the property of Jews belonged to the ruler, who could therefore remit debts due to Jews as being owed to himself.

6. Nevertheless, as we shall see, he was prepared to resume his armor as a knight in the service of the Church.

With a smile he replied, "I deserve your rebuke. I must admit that I am a coward." He immediately re-entered the room, "bent his head down against the sick woman's body and spread the bedclothes over his head and her side, that the stench might not escape and his nose might get the full measure of it. And he spent some time in this posture." The matron changed her tune and said he had been too hard upon himself. But he replied, "I must tell you, dear friend in Christ, that now the stench is fragrant and delightful as the scent of spices. For what you told me is true. It was my sins that stank so foully."

These are acts of heroic charity—Franciscan as any deed of St. Francis. But John also overcame natural repugnance for the sake of doing so and surely to excess, when he had his face washed by the nurse who washed the filthy heads and bodies of the sick paupers, used the comb used on their "scabby" scalps and the utensils from which they ate and drank.

Informed that a destitute woman on his estates had just given birth to a child, John hurried off to her hovel, placed woman and baby in a large basket and carried them to the hospice on his shoulders. We always hear of him hurrying, rushing off, leaping from his horse. From first to last, whether as the King's knight or God's, he was impetuous, acted on impulse. St. Francis too was impulsive.

Again like St. Francis, John had a special devotion to lepers. Riding once at the head of a troop of horsemen[7] he met twenty-five lepers. He dismounted, went among them, gave each leper five *solidi*, knelt before each and kissed his hand. One of the band, too infirm to keep up with his company, when John reached him, asked an alms. John had given away all his money. He asked the leper for his shirt. He stripped off his own—still a valuable garment—and put it on the leper, then above it the leper's own shirt. On this the biographer comments, that John's charity was even greater than St. Martin's. For, whereas Martin gave the beggar only half his cloak, John gave his entire shirt.

7. In some of these stories John is still the feudal lord clad in armor—in others dressed like a pauper. The former no doubt belong to the early days of his conversion. Chronological sequence, however, cannot be even approximately established.

The rest of that day John must spend settling disputes among his vassals. He found himself quite unable to grasp what they said or reply and was obliged to hand over the business to his bailiff. Later he explained that the cause of this disability was the attraction of a lovely countenance seen in the air. The following day he passed in retreat at a monastery.

He was told of a leper at Provins hideously disfigured by his disease. He visited him, entered his hut, knelt down, and kissed him. He spent an entire day waiting upon him and at his departure left a large alms to supply his needs.

On a journey he would always seek out lepers, kneel down and kiss their hands and disfigured faces. When he had no money to give, he would even give them his gloves.

This love for lepers remained with him in later days as a monk. One day when the community had gone out to work in the fields they met a leper "hideously disfigured, a loathsome spectacle." John kissed him; but, since he was no longer his own master, it was a furtive kiss.

We should notice the psychological value and the theological depth of John's treatment of these unhappy outcasts. His attitude of personal homage—to kiss the hand kneeling was the feudal homage to an overlord—gave the sufferer what he needed most, a sense of his human dignity, made him feel that he was not after all just the off-scouring of society, shunned by other men and the object of their disgust. For here was a great nobleman humbly paying homage. Theologically the gesture penetrated to the very heart of Christianity, the truth that the most despised and outcast of human society is mystically identical with Christ, so that Christ may and should be worshipped and served in him. John probably knew little theology, was certainly incapable of seeing what was unchristian in the code accepted by contemporary society, ecclesiastical as well as lay. But the intuition of a saint's charity saw the divine-human Christian fact.

John regularly entertained poor men at his table. Once when he was dining with them at Crevecoeur, a blind pauper burst out in praise and thanksgiving to God and his host. "The blessing of the heavenly King be yours, reverend John," he cried out, "for I have received from you more benefits than I can fairly tell." Asked what they were, he replied that he had been a thorough-paced scoundrel, a robber guilty of sacrilege and many other crimes. Barons, often even lesser lords of a manor, had their courts of justice with rights even of life and death over their subjects. In the exercise of his seignorial jurisdiction John had had the man blinded, the eyes put out, which he said "were my guides to the crimes I committed and intended to commit." His words were repeated to John. He rose from table and prostrate before the blind man begged his pardon with tears. The man, however, told him he had no need to do so. For he was greatly indebted to him for having saved him from the gallows and everlasting perdition.

It was John's custom, when his household had gone to sleep, to place poor men in his bed, there to enjoy the unwonted luxury of a comfortable night's rest, while he himself slept on the ground. When at Crevecoeur the number of retainers present prevented this, a poor child complained that their presence was a great nuisance to himself and his friends. For it deprived them of the soft bed they would otherwise have enjoyed. In this way John's practice was betrayed.

In the coldest days of winter he would hear Matins in church, unheated of course, wearing nothing under his cloak but a shirt and drawers of haircloth, wrapped in prayer and bedewing the ground with his tears. This absorption in prayer is, I think, the sole indication which has reached us of the profound and intense prayer which nourished his heroic humility and charity.

At Soissons he asked his host whether he knew of any religious person with whom he might converse. He told him of an anchoress renowned for her sanctity. He asked to be taken to her. "Surely, my Lord," his host expostulated, "you cannot go on foot to visit a pauper, through our streets and public places. Such unheard-of behavior would not be respectable or becoming a man in your position."

"What," he retorted, "is worldly glory, what are monarchs, princes, or John of Montmirail but a rotten corpse doomed to feed worms?" The objector was silenced.

One day, as he was travelling in his humble garb, he met a large party of kinsmen. They expressed their indignation at the sight of the head of their noble family clothed like a pauper. "Your conduct is a perfect disgrace. It shames and humiliates us your kinsfolk exceedingly." "Would that you, my dear relatives," he replied, "might reach the Lord Jesus by any way, no matter how ignominious."

John the overlord of many communities[8] would now say he could wish himself the son of the meanest serf.

It was no doubt his impulsive temperament which made him once utter the prayer to our Lady that she might address him from her image and inform him that he would never possess her Son, but that it might not be true. For the false belief would move his heart to contrition for his sins. In punishment, so he thought, for having asked our Lady to lie, an evil spirit was permitted to torment him for four years with a pain in his side. Mediaeval men were apt to attribute disease to a demon, not however without support from the Gospel: "This daughter of Abraham whom Satan has afflicted." At the end of that time the anchoress Marie de Goignelieu paid him a visit. As the biographer here informs us that she was still alive, she was presumably his informant. He asked her if she knew or had ever seen him. "Not," she answered, "in the flesh." He understood that she had seen him in the spirit, telepathically we should say. The thought of such communion in God thrilled him with joy. The pain ceased and did not return.

A charming story is told of John's devotion to our Lady. Riding one day with a troop of horsemen he passed a wayside Madonna unnoticed and therefore unsaluted. He must, however, have been subconsciously aware of it. For shortly afterwards it came into his mind. He leapt from his horse, walked back and begged pardon on bended knee. In the presence of many witnesses the image turned its face towards him.

It was John's intention to dedicate his military prowess to the service of God by joining the Crusade led by the elder Simon de Montfort[9]

8. Lit., "peoples." It is not clear whether when he said this he was still overlord or had resigned his possessions.

against the Albigenses, the Catharist heretics of Languedoc. Though, unlike many of the crusaders, he had no motive of personal gain, one could not wish our saint associated with the atrocities committed in the Crusade. It was not to be. John had expended so much, first on worldly display, later in lavish alms, that he could raise the necessary funds only by the sale of property. He therefore arranged to sell some woods, whether for timber or sporting rights, to the value of seven thousand livres. They must, I think, have formed part of his wife's dowry. For the prospective purchasers required her consent. Helvide, as we shall see, a strongminded and determined lady, stoutly refused to give it. The sale therefore fell through and John was obliged to abandon his intention. Evidently our Lord required some other form of service. What was it to be? In his perplexity he discussed his problem with a confidential retainer. As the Bollandist suggests, he was probably Amand, the faithful servant who accompanied his master to Longpont, as de Rancé's valet was to accompany his master to La Trappe four centuries later. He suggested that John should embrace the life of a hermit. They could share a hermitage and he would wait upon his master. Delighted by the suggestion, John bade his servant look for a suitable hermitage. He went into the diocese of Liege to consult a hermit renowned for his holiness. The hermit strongly dissuaded John from following his example. He had found it too much for his strength to be exposed single-handed to the assaults of Satan. If John would be advised by him, let him join the Cistercians—"the holiest of the orders." "Indeed I know of no safer or more direct road to heaven." "If your master does not believe me, let him consult the theologians of Paris." Already Paris had become what it would long remain: the intellectual and theological center of Latin Christendom. John did consult the Paris theologians, giving a welcome tip for their pains, in particular three of outstanding eminence. They unanimously advised him to become a Cistercian.

Though we must not forget that this is the biased report of a Cistercian, it is perfectly credible. For St. Bernard's prestige still overshadowed

9. Father of the English statesman and Parliamentarian.

the Church and the Cistercians were still the *dernier cri* in religion. But the friars were on the doorstep.

John accordingly received the habit at the Abbey of Longpont from the hands of its Abbot Walter (1200–1219). It was on Ascension Day, probably in 1210.

At that time the Church did not require, if a married person wished to embrace the religious life, that his partner should do the same. But she did require his or her consent.

We are not told of Helvide's consent being asked or given. But we may take it for granted. No doubt she gave it gladly. She was, I am sure, only too pleased to be rid of her husband.[10] In fairness we must consider her point of view. A haughty chatelaine, she had made a match befitting her nobility. She had married a peer of France, the King's personal friend, a man renowned for his exploits on the battlefield and in the lists. Now, she found herself tied to a husband who dressed like a tramp, kissed lepers, invited filthy beggars to his table, even gave them his bed. It was intolerable. She would be delighted when the gate of Montmirail closed behind him for the last time and the castle under her son and herself would be once more what a nobleman's castle should be.

Away in Thuringia a young girl was growing up who would have understood John's way of life and sympathized with it—the future Landgraefin St. Elizabeth. For it was her own way of life. But Helvide could not be expected to understand.[11]

When, as custom required, the Abbot warned his postulant of the rigors of the Cistercian life, John replied, "I could not have any greater joy in the world than to eat bread made of the bran which is fed to dogs." Not satisfied with the austerities of the rule, he sought out the coarsest food and stinted himself even of what is necessary for health.

10. This view of Helvide's sentiments is not merely a presumption. It is verified by her later conduct (see below, p. 98).

11. Charters prove that Helvide was willing enough to make religious and charitable foundations, but not that a peer should live like a pauper.

And to make the dishes more unpalatable he poured cold water into his portion.

The Abbot, informed of this indiscreet abstinence, rebuked John and commanded him in virtue of obedience to eat as much as he could of the bread served to him. He took the obedience literally and devoured the entire loaf[12] set before him "with the utmost difficulty"—not leaving even the crumbs. He thus made what was meant to be a compulsory alleviation an additional penance. Aware, however, that even he could not endure to repeat the gastronomical feat, he asked the Abbot to remove or at least lighten his obedience. The Abbot replied, "I bid you eat a loaf a day and for the rest to eat all you can." John, however, persuaded him to leave the amount of food to his discretion or indiscretion.

He behaved in the same way—reminiscent of Brother Juniper—when the Abbot sent him a fish with orders to eat the whole of it. He devoured the entire fish, head, tail and bones.

One day a party of monks going out to work in the fields came upon the stinking carcass of a dead animal. They hurried past, stopping up their nostrils with hand or sleeve. John, who had long ago conquered his sense of smell, went up to the carcass and drew it out of the monks' path.

Amand the retainer who had followed John to Longpont, still eager to serve his old master, carried off his shoes one night, polished them and returned them to his cell. We might have expected John to be touched by this proof of a faithful devotion. Not at all. He rushed off in a rage to the Prior and threatened to leave a monastery where he was waited upon. In this imperious gesture, surely, this proud humility or humble pride, this slight to Amand's affection and loyalty, the old Adam gave a sign of life. The tactful Prior, however, smoothed the matter over by advising John the following night to polish Amand's shoes, which he accordingly did. More attractive is the story of John's loving attendance upon a monk taken violently sick.

12. How large the loaf was I do not know. As the Carthusians (see above, p. 69) were given a loaf for their weekly ration, it may have been very large.

From the stories told John would appear to have been absent from his monastery more often than was usual for a simple monk. Possibly his superiors, proud to possess in the community so renowned a nobleman, made an exhibit of him to the outside world. Or they may have considered him the most suitable monk to deal with a world with which he was so well acquainted and where he was personally known to so many.

Once John was at Cambrai with a monk, Gilo the cellarer. On their way to visit an anchoress they came upon a party of men playing a game in the town ditch, who shouted after them in derision, "Hauy, hauy!"—"Hoy, hoy!" Gilo blushed and hastened his steps. John turned back, told the men his name, and asked them to continue their jeers at a sinner worthy of their contumely.

A little later he was once more at Cambrai, presumably before his solemn profession, when the novice settles his financial account with the world. For he came to satisfy all claims on his estate—make restitution to any he might have wronged. A woman complained that she had been seriously wronged by him. But he had spent every penny and could but assure her that were it in his power he would repay her without delay, were it at the cost of his own eyes, nose, and ears. However sincere the assurance, it could hardly have been satisfactory to the woman had she a genuine claim on his estate.

He was riding out on business with a "serving lad" of the monastery. The youth grew hungry, called at a monastery, and asked for food. The inhospitable monks refused him, whereupon he returned in a rage to John and poured out abuse of the churls. John leapt from his horse, and prostrate before the young man begged him to desist. His humility touched him and he obeyed.

John had given Longpont a grange attached to a castle called Grandeluz. But his eldest son William, now Lord of Montmirail, refused to allow the monks to use it or repair it. Informed of this, John brought a party of labourers to Grandeluz to do the repairs, working among them himself and carrying on his shoulder tiles for the roofs. He had also given Longpont the lesser tithes, *decima minuta*, of Grandeluz.

Again William interfered, forbade them to be collected, and attacked the monks who attempted to do so. Hoping that his son would respect his father, John collected the tithes in person from house to house. Whether or no with William's connivance, perhaps to curry favour with him, "a tough"[13] followed John around, tore from his shoulder a bunch of leeks—no doubt part of the tithe, which was paid in kind—pulled off his hat and flung it into the mire. John quietly picked it up and went on has without even giving his assailant a look.

Riding with the Prior and another monk. John noticed that the monk was carrying the bag containing their clothes. He insisted that it should be transferred to his own horse.

We have noticed William's hostility to his father and the community to which he belonged. It was displayed even more plainly when John had occasion to visit his old home in company with the Prior. His son being away from home, he asked his retainers to put them up for the night. Knowing no doubt it was what their lord would wish, they refused with flimsy excuses. As on the occasion of the shoes, the Prior was tactful. "Do not be put out," he told John. "Remember our Lord came to His own and His own received Him not." John's anger subsided. He rejoiced and thanked God and an "outsider" gave them hospitality.

On another occasion John revisited Montmirail. This time his wife was at home and was told of her husband's arrival. It was most unwelcome and she made it plain. For she sent back a curt message: "My lady is taking a vapour bath[14] and is therefore unable to see you or speak with you." John seemed unmoved. "May God," he said, "give her benefit from her bath," and went away. He turned for hospitality to his stepmother, a Countess. She at any rate gave him a welcome, but asked why he had not gone to his old home. "You, my lady," he answered, "are not taking a bath."[15] In this reply I detect an acid flavor which suggests that he resented his wife's treatment.

13. Lit., "one of those known as Ribaldi." We must discuss later the meaning of the term.

14. "*Domina sudat*"—"My lady is sweating." This vapour bath, a legacy from the Roman Empire, returned later to Western Europe as the "Turkish" bath.

He took advantage of this visit to his stepmother to persuade her to remit a sentence of mutilation or blinding she had pronounced on a robber, on condition that the culprit took the cross.[16] She consented.

One day the Prior asked John if he were glad he had become a Cistercian. He replied that although he would not have chosen any other order, were he now free, he would not become a monk. For he found the respect paid him by the community intolerable. It is surprising that he had not foreseen that this would be the case. When the Prior asked what then he would do, he answered he would be a "ribald" (*ribaldus*). Though "ribald" has survived as an adjective—ribald laughter, a ribald jest—it is practically obsolete as a noun. If used at all, it means one who uses ribald language. In its original, its mediaeval sense, it can hardly be translated. For it bore a double connotation, social and moral. Socially the *ribaldus* was the down-and-out, the vagabond, the outcast, the displaced person of mediaeval society, the man who had no place in the established feudal hierarchy, as it ranged from the tenant-in-chief down to the serf. Morally he was a rogue, the addict of every vice and crime. And, as always, the respectable member of society was glad to insist upon the immorality of the disreputable, conveniently forgetting that it was largely due to the conditions in which the society which condemned him compelled him to live. Such was the attitude of our good Prior, amazed and shocked by John's reply. "What," he exclaimed, "would you swear and perjure yourself, dice, take a whore around with you, be constantly drunk?" "Heaven forbid," was John's answer. "But the outcast need not be a rogue" (lit., "There are different kinds of *ribald*"). "Not all these 'ribalds' are evil livers. There are those who clean out stables, cart dung, perform in humble obedience the most abject tasks and are therefore treated as the scum of humanity and earn a crust of bread by the sweat of their brow. But although men despise their life as worthless and contemptible, in the eyes of God it is praiseworthy and of great

15. "*Tu, domina, non sudas*"—"You, my lady, are not sweating."

16. If, as the biographer infers, this happened on the occasion of this visit, it must have been for the Crusade against the Albigenses. The Fifth Crusade did not begin till some years after John's death.

price." "But," insisted the Prior, "your fellows would persecute you for not takng part in their misdeeds." "What joy it would be to endure any injury they might do me, any insult they might put upon me."

I have chosen these for John's last recorded words. For more than any others they express his truly Franciscan sanctity.[17] He will have none of the smug and willful pretense which confounds destitution with sin because the former so often produces the latter, though its pressure diminishes the malice. He sees in the pauper's life, if lived for Christ, a life more Christlike even than that of the religious secured against the world's buffets. He sees in the social outcast Christ Himself.

The student of history knows that movements of thought or feeling arise at the same time in many different quarters and spread beyond the range of direct communication. So it was now with the Franciscan ideal of poverty, the poverty of the destitute and despised Christian following the poor Man who died, naked and bereft of all, the reviled outcast. St. Francis and his first following; the poor men of Lyons, though they soon revolted against the Church; St. Elizabeth and Blessed John: all were moved by the same spirit, pursued the same ideal. And the same movement is astir again today, the same ideal emerging into view. The ideal cherished by Blessed John to be a social outcast, a ribaldus among the disinherited, is the ideal today, not only of the priest-worker[18] but of many other Catholics who would win back to Christ the godless proletariat of our great cities, the *ribaldi* of the twentieth century, by becoming, as he desired to become, a member of this suffering and destitute humanity, living among the ribalds a ribald's life, themselves ribalds of Christ.

The Matins of Michaelmas 1217 were being sung. Prior Hugh, overcome by fatigue, dozed in his stall. During his snatch of sleep he dreamed. Before the stall of each monk he saw a burning candle. One candle was taller and brighter than the rest and lit up the choir. Then it rose from the ground and disappeared through the roof.

---

17. The resemblance to St. Benedict Joseph Labre, the saintly tramp of the eighteenth century, has been pointed out to me. It is indeed most striking.

18. That incidental mistakes have been made cannot detract from the Christlike spirit which inspired the experiment.

About the same time a lay brother dreamed much the same dream. But the candle did not rise of itself. He saw our Lord descend and take it up with Him. In the course of the morning the significance of these dreams became clear. While the Prior was singing Mass, he heard the sound of the wooden tablet being struck which announced a monk's death. It was the death of Blessed John.

His name is mentioned as a Beatus in the Cistercian Menology and the Benedictine Martyrology, even more appropriately perhaps as Humilis (humble) in a Gallican Martyrology.

> His relics have survived the Revolution. An attempt to canonise him shortly after his death came to nothing. In 1891, however, his cultus was officially approved and in 1908 his Mass and Office were granted to the diocese of Châlons for October 5. He is also commemorated at Soissons and Arras.[19]

19. *Vies des Saints et bienheureux* by the Pères Benedictins. Septembre, p. 615. I am indebted for my acquaintance with Blessed John to this admirable compilation.

BLESSED JORDAN OF SAXONY [DIED 1237]

BLESSED DIANA D'ANDALO [CIRCA 1201–1236]

WHEN ST. DOMINIC died in August 1221, his Order, as Dr. Altaner has pointed out, though firmly established, was comparatively small and uninfluential. There were barely thirty convents and some few hundred members. The Franciscans, on the other hand, already counted many thousands. Though in any case they would no doubt have survived, the Dominicans might well have been of no greater extent or importance in the life of the Church than the Trinitarians or Servites. That they increased so rapidly and attracted some of the greatest intellects of mediaeval Europe was due to St. Dominic's successor as Master General, Blessed Jordan of Saxony. When he died, the Blackfriars, for numbers, influence, and the quality of their members were on the same footing as the Grey—both together the intellectual and the spiritual leaders of the Church, the right and left arms of the Papacy.

We must therefore agree with Dr. Altaner that Jordan was in truth the second founder of the Order who brought St. Dominic's work to a successful conclusion.

Unfortunately there is no early life of Blessed Jordan. The fifteenth-century life adds nothing, and at that late date could not add anything, to our earlier sources. There is an account by Jordan himself of the origins of the Order, scattered notices in chronicles, a book by Thomas of Chantimpré entitled *The Book of Bees* (*Liber de Apibus*), also an early compilation of stories about the earliest brethren, the *Vitae Fratrum*, which, however, like the Franciscan *Fioretti*, blends fact with legend. Fortunately, however, there is a source which of its nature could not be surpassed for authenticity or personal revelation, Jordan's surviving correspondence. A learned edition—in most cases the letters have been dated—has been given us by the writer to whom I have referred already, Dr. Altaner. It has provided the greater part of the material for this study. I have also used Père Mortier's account of Blessed Jordan in his *Histoire des Maîtres Généraux.*[1] And I have consulted the *Vitae Fratrum.* Anecdotes from that source are told with due reserve. They cannot possess the certainty attaching to the correspondence. The pithy "sayings," however, bear the indubitable stamp of Jordan's humorous common sense.

Of the fifty-six surviving letters no fewer than thirty-eight are addressed to one correspondent, the nun whose name I have therefore joined with Jordan's, a beata with a beatus, Blessed Diana d'Andalo of St. Agnes' convent at Bologna; and of the remaining eighteen, twelve are addressed to the community in general. Only six, therefore, are addressed elsewhere. What little we know of Diana apart from Jordan's letters we owe to a chronicle of the convent by a nun, Sister Angelica, who wrote between 1264 and 1283.

Jordan was a Saxon. He may well have been of noble birth, was certainly of good family. Our first information about him is of his meeting with St. Dominic in 1219 at the University of Paris. Since he would so soon be St. Dominic's successor, he must, I think, have been already a master. It has indeed been suggested recently that he is to be identified with a celebrated mathematician, Jordan Nemorarius. If so he was a much older man than has been supposed hitherto. But we do not know. On Dominic's advice he was ordained deacon. He also made the acquaintance of Dominic's disciple, Blessed Reginald of Orleans, on his arrival as Prior. The following spring, February 12, 1220, influenced by the preaching of Reginald, who however died

1. Volume 1.

shortly before his clothing,[2] he entered the Order at Paris. Their convent was the convent of St. James, destined by the irony of history to give its name to the Jacobins of the French Revolution, whose club met at the dissolved Priory. Jordan was now a bachelor of theology. As he had asked our Lady to grant, his friend Henry, later to become Prior of the convent at Cologne, was clothed together with him. Though urged by his friend to join the Order, Henry was reluctant to take the step. Jordan opened the book of Isaiah, and reading the passage he found a warning not to refuse God's call. A few lines below he read the words *Stemis simul*—"We must keep together." (Years later, when their duties kept them far apart, Henry would ruefully remind his friend of these words. Jordan would but reply, "What greater glory than to share the poverty of Christ?") Then one night at Matins Henry saw our Lady praying that he might yield, a vision or dream followed by a vision of the Judgment when one of our Lord's assessors pointed to him and cried out, "You there below, what have you given up for our Lord?" Henry was terrified, and shortly after surrendered to grace. The friends were clothed on Ash Wednesday. As they entered the church the brethren were singing the antiphon "*Immutemur habitu*"—"We must change our garments."

On May 17 the same year (1220), as one of four deputies elected by the Paris convent, Jordan attended the first General Chapter of the Order held at Bologna. At its conclusion he returned to Paris. It was on this occasion perhaps that he first met Diana. He must in any case have heard much about her. There had been a convent of friars at Bologna for the past two years, since St. Dominic in 1218 sent friars from Rome. The first Prior had been the man who had won Jordan for the Order, Blessed Reginald of Orleans. He was equally successful in influencing Diana, a girl who belonged to one of the noblest and wealthiest families in Bologna, the Carbonesi. Pier father's Christian name, Andalo, was, however, attached to his children. Diana therefore was known as Diana d'Andalo, Andalo's Diana. Pier father befriended the friars and his financial aid

2. Reginald died on February 1, 1220.

made it possible to build a convent. When St. Dominic came in person to Bologna in August 1219, Diana, about the age of eighteen, placed herself under his direction and took the vows of a religious. She thus lived a nun's life in her father's house. Other women of noble Bolognese families followed her example. A convent was clearly needed for these women, and in 1220 St. Dominic sent four friars to arrange for its foundation, among them Blessed Guala.

Unexpectedly, Diana's father and brothers strongly opposed her leaving home. She took refuge from her family at an Augustinian convent at Ronzano. Her relatives pursued her and carried her off with such violence that one of her ribs was broken in the scuffle. This must have occurred in 1221. For more than a year she was a prisoner in her father's palazzo—for most of the time a crippled invalid. St. Dominic, however, contrived to smuggle letters to her. He had, however, been dead over a year when on her recovery Diana once more fled to the Ronzano convent, November 1, 1222. Meanwhile the second General Chapter held at Bologna in May 1221 had elected Jordan in his absence Provincial of Lombardy, Northern Italy, and he came from Paris to assume office. We are not informed if he was present at St. Dominic's death in August. But he was certainly at Bologna in October. From the tone of his first letter to Diana it seems clear that he must have met her at this time, if not before. On May 22, 1222, at a General Chapter held in Paris, he was elected to succeed St. Dominic as Master General.

Diana's persistence was at last successful. After her second flight from home her family abandoned its opposition. According to Mortier it was Jordan who overcame her father's objections by pointing out to him that, if he gave a site for the convent adjoining his palazzo, he would have the comfort of seeing her in his old age. In Advent Jordan wrote the first of his letters to Diana, the first at any rate we possess (LI).[3] He exhorts her to set her desire on heavenly things and tells her that her ignorance of his own German language affects only earthly

3. The accepted numeration bears no relation to chronology. I shall follow the order established by Dr. Altaner.

matters. We may notice his emphasis upon desire as the motive power of ascent to God.

Jordan had obtained leave from the Bishop for the foundation of a convent for Dominican nuns at Bologna. On the octave of the Ascension, 1223, Diana and four other Bolognese girls entered their convent of St. Agnes. Jordan presided at a Chapter General which opened at Bologna on June 11, and on June 29 he clothed the five nuns.

Throughout Jordan's term of office the General Chapter met in alternate years at Paris and Bologna, at Paris because it was the intellectual capital of Catholic Christendom, at Bologna to honour the founder's tomb. It is worth notice that it never met at Rome, though there is evidence of Jordan's occasional visits to the Curia. The state of the city was too perturbed, the Pope's hold upon it too precarious, for mediaeval Rome to be more than the juridical metropolis of the Church and the uncertain residence of the Pope; it was by no means a suitable place for the regular sessions of a General Chapter.

Already, though a little more formal in address than later, Jordan's first letter to Diana proves that the friendship between them was already well established. These particular friendships—spiritual unions in God between holy men and women—are by no means uncommon in the lives of saints. We have but to think of St. Teresa and Father Gratian, St. Francis de Sales and St. Jeanne Chantal—St. Vincent de Paul saw their souls ascend to heaven blend in one flame. And we shall encounter another instance in the spiritual bond which united another Dominican, Blessed Osanna of Mantua, and her Olivetan director, Father Girolamo Scholari.

Such a bond is as strong as that between man and wife in a happy marriage, the union as close. The bond indeed is stronger, the union closer than marriage in its natural aspect. For it is forged by God and founded on Him. But it is pure, limpid, radiant as light dissolved in clear water. For it is raised above the order of biological sex. That rationalists, those in particular of Freudian views, should see in it but disguised sexuality is intelligible enough. For they recognize only the biological. It is stranger that many convinced of the spiritual order and its transcendence of the biological, many of them ecclesiastics, should agree on this point with the Freudians and regard with suspicion and disfavour these spiritual friendships between a man and a woman, the marriage not of two bodies nor even of two minds but of two spirits. For they prove that the differentiation of the sexes exceeds physiological sex, and, despite St. Thomas—had he, one wonders, read Jordan's correspondence or pondered its meaning?—that in the order of spirit also, woman is man's complement and helpmeet. This is not to say that the body plays no part.[4] But it does so not as it is ensouled, on the biological plane, but as it is already inspirited, a vessel and vehicle of the spirit.

As regards the expression of this friendship in terms of warm affection, we must remember that the style of Latin letter writing descended from the rhetorical conventions of Latin literature which would never use a positive where a superlative could be employed. For this reason I translate Jordan's frequent address *carissima* as not literally "dearest" but "beloved." That is to say, present convention would not permit Jordan's expression of his love for Diana. Even in this correspondence it comes to the surface only occasionally, at times no doubt of particular emotional stress. Its depth, however, is as certain as its spirituality, its spirituality as certain as its depth.

Particular themes recur in these letters. One of these has been struck already in the first letter—the primary importance of desire for heaven, its everlasting union with God. And, in that heavenly union there will be everlasting and inseparable union between Jordan and Diana. This in fact will be the subject of his last letter to her. *Inter mundanas varietates ibi fixa sint corda ubi vera sunt gaudia.*

Constant also is the insistence on the need and value of Diana's prayer and the prayers of the community if Jordan's apostolic work to enlarge the Order in numbers and quality alike is to be successful. He informs her of his successes, also of occasional failures, and attributes

4. Cf. D. Divo Barsotti, *Il Mistero Cristiano nell' Anno Liturgico. II Santorale. La Verginita* (p. 398). This is a book of outstanding value—despite occasional exaggerations of statement, rich in profound and comprehensive insights. It has been my privilege to translate it into English.

the former to the nuns' intercession. Is there any lesson more necessary today?

Another theme might be summed up: "Love, not asceticism, the substance of sanctity." It is not that Jordan overlooks the need for asceticism. But it must be kept within bounds. Moderation, the due measure, *modus*, must be observed. Otherwise excessive bodily weakness must lame the exercise of aspiring love rising to God. And this is the substance of religion. On this point Jordan supports the wisdom of our English master of prayer—Augustine Baker.

This moderation, indeed, expresses a quality eminently distinctive of Jordan, a quality we English people like to regard as peculiarly our own, common sense. It was exemplified when in reply to the question, which is better, studying Scripture or praying, he said, "You might as well ask which is better—eating or drinking"; also when he answered another questioner: "The best way to pray is the way in which you can pray most fervently."

Another quality evident in these letters is Jordan's gentleness. Not once does he speak bitterly of those who opposed the designs he had most at heart—never a word of abuse. In this respect his correspondence contrasts strikingly with St. Bernard's, in which invective is frequent and the character and conduct of those with whom he is in conflict are seen and displayed in the worst light. This undeniable defect has no place in Jordan.[5]

As with St. Francis, his gentleness was appreciated by animals. Once as he was travelling in Switzerland on foot, staff in hand, among his companions, they called his attention to an ermine which had scuttled into its hole. Jordan invited it to come out. "Come out, lovely little creature, and let us see you." Immediately it appeared at the entrance of its hole and gazed fixedly on Jordan. He took it up, one hand beneath its body, and fondled its head and back with the other hand. The animal showed every sign of pleasure. Then he said, "Now return to your

5. In this respect St. Thomas resembles Jordan. He combats opinions, not persons, and, if possible, avoids mentioning the names of opponents.

lair—Blessed be the Lord who made you." At which the ermine disappeared underground.

Diana was fortunate indeed in his spiritual guidance.[6] Within a month of the clothing in July 1223 Jordan writes to her from Venice (XXXV). He is going to Padua to hunt for subjects at the University and asks her prayer. Brother Arcangelo, he says, is sorry that pressure of business prevented him from visiting her before he left Bologna.

From Padua in August Jordan writes three letters, one to the community, two to Diana (XIX, XX, XXI). At first, he says, his preaching was unsuccessful, his audience cold. He had in fact decided to leave and look for a more promising field when "God suddenly touched the hearts of many… Ten have already joined." Among them are two Germans, sons of Counts. One occupied an important post besides holding many other dignities and possessing great wealth, the other is well-to-do and noble in body and spirit. One of the two was the teacher of St. Thomas, the thinker who did much to incorporate Aristotelianism into Catholic philosophy, also one of the fathers of modern science, St. Albert the Great. Jordan in a sermon had laid his finger on an unspoken difficulty entertained by Albert and made his vocation clear. Another letter from Padua comforts Diana for a trouble from which she is suffering and brings more good news of his successful mission. "I have received thirty-three brethren…laymen of excellent character, among them many of noble birth… More are expected." "Do not be afraid. I will be a father to you, you a daughter to me."

Consistently Jordan will choose universities for the field of these recruiting campaigns. He thus established a close contact between the Dominicans and the centres of intellectual life, planted his friars at these centres and obtained men capable not only of sharing but very soon of dominating (together with the Franciscans) the thought and work of the universities. In pursuance of this purpose Jordan introduced

6. One cannot but wish that her contemporary, St. Elizabeth, could have been directed by Jordan instead of the fanatical sadist Conrad of Marburg. He would not have beaten her or parted her from her devoted maids and children.

afternoon sermons at universities—devoted to recruiting for the Order and usually with great success.

He found, it seems, more novices among bachelors and masters of arts than among theologians and canonists. This he explained by the fact that to the former theology came as something new with the full impact of spiritual reality. The latter, on the other hand, had been accustomed to handle theological doctrine and scripture not as the concrete and living word of God, but as intellectual abstractions little better than counters in a professional game. To the "artist," on the other hand, theology was a generous wine following the water of Aristotelian philosophy.

Sometimes parents objected—violently—to their sons' vocations. Count Flankenberg, for example, gathered a band of relatives to drag his son Albert by force from the Paris convent. The novices were too many for the attackers, and an uncle was himself converted and took the habit. Travelling through Lombardy, Jordan met a band of knights. "Where," shouted their leader, "is Master Jordan? He has robbed me of my only son." "I am Master Jordan," he replied with his disarming gentleness. The father repented of the intended murder and for penance promised a pilgrimage to the Holy Land. A knight had stolen a cow belonging to Jordan's mother. When he complained that Jordan had stolen his son for the Order, he replied that the man who had stolen his mother's cow could not complain if he took a calf from him.

He knew how to keep as well as win men. We do not know whether it was at this early stage of recruitment or later that a revealing episode occurred. He had gathered a band of novices and they were travelling with him. In his lodgings he began Compline. Under the emotional tension the young men broke into a titter. An angry friar made signs to them to cease. Jordan took no notice and unconcernedly proceeded with the office. When it was over, he turned to the indignant friar. "Who, pray, appointed you novice master?" Then to the novices, "Laugh on! You have good cause for laughter. For you have escaped from the bondage of the devil. Laugh away, dear sons." Though one might suppose that not only the religious but the baptised Christian had escaped the bondage of Satan, Jordan's charm and understanding sympathy even as recorded over the ages are irresistible.

Of all he received into the Order he did not, it is said, lose one. A novice who insisted on returning to the world left the Chapter to change into his secular clothes. Led by Jordan—it was Pentecost—the friars prayed fervently for him. He suddenly returned and, penitent, entreated to be allowed to remain. At every house he visited Jordan made a point of seeing the novices and listening to their difficulties, and would invite them to his table.

A young man lived with little practice of religion. He fasted only on Good Friday, never went to confession, and knew no prayer except the Pater Noster. On a passing impulse he joined the order. He soon repented, and rebelled so violently against the religious life that he struck with his Psalter the superior, who had persuaded him to join. Jordan led him to an altar and asked him to kneel and say the Lord's Prayer—the one prayer he really knew. As he did so his heart was touched and he became an exemplary religious. A friar at a Chapter stood out against Jordan's proposal to re-admit a penitent friar who had left the Order. "If you, my brother," he said, "had shed a single drop of your blood for this man for whom our Lord shed His blood, you would think very differently." He withdrew his objection.

The same autumn (1223) Jordan is writing from Milan (XXXVIII) lest Diana be made anxious by unconfirmed rumors. On his way to Milan he had visited Brescia, where he had taken part in a translation of the relics of the local saints, Faustinus and Jovita.[7] He had fallen ill but had recovered his health.

From Milan he went on to Paris and writes from Paris in Advent (XXXIV). He informs Diana of his arrival. He urges her to desire heaven—"the treasury of universal joy," the place filled with the "light of universal beauty"—and asks her prayers that he may win subjects from the university. Another letter (XVII) was written between the autumn of 1223 and June 1224. St. Agnes' convent was in need of nuns already

7. Their feast is kept on the same day as Blessed Jordan's, February 15.

experienced in life according to the Dominican constitutions.[8] Pope Honorius had refused to permit nuns to be sent from the convent of St. Sixtus in Rome re-founded by St. Dominic. Jordan informs Diana that "suitable" nuns will be sent from St. Dominic's first foundation for women at Prouille. The Prior of Montpellier has written to that effect. The remainder of the letter is a panegyric of poverty, charity, and humility.

About Easter (April 14) 1224 Jordan tells Diana he had suffered from "tertian" fever at mid-Lent. His campaign at the university has been successful. Between Advent and Easter he has received some forty novices, some masters, others reasonably instructed. "Be rooted in humility, grow in charity." In view of his desire to recruit men of learning, it is not easy to credit Thomas of Chantimpré's charge that he received sixty scholars so ignorant that they could hardly read a lesson at Matins. But he may of course have perceived possibilities in them.

Jordan's next datable letter (XXVII) was written to the community in January or February 1225. He admonishes the nuns to keep the flesh in subjection, but with moderation. They must not attempt to fly but climb the ladder of perfection step by step. In all things the mean must be observed. Only the love of God must have no mean. We ascend to God not by tormenting the flesh but by holy desires. After all he has been unable to obtain nuns from Prouille. The reason he will explain when he arrives at Bologna. He opened the General Chapter at Bologna on May 18. It was followed by a preaching tour in the cities of northern Italy.

We possess three letters written at this time, in June or July 1225. One (XXX) was written to comfort Diana and her relatives on the death of her brother Brancaleone who had become Podestá of Genoa.[9] They must rejoice in his heavenly bliss. He is sending a nun called Jordana cloth to make a tunic and hood. The next letter (XXXI) pursues the same theme of consolation. Jordan congratulates Diana that she does

8. Strictly speaking there is no Dominican rule. The Dominicans follow the rule of the Augustinian Canons with special constitutions.

not grieve immoderately for her brother's death. Once more he warns her against excessive abstinence from food, drink, and sleep. "In all matters behave with moderation and patience." The third letter (XLV) addressed to the community asks the nuns to give spiritual comfort to Brancaleone's widow. They must make the journey northwards, which he, Prior Henry of Cologne and other companions are about to undertake, the subject of their prayer. When the next letter was written (XXXIII) on August 16 Jordan had already reached Trent. Though he had been ill, his doctor had allowed him to leave Verona on August 10. At Trent he had preached to the people on the Assumption, to the clergy the following day. "I am quite sure," he remarks, "that I cannot repay you equal affection. For I am dearer to you, than you to me."

The next letter (XXXII) was written to Diana shortly after his arrival at Magdeburg on September 24. He expresses his satisfaction with the state of the Magdeburg convent. Once again he insists on moderation in bodily penance.

From Germany Jordan proceeded to Paris where he wrote to Diana soon after March 25 of the following year, 1226 (XXVIII). He sympathizes with the troubles endured by the citizens of Bologna and in consequence by the community. Dr. Altaner believes he is referring to an attack by the Emperor Frederick II. Your Bridegroom, Jordan writes, will be with you through all you may have to suffer. "I am not coming to you at present. For I am certain it would serve no good purpose. But, if God will, I will come before the year is out. We shall see each other again and our hearts will rejoice. At present we experience in turn joy and sorrow. But in a little while the hour will come when our joy will be perfect and will never be taken from us." He has good news of the growth of the Order in Paris. Within the space of four weeks twenty-one novices have been received, among them six masters of arts. The Bishop of Paris came to hear his sermon and dined with the friars. And on the Annunciation the Papal Legate dined with them. The Queen, Blanche

9. It was a common practice for the better preservation of peace to import the chief magistrate from another city.

of Castile, once as a girl bride visited and comforted by St. Hugh, "shows great affection for us and has conversed with me familiarly about her affairs."

The next letter, addressed to the community, was written about Whitsun, June 7, either from Paris or on a journey through Germany. They must take heart in the troubles besetting them—no doubt the war with the Emperor—and trust in our Lord. They must do this even in times of aridity. What matters is desire.

We hear no more till January 1227, when Jordan writes to Diana from a town in northern Italy (VIII). He had carried out his intention to visit Bologna the previous year and will return for the Whitsun General Chapter. He informs her of a Bull obtained from Pope Honorius, December 17 last, placing St. Agnes' convent under the protection of the Master General. Shortly afterwards in another letter written in January or February (XXIII), Jordan congratulates Diana on the Bull. The Pope moreover had at last withdrawn his refusal to permit nuns to be sent from St. Sixtus. A group had arrived at St. Agnes' headed by Caecilia, of the noble Roman family of Cesarini. She was now Prioress of the convent. Diana has told him that, since the convent has thus been secured, she no longer desires to live. Jordan approves her desire for heaven but warns her not to shorten her life by immoderate penance. He is entrusting to her care a little German girl, presumably a poor orphan. It is his wish that a German friar should visit her at least once a week lest she forget her native language. The Prior of the convent must be told to arrange this. Since Easter she has been with a priest, Gerard by name, who could speak only the Lombard dialect of Italian. He says she is a good girl and he was loath to part with her. Jordan recommends to Diana's prayers the fruit of his recent preaching, twenty-eight suitable novices.

It is remarkable and somewhat surprising that, though he sent her occasional greetings, we do not possess a single letter addressed to the Roman Prioress Caecilia. Had any such been written it would surely have been preserved with the other correspondence by the convent. It must surely have been a slight to the Prioress that the Master General corresponded so regularly with one of her nuns and passed her over. For once, I cannot but think, Jordan was lacking in his usual kindly tact. That there is no evidence of resentment on Caecilia's part is a proof that she deserved to share, as she did, Diana's tomb and cultus.[10]

On May 30 Jordan opened the Chapter at Bologna. He writes to Diana from Paris before Christmas, 1227 (XXXIX). "Since I cannot see you, beloved, in the flesh as often as I would wish, I am deprived of the mutual happiness of our company. But my heart's desire obtains some satisfaction when I am able to visit you by letter and inform you how things are going with me. I would have written long ago could I have found a messenger." He had reached Paris a fortnight before Christmas. He asks the prayers of the community, that he may be successful in obtaining novices at the university, and repeats his warning against excessive mortification. "In watching and abstinence it is easy to exceed the mean. But we can never have too much of virtue, humility, patience, kindness, obedience, charity, and modesty."

The next letter (LIII) is addressed to an unnamed German nun, a Canoness of Oeren at Trèves. It was written after Christmas, 1237. Though we possess only three letters written to her, it is clear that she too was Jordan's close friend. He would, he says, console her (by a personal visit) for the tears she had shed at his departure from Trèves the previous autumn.[11] Unhappily he is unable to do so. For he has been plunged into the depths of sorrow by the death at the Cologne convent of its Prior, his intimate friend Henry. "I mourn a most dear son, a friend deeply cherished, a most beloved brother." Our Lady had heard his prayer that Henry should enter the Order along with himself. About the same time he wrote in the same strain to Diana and the community (XLIV). God will wipe away the tears she had shed at his departure. He tells her of his loss and the general mourning at Cologne for

10. Also shared by another nun from St. Sixtus, Amata. Nothing, however, is known of her.

11. We must remember that in the Middle Ages tears came easily. Members of Henry I's council—corresponding to modern Cabinet Ministers—wept when one of their body departed on a journey. Can we imagine Sir Winston Churchill weeping as he bids Mr. Eden goodbye at the airport!

Prior Henry. "We must hasten to enter his rest, but not too quickly, for we have a long journey before us. If however you grow weary, your Jesus was weary from His journey and sat down by the well to rest His fatigue." Nor must she mourn too bitterly the death of her brothers and her sister Otha. They and Prior Henry are happier than we.

Still in Paris, somewhere about Easter, March 26, 1228, Jordan wrote again to the same Canoness at Trèves. His thoughts are still engrossed by his friend's death last year. He describes it in detail. The night of his death, he tells her, "I visited him before Matins. He asked to be anointed. We then went to Matins. I remarked how applicable were the lessons read. When I returned, I found him speaking loudly, even chanting, about God and with God, expressing his desire for heaven. Later on he died while the prayers of commendation were being said." Jordan no doubt remained in Paris at least until the General Chapter of 1228.

In February or March, possibly June or July 1229, he is at Padua. He writes to the community of St. Agnes. He congratulates the nuns on their single-hearted search for God, but must yet again warn them against indiscreet and immoderate penance and weeping. Thanks to their prayers he has recruited twenty excellent novices from the students at the university. Jordan in fact haunted universities and seems never to have been long away from a university. He founded four Dominican houses of study at universities, with chairs of theology, one at Oxford, one at Toulouse and two at Paris. And he organized the studies of the Order to culminate in a general house of higher studies, a *studium generale,* at Paris, for picked students throughout the Order. How wise he was in this would very soon be shown by the intellectual achievement of the Blackfriars.

The next letter was written to Diana from a city in Upper Italy in the summer of 1229 (XIV). He tells her of his success at Vercelli, of the many well-educated men of excellent character given him by the Lord. Three Germans of the highest standing in the city, four Provencals and three Lombards had joined the Order at the same time. He is in good health. "Do not take it too much to heart, beloved, that you cannot always have my bodily presence. For my spirit is always with you in the most sincere charity. All the same I am not surprised that you suffer from my absence, for I too cannot but suffer from yours. But I am comforted by the thought that our separation will not last forever. It will soon have an end and we shall shortly enjoy everlastingly each other's company in the presence of Jesus Christ the Son of God. I send a special greeting to the novice Juliana."

Two letters were written shortly afterward from Genoa, probably on the same day (XLVIII and XLIX). The former, addressed to Diana, is being written to relieve her anxiety about a constitution passed by the General Chapter at Paris the previous year forbidding friars to clothe women or undertake their direction. It was not, he explains, aimed at the regular convents but forbade the indiscriminate clothing and direction of isolated individuals. She has therefore no cause for alarm. Nevertheless the future would show that there was an influential body of friars who were opposed to convents of women. Again he bids her not to be depressed by their separation. Jesus Christ is the bond uniting their spirits. "In Him I always enjoy your presence wherever I go." The second letter was addressed to Stephen, the provincial Prior of Lombardy. Jordan explains the new constitution as he had explained it to his friend. He informs him of his success at Vercelli, a more detailed account than he had given Diana. In despair of results he was on the verge of leaving the city when recruits began to come in. The first to join was a German, Martin Walter, a master of logic at Paris where he was in the first rank of teachers. He had warned colleagues and students not to attend Jordan's dangerously seductive sermons. Curiosity too strong for consistency, he went himself and was captured. Beating his sides he exclaimed, "Master Walter, you will go, you will go in spite of everything." He was followed by two bachelors of arts, one a Provencal, the other a Lombard. It was then the turn of a German canonist, a Canon of Spiers, rector of the German schools at Vercelli. Of the two Provencals who followed, one lectured on canon, the other on civil law. He thus obtained in all some twelve or thirteen novices. He had brought almost all with him to Genoa. Two would accompany him to Montpellier. The rest would await orders at Genoa. Possibly the giggling novices belonged to this group from Vercelli.

It was from Genoa, Mortier thinks, that he visited the Emperor Frederick and rebuked him to his face. "It is said that you oppress the churches, make light of ecclesiastical censures, practice augury, favour Jews and Saracens, turn a deaf ear to good advice and show no respect for Christ's Vicar." Though not converted, the Emperor was impressed by Jordan's holiness—very few in the Middle Ages were not impressed by evident holiness. He heard him out in silence and after his departure said, "I feel great respect for this friar who has come here to speak to me in God's name."

From Montpellier through Auvergne, Burgundy, and France, Jordan travelled to Paris, and from Paris wrote to the community of St. Agnes after October 9, 1229 (X). He has found the state of the Paris convent everything he could wish. They must pray for the threatened peace of the Church. He no doubt had in mind the struggle with Frederick. But they can and should preserve inner peace.

The next letter, addressed to the community (XVI), was written from England. As we should have expected, Jordan is at a university, Oxford. The letter was written just before the Purification, February 2, 1230. He urges the nuns to bear their troubles in confident hope of heaven. But once more he warns them against immoderate penance. "The Lord," he says, "has given me hope of a good catch at these Oxford schools." At Oxford he presided over the first English Provincial Chapter. It was the custom of the English friars to say *mea culpa* for the least infraction of the rule. The devil, it is said, appeared to Jordan and told him that this *mea culpa* robbed him of all his profit from the fault.

In London Jordan visited the Franciscans, where he found a friar suffering badly from a diseased leg. "Are you not ashamed, brother," he said in jest, "that the Father of our Lord Jesus is dragging you to Him by the foot?"

A considerable gap follows in the datable letters. Jordan opened the General Chapter at Paris on May 26 and the following year at Bologna,

May 11, 12 31. It was probably during this summer of 1231 that he wrote to Diana (XLVI).

> When I must bid you goodbye it is with a heavy heart, and you add to my sorrow. For, when I see you so disconsolate, I cannot but grieve not only for our separation but for your inconsolable grief. But why do you grieve so sorely? Am I not yours, am I not always with you, yours at work, yours at rest, yours when you are present, yours when you are absent, yours in prayer, yours in merit and yours, I trust, in the heavenly reward? What would you do, if I should die? You should not mourn disconsolately even for my death. For you would not lose me when I died but send me ahead of you to those abodes of light where I could pray for you to the Father. Living with God I could do you far more good than I can lingering out a dying life here below.

There is another long break in the datable correspondence; and it is not until Christmas time, probably in 1232, that we can date another letter (L). A German notice from Lille makes it likely that Jordan was in Paris at the end of 1231. And he certainly presided over the General Chapter which opened at Paris on May 30, 1232. As the result of her prayers, he writes in his Christmas letter to Diana, Jesus has given the Order many excellent members of the University of Padua and touched the hearts of many more, so that, if the nuns persevere in prayer, there is good reason to hope that they too will join.

Jordan was in a city of upper Italy when in the early spring of 1233 he wrote to Diana (V). Their hearts, he tells her, are one in our Lord. He had rather suffer himself than see her suffer. "Meanwhile take comfort. By God's grace I will be seeing you shortly in the flesh who are always in my mind's eye. Of all the cities of Lombardy, Tuscany, France, England, I might almost add Germany, Bologna is nearest to my heart."

About the same time, between April 3 and April 10, Dr. Altaner concludes, a day in Easter week, Jordan wrote again from Padua to

Diana (XXVI). Her prayers and those of the nuns, he informs her, "have produced thirty novices of excellent character, learned and of noble birth. Many are masters in the university. Master James, Archdeacon of Ravenna and Provost of Bobbio, one of the most expert lawyers in Lombardy, who had refused a bishopric, was clothed and made his profession on Wednesday in Holy Week, and with him another Archdeacon, a member of one of the noblest and wealthiest families in Hungary. And, as I am informed, throughout the world our brethren are being multiplied, increasing in numbers and virtue."

On the same day he wrote to the Prior and convent at Paris. He is delighted to hear of their prayer, charity and peace. "You have risen with Christ. Pray, work and do your utmost that, so long as it is not granted you to behold the heavenly Jesus in Galilee, He may come to visit us even in this present life, appearing to us as He once appeared to His disciples." This is the nearest approach to mysticism in Jordan's letters—though his prayer was no doubt contemplative. These appearances however are reserved for those who belong to the community. He then tells the Prior as he had told Diana of his success at Padua.

Jordan was at Bologna for the General Chapter, which opened on May 22, when, in view no doubt of his approaching canonisation, St. Dominic's body was translated on May 24 to a more honourable tomb. Hitherto afraid of presuming upon the Church's judgment the friars had actually neglected the tomb. On this occasion Jordan was aware of a delicious scent emanating from the saint's body which, as he spent long hours beside it, refreshed his spirit. Though he little knew it, this was probably the last time he would see Diana on earth.

From Bologna he went to Modena and from Modena to Reggio. From Reggio he travelled northward from convent to convent, and in June or July from some city of northern Italy he wrote to the community (XXXVI). He had, he said, spent eight days at Modena. But his preaching had borne little fruit. He went on to Reggio where, as we learn from a later letter, he had better success. Since he wishes to cross the Alps before winter sets in, he is unable to return to Bologna. Indeed had he returned, it would have meant but another parting with its tears.

A little later Jordan is at Vercelli where he writes to Diana (IV). Here he has obtained but one novice, though an excellent subject. But he hopes for better things shortly. Father Henry has been dangerously ill, at death's door. She must not be anxious about his safety. God will guard him on journeys undertaken for His service. From Vercelli he proceeded to Milan where he was detained by a long illness and was unable to leave before the following Spring (1234). We have four letters to Diana written from Milan (VII, III, VI, II). He informs her that he had brought eight novices from Vercelli. But a tertian fever followed by three further attacks of illness had prevented him from crossing the Alps as he had intended. His illness, however, is not dangerous. He wishes to assure her of this, lest she should hear a rumor to the contrary. Father Henry has recovered and gone on to Germany. In the following letter (III) he reproaches her for taking his illness so much to heart. "You could not wish me to have no share in the Passion of Christ." He admits, however, that he had after all been in danger, though the danger was past. In the next letter (VI) he tells her he is definitely convalescent, though still weak. He is, however, too weak to undertake a journey to Bologna before leaving Italy. He must be at Paris for the General Chapter. "But I am no less present with you in spirit. Wherever I go, I remain with you and take you with me spiritually" (II). The last letter was written in the spring of 1234.

From Milan Jordan went on to Zürich. But a return of illness detained him in that city. For the first time he was unable to attend a General Chapter. Here, we are told, he cured a smith of nosebleeds which had troubled him for years. He was still at Zürich in the middle of July (1234) when he wrote to Diana (XLVII). He informs her that a serious illness had made it impossible to attend the Chapter in Paris and that in his absence the definitors had passed constitutions hostile to her convent. The party opposed to Dominican nuns had no doubt seized the opportunity to expel them from the Order. When, however, he was informed of this, he had made use of his authority as Master General to annul the objectionable constitutions. She must not be troubled but exercise patient trust in God. He is now much better in body and mind (literally, "brain") and is preaching both to clergy and people. He has not however recovered his former strength.

Shortly before August 5 Jordan arrived at Strasburg and soon after that date wrote to Diana (XLIII). "Your letters, beloved, told me 'the good news' that our blessed father [St. Dominic] has been canonised and expressed your joy. I too rejoice and thank God." "The messenger from the provincial Prior found me at Strasburg on the vigil of St. Sixtus" (August 5). St. Dominic had been canonised on July 3. "I had, however, already been informed of the canonisation of our holy father by a letter from Father Raymund who is with the Roman Curia. And the brethren of the Strasburg convent had also been informed by a letter from Father Godfrey written from the Curia. We kept the feast with joy on this vigil of St. Sixtus[12] to the honour of God and our blessed Father." "I am on the point of setting out for Lombardy and hope to see you shortly. I feel the suffering you feel from the injury to your foot but warn you in future to take better care not only of your foot but your entire body." There is no evidence that Jordan's hope of seeing Diana was fulfilled. And he was certainly prevented by illness from attending the General Chapter which opened at Bologna on May 27, 1235.

Shortly afterwards he wrote to the community (XXX–VII).

> As you see it has not been God's will that I should be present at the General Chapter. If for no other reason, I should grieve for your sakes alone, that I have been unable to see you and enjoy the comfort of your presence. But we must patiently accept what God ordains for us. In every possible way He makes it plain to you that in this life we must not put our trust in human beings nor look to them for comfort. We must love Him with all our heart, soul, and strength. For He alone can and ought to suffice the soul, in this present life by His grace, hereafter with His glory.

12. Later, to keep August 5 for our Lady of the Snows, St. Dominic's feast was transferred to August 4.

Before we pass on to the last two letters we must consider eleven letters which cannot be dated to any particular year.

Letter IX strikes a note often heard. This world affords no stability. Our trust must be in God and, in prosperity and adversity alike, so far as we can, we must imitate His unmoved tranquility. "For your comfort, however, I will tell you of my dream…I dreamed that you appeared to me and said: 'Our Lord has spoken to me after this fashion: "I, Diana, I, Diana, I am good, I am good, I am good.'" These words were repeated many times."

In Letter XII Jordan tells Diana that, though he is unable to write at length, he must write a few words for her comfort. "For you are impressed so deeply on my heart that I cannot forget you, but must think of you as often as I call to mind the genuine and wholehearted affection you feel for me. For the love you bear me kindles the flame of the charity I have for you, touches my spirit to the quick.[13] May the Paraclete, the Spirit of truth, possess and comfort your heart and grant us to be together forever in the heavenly Jerusalem."

Letter XVIII to the community of St. Agnes is yet another warning against extremes, too much ease or too much austerity. And Letter XXIV is written to the same nuns. "Do not weep for yourselves, because I have left you in the flesh, but rejoice that your Bridegroom is in your midst. Soon all your sorrow will be turned into joy."

Letter XI, also to the community, rubs in the warning against excess in watching, abstinence and tears.

Letter XV to Diana asks why he need write notes to comfort her, when she can obtain better and more delightful consolation by reading every day the book of life, the law of charity made visible in Christ crucified.

Letter XXV was written to Diana on the occasion of her father's death. Those who are already dead do not mourn for those who die after their own decease. "But you, beloved, predeceased your father and

13. *Diligere, afficere, amor, caritas.* Though a translator must distinguish, the meaning of all these words is here substantially identical.

have been a long while dead, your life hidden with Christ in glory.[14] Now therefore that, as I have just learned in Milan, he has died, it is not fitting to mourn for him. If you do, it is proof that you are not wholly dead. I do not say this because his death leaves me cold, but chiefly on your account. You should be impressed by God's loving kindness in depriving you of the temporary parents of your body that you may find in Him a spiritual and everlasting friend."

The tone of this letter, I confess, surprises me, strikes me as rigid, almost unfeeling. It seems in fact to betray a human inconsistency. When Diana grieves for his absence, Jordan feels and shows a warm sympathy, but when her father dies she ought to be too mortified to grieve. On the other hand, she could hardly perhaps be expected to feel a deep sorrow for the loss of a parent at least partly responsible for her broken rib.

In Letter XXIV, Jordan informs Diana that almost thirty novices, suitable men and well educated, have been received. He is about to set out for Rome.

Letter XLI is a note of greeting hastily scribbled at Christmas.

Letter LIV is addressed to the German Canoness of Oeren. "Abide, beloved, an immovable column[15] in the fear of God… As far as you can, avoid useless conversations and unite yourself to God, cultivating His friendship by constant prayer."

The addressee of Letter LV is not named. "The strong and sincere love you bear me according to God in Christ makes you believe I too love you. I do. Otherwise I would not imitate Him who said: I love them that love me. I am, however, aware that you love me more than I you. I am sorry thus to defraud your affection. But neither do I repay Christ's love with a love equal to His." "I know that you wish to leave your

14. Evidently a conflation by memory of two texts from the same passage of Colossians—the Epistle for the first Mass of Easter. "You are dead and your life *hid with Christ in God*…You will appear *with Him in Glory*."

15. The phrase was probably suggested by an antiphon in the Office for St. Lucy (December 13): *Columna es immobilis Lucia, Sponsa Christi*: "An immovable column art thou, Lucy, Bride of Christ.

country and kin. That I dare not advise for the moment. But you are in truth no longer in this world but have ascended to Christ. Already you are a foreigner on earth and it will not be long before you are following the Lamb in heaven, whose love can never fail you."

Because this letter has come down to us with three addressed to the Canoness of Oeren, Dr. Altaner believes it was written to her. But there could surely have been no question of advising her to leave her home. Could it have been written to Diana when she was still in her father's home but eager to leave it for a convent? It might, however, have been written to the Canoness before she left home.

That in another letter, certainly addressed to Diana, Jordan uses the same language—his affection for her cannot equal hers for him—suggests that, though the sentiments expressed are wholly sincere and deeply felt, the expression itself is in part conventional, clichés of a particular literary genre—the love letter in the widest sense of the term "love." Textbooks were in fact compiled to teach the art of writing letters and arranging them in a series of models for each genre. Something of the kind, I suspect, lay behind many mediaeval letters.[16]

In addition to the itinerary made known by Jordan's letters, we have information of at least two visits to Rome, one of them certainly before the death of Honorius III in March 1227. We also know that he visited Naples, and the Cistercian convent at Aywières near Brussels where the mystic St. Lutgardis was a nun.

It was Jordan, we are told, who introduced the solemn singing of an Antiphon of our Lady at the end of Compline—the *Salve Regina,* which is still the sole antiphon sung by the Dominicans. It was first instituted, it is said, to rid the convent at Paris from persistent diabolic manifestations. He thus unknowingly started a devotion which would finally give birth to Benediction of the Blessed Sacrament. He also practiced, though he did not invent, a devotion in honour of our Lady in which the *Ave Maris Stella* was followed by the *Magnificat* and three psalms, the

16. One such textbook, in its day widely used, Franciscus Niger's (Franceso Neri) *Ars scribendi Epistolas,* is in my possession: the first edition published at Venice in 1489.

initial letters of the four composing the name *Maria*, a mediaeval devotion as baroque as any "device" of the sixteenth or seventeenth century.

Jordan loved poverty. On his journeys the band of travelers was supported by the alms they begged. Once he was sitting by a spring when his companions returned empty-handed. Jordan communicated to his companions the joy he felt and they broke into song. A lady passing by was scandalized by their mirth but when informed of its reason her edification took the practical shape of ordering provisions and wine. On another occasion, after dining at Pope Gregory's table, Jordan was delighted to spend the night supperless in the hovel of a Campagna peasant when the parish priest had turned these disreputable beggars from his door. Nor was he distressed when a beggar to whom he had given his cloak sold it for a drink. Better, he said, a gift wasted than charity refused. There are stories of food multiplied and the undrinkable wine proffered by the churlish husband of a hospitable wife given a delicious flavor.

As Jordan walked along he would sing his favourite chants, the hymn *Jesu nostra redemptio* or the *Salve Regina,* and like St. Hugh would be lost in contemplation. And sometimes he lost his way. It did not trouble him. "We are on the right road to heaven."

A dark shadow, we cannot deny it, is cast on Jordan's term of office by the activities of the Dominican Inquisitors, such as those who at Toulouse burned for her obstinate Catharism a bedridden old woman; and in particular by the reign of terror set up by the notorious Inquisitor Robert le Bougre, when parents denounced their children for heresy, children their parents.

In this connection, however, Père Mortier calls attention to an unexpected and significant fact. All Papal documents concerning the Inquisition and its procedure are directed either to individual Dominican Inquisitors or to Provincials, not a single one to the Master General. We may surely agree with his explanation that it was because the Pope was aware how incompatible with the temper and activities of an Inquisitor was Jordan's gentle charity that he passed him over and dealt directly with his subordinates.

But we must return to the last letters and the last days.

From the Advent of 1235 Jordan was in Paris. It was from Paris that he wrote the following Spring, 1236, to Diana (XLII).

"The longer we have been parted" (it was probably almost three years) "the greater our desire to see each other. I believe, however, it has been God's will that up to the present has prevented me from coming. If it is His will we should sincerely bow our wills to His. I have been in Paris all winter since Advent. By God's grace many men of excellent character and high standing, learned and of good birth and masters in the schools, have joined us. This very day I am writing this letter, I have been informed that seventy-two novices have been received. You and your sisters must thank God for them. Pending my arrival, I would have you know of my health. For a long time past I have been wholly free of fever, but I suffer greatly in one eye and am in danger of losing the sight of it." He did in fact become blind in one eye.

At Whitsun (May 8) Jordan presided over the General Chapter in Paris. It was decided that he should visit the convents in the Holy Land.

It was about this time that he wrote his last letter to Diana (XIII). He does not mention the projected journey to the East. If it had actually been decided, he must have hoped to embark from an Italian port and visit Bologna on his way.

> I cannot, beloved, see you in the flesh as often as you and I would wish and enjoy the comfort of our meeting. But my heart's desire receives some alleviation when I can visit you by letter and inform you how things are going with me, even as I would fain hear how you are faring. For your progress and your happiness rejoice and refresh my spirit. But you do not know to what part of the world I may be going, and even if you did, you would not have any messenger at your disposal by whom you could make the enquiries you would wish to make. What, however, we have written to each other, beloved, is after all of little worth. Hidden in our hearts is the burning love of our Lord whereby you and I always converse by the sentiments

> of a love no tongue can worthily utter or letter convey.[17]
>
> Unhappy, Diana, is the lot we endure at present. Here below our love cannot be without sorrow and care. For you grieve and suffer that you cannot see me constantly, I too that I may so seldom have the joy of seeing you. Who will lead us into the citadel, the city of the Lord of hosts which the Most High has founded, where we shall have nothing more to desire from Him or from each other? Here we are tormented every day, our heartstrings wrung and our griefs draw from us the cry: "Who will free us from the body of this death?" But we must bear these things patiently and, so far as the necessities of daily life permit, fix our minds on Him alone who is able to set us free from our afflictions, in whom alone rest can be found. Apart from Him whatever we see will prove a source of suffering and much sorrow. Meantime we must accept joyfully any unhappiness we may meet. For the measure of our sufferings will be the measure of the joy we shall receive from Jesus Christ, the Son of God, to whom be honour, glory, power and majesty forever and ever.

We do not know whether Diana received this last letter from Jordan. For she died on June 10. It may well have been the news of her death that altered his plans. For he did not pass through Italy on his way to Palestine but sailed from a French port, possibly Marseilles. When he had completed his visitation, he embarked early the following year, 1237, on his return journey. His successor as Master General, St. Raymond of Peñafort, has been credited by legend with the feat of walking over the sea from Majorca to the Spanish mainland. Jordan at any rate lacked this power. When his ship was wrecked off the coast of Syria and went down with all hands, the crew, two friars accompanying him and sixty-six pilgrims, he was drowned with them. It was February 13, 1237.

17. As Dr. Altaner has pointed out, these words were an adaptation of a verse from the hymn: *Jesu dulcis memoria.*

His body was recovered and buried at Acco. He would not have wished to live. For he had laid securely the foundations of his Order as the mighty intellectual and spiritual power it has proved. And he was united to Diana in the bliss of God, never more to be parted.

A Carmelite was tempted by the news of his death. Either this Jordan was not after all a good man or God has no care for the good. Is, then, my service of God worthwhile? A vision of Jordan in glory reassured him and confirmed him in his vocation.

Before his death was known in Europe a friar at Limoges saw corpses lying on the seashore. Suddenly Jordan emerged from the water fixed to a St. Andrew's cross. He spoke to the friar: Unless I go away the Comforter will not come." And so he ascended on his cross into the glory of heaven.

To his friend St. Lutgardis, Jordan appeared in such glory that she could not recognize him. "I am Brother Jordan," he told her, "of the Order of Preachers. I have passed from the shadows of an evil world into the glory of the heavenly mansions. I have taken my place on the summits among the Apostles and the Prophets."

Jordan's cultus was approved in 1826. The Dominicans keep his feast on February 15, February 13 being occupied by St. Catharine Ricci, and on June 9 the feast of Blessed Diana, Caecilia and Amata. Though their cultus has been approved, they have not been formally beatified.

BLESSED OSANNA OF MANTUA

[1449–1501]

FOR ALL THE neo-paganism, worldliness, vice and crime which disfigured so sorely both the Church and society, the Italy of the Renaissance was lacking neither in saints nor in Christian humanists. Too many are obsessed by the Borgias, whose authentic misdeeds moreover have been exaggerated, at first by political enemies, later by a crude sensationalism. They would be well advised to read the life of a contemporary Mantuan Beata. Nor was she the only Mantuan of outstanding holiness. We are told of a priest favoured with sublime gifts of prayer. Born the year before and surviving her fifteen years was another beatified Mantuan, Blessed John Baptist Spagnuolo. He became General of the Carmelites. But he is better known to posterity as an eminent humanist, "the Mantuan" whose Latin poems—he wrote over fifty thousand lines—were long studied in schools together with the greater Mantuan, Virgil. And this was but one small city state of Italy.

Our authorities for Osanna's life are excellent. Her confessor Silvestri wrote a biography. His sources, he specifies, were Osanna's letters, personal knowledge, and the relation of eye-witnesses. It is supplemented by the reminiscences of Girolamo Scholari. Girolamo was an Olivetan monk[1] who for many years was her disciple and intimate friend. She confided to him secrets of her interior life and graces of prayer to which no one else was admitted. For there existed between them the bond which so often links in God a holy man and woman, in which the mutual complement and bond of the two sexes is raised above the sphere of biological sex but is therefore all the deeper and more enduring. Girolamo often said Mass for Osanna in her room when she was, as often, too infirm to go to church. It would be followed by long conversations during which from time to time he questioned her about her experiences in prayer. They frequently continued for hours. On one occasion a messenger from the court interrupted the conversation. Another time Osanna's meal was delayed so long that the servants, tired of waiting, broke in upon it.

Osanna intended her confidences for Girolamo alone and asked him to destroy her letters. On one occasion she desisted from writing a confidential letter for fear a servant might find and read it. Girolamo, however, after her death published not only the substance of many private conversations but also forty-three letters she had written to him. Whether the breach of confidence was justified by a duty to make known her holiness and the divine gifts lavished upon her is one of the many moral problems to which no certain answer can be given—so evenly balanced are the arguments on either side. We may, however, be thankful that Girolamo did enrich posterity with his unique contribution to our knowledge of Osanna.

Many, perhaps most, of the events related by Girolamo are to be found in Silvestri's life—indeed he himself at times tells the same story twice. But his account often contains details and personal explanations by Osanna lacking in Silvestri's more jejune and comparatively superficial accounts.[2] Where therefore they overlap Girolamo is a better source than Silvestri, though the latter sometimes adds details in which Girolamo was uninterested. Our informants, however, do not conflict. To the

1. The Olivetans are a branch of the Benedictines.
2. These sources are to be found in the Bollandists (June 18, Vol. 2, pp. 552–667). There are additional sources unfortunately inaccessible to me. They are utilized by Bagolini and L. Feretti, *La Beata Osanna Andreasi da Mantua* (1905), which in Fr. Thurston's judgment is the most satisfactory life of the saint.

extent of his information Silvestri agrees substantially with Girolamo—an agreement which is a further guarantee of reliability.

Osanna Andreasi was born of a noble Mantuan family. Her mother Luisa[3] was a Gonzaga, a relative therefore of the ruler of Mantua, at that time a Marquis. The relationship explains Osanna's entrée at the Mantuan Court which became a close friendship, first with Marquis Frederick, later with his son Francis and their respective wives, Margaret and Isabella. Osanna therefore was related through her mother to the future St. Aloysius.

She was born on January 17, 1449. Her parents had a residence at a village on the Po, Carbonaruola, where they escaped from the summer heat of the city. It was there that, at the early age of six, Osanna was initiated into the contemplative and mystical prayer which would be the outstanding feature and the heart of her life. As she walked by the river an angel showed the little girl the heavens and their operations as God's praise and service—"how every creature by its very being did nothing but cry out…'Love God, all you who live on earth, for He has made all things for no other end than to be loved by you.'" "God," she says in a letter to Girolamo,[4] "infused into my soul a knowledge and light—such that whatever I saw or heard presented God to my mind with such knowledge and sensible taste of the divine sweetness that my spirit was very often rapt in Christ. In my heart Christ constantly spoke, whether I was walking or at rest or engaged in conversation, so that I could neither eat nor sleep. My soul, whether in or out of the body I know not, saw a great brightness and understood that it was the Father, the Son, and the Holy Spirit." She also saw the divine Child, but often, it would seem, as crucified—"*parvulus*, a little boy, nailed to a cross." Thus subconscious imagination fused two popular devotions—devotion to the divine Infancy and devotion to the Passion. Once Jesus placed His

3. Silvestri, at any rate as printed by the Bollandists, calls her Agnes with no family name. Thurston's Butler (supported so far as Gonzaga is concerned by the French Benedictine *Vies des Saints et Bienheureux*) must no doubt have good authority for the name Luisa.

4. Letter 2.

cross on her shoulders. Once she heard His voice saying, "Dear daughter, put away your love for your bodily parents and attachment to them, and I will unite you to your heavenly Father, your eternal God, and my most holy Mother, the Virgin Mary." She was filled with consolation and the desire to leave the world and her family. Later, however, she recognized that this was not God's will. The subjective factor of the novice's unrestrained fervour was evidently at work.

Thus, as a little girl Osanna began to enjoy the passive contemplation in which God communicates Himself to the soul by infused images and concepts drawn from the subject's subconscious. Indeed, there could hardly be a more "ecstatic" saint. Till her death fifty years later she was frequently the subject of trances which commonly lasted for hours, sometimes, at least in her youth, two or even three days. Unfortunately, neither Silvestri nor Girolamo was interested in chronological sequence. What hagiographer was? Her experiences therefore can seldom be dated.

It is not surprising that her parents were perplexed and dismayed by this abnormal child in a family of normal boys and girls. What were they to make of these queer states in which for so long she was completely unconscious of her surroundings? "You will be the death of me," complained her mother, "and bring disgrace on our family. I can't think what is the matter with you or what will be the end of all this." Her father put down the ecstasies to epilepsy, "the falling sickness"—these Catholic parents, be it remarked, were not ready to cry miracle—and being of sterner stuff than her mother tormented his daughter—no doubt by blows—to rid her by this rough treatment of her supposedly morbid condition. Now indeed or later, burns and other wounds were inflicted, and once in church a woman drove a sharp needle into Osanna's flesh. She felt nothing till she returned to normal consciousness and with it to the pain of these wounds.

At the age of fourteen Osanna was clothed with the habit of a Dominican tertiary. She was given to understand by our Lord that it was His will that she should not become a nun but remain in the world for the good she would do there to souls. She was in fact to share the vocation of St. Catherine of Siena. She did not, however, make her tertiary profession until she was a woman of fifty—not many years before her death. Silvestri attributes the delay to her fear that her household duties, together with her lengthy periods of ecstatic unconsciousness, would prevent her carrying out her tertiary obligations. Girolamo, however (but merely as his personal opinion, "*credo*") thinks the reason was God's will that she should pledge her obedience to none but Himself.

Whatever the reason of its long continuance, the delay was due at first to the friars' distrust of a visionary, their dislike of her public ecstasies. "The Order of Preachers," comments Silvestri, "entertains an ingrained contempt and abhorrence for any devotion which attracts publicity." They put her ecstasies down to shamming, illness, or diabolic possession and even contemplated depriving her of the tertiary habit.

Not only was Osanna liable to ecstasies in church, some of which continued from Mass until it was closed in the evening. Once, as she was riding through the streets on her way to embark for a visit to medical baths, an ecstasy took possession of her on horseback and she sat a whole day motionless in the saddle, even when the horse stumbled. Only when it was being led on board the boat did she recover consciousness. An ecstasy would catch her in the rain or out in the garden at night.

Because Osanna was thus an ecstatic from childhood, we must not conclude she was holier, united more closely to God than holy persons who never experience an ecstasy or but seldom, or, like St. Teresa, not until middle age. Whether union with God is conscious or unconscious, and if conscious how intensely it is felt, does not depend solely on the intimacy of the union. A man or woman—and women are more transparent than men—of transparent temper, that is to say of a temperament so sensitive that events which take place in the central spirit come easily to the conscious surface, will be aware of a central union with God when a person of more opaque, less sensitive temper will be altogether unconscious of it, or his consciousness will be less intense.

Osanna was extraordinarily sensitive and transparent, which is not at all the same thing as morbid or hysterical, though hysteria also may be transparent and all forms of transparence are pre-eminently suggestible.

During their many conversations Father Girolamo, after he had said Mass in her room, would often press Osanna to tell him of her graces of prayer and explain her prayer. What did she experience in those protracted ecstasies? These conversations belong to the latter part of her life and are therefore concerned with heights of contemplation presumably never reached in earlier years. Her experiences seem, however, to have been of the same type from first to last.

Osanna is insistent that these states of prayer can be understood only by those who have experienced them. "The things of God He has shown me in this union are so sublime that I cannot even make them clear to myself." "What splendour did I see! What joy did my soul feel in that union. Such splendour and light unbounded[5] can neither be uttered nor understood save by those who in this holy union have tasted, seen and felt it. They alone conceive it, but even they cannot find words, likeness or form as means by which to communicate what they know to mortals who have no experience of such grace."[6]

5. Cf. the "*luce eterna*" of Dante's *Paradiso*.

6. We may compare the words which introduce Dante's vision of Paradise:

> La gloria di colui che tutto move
> per l'universo penetra e risplende
> in una parte più e meno altrove.
> Nel ciel che più de la sua luce prende
> fu io, e vidi cose che ridire
> ne sa ne puo chi di la su discende.
>
> ***
>
> Trasumanar significar per verba
> non si poria; pero l'esemplo basti
> a cui esperienza grazia serba.
>
> ***
>
> His glory, by whose being all things move,
> Pervades creation and no more, no less
> Resplendent shines in every part thereof.
> Within the heaven his brightest beams caress
> Was I, and things beheld which none returning
> To earth hath power or knowledge to express.
>
> ***
>
> Since words may tell not what it means to outsoar
> The human, let the example [of Glaucus defied] satisfy
> Him for whom grace hath fuller proof in store.
>
> (Translated by Geoffrey Bickersteth—one word altered.)

> I could not possibly explain to you the fashion of this union nor point to any form like it nor find language to express such knowledge… Such was this more intimate union whereby my soul saw and knew all things created…and enjoyed more fully than ever before splendour, sweetness, and eternal Majesty. To tell you, however, the nature or extent of this unbounded light is utterly impossible. For it cannot be expressed or understood save by those accustomed to fix the eyes of the understanding on the form the soul sees and knows. For it is not the faculties of the body that know and understand but the soul united to the God she beholds. She understands after her own spiritual fashion things past, present, and to come, but cannot explain what she sees. All her bodily faculties are put to sleep and cease to operate. But the soul ascends to that unfathomable vision man's eye has never seen nor his ear heard. That divine spectacle holds the soul fast at an altitude so dizzy, that it is as though she were in the air, supported only by that intuition of God which draws her to itself in which she remains fixed and which she is enjoying… I would like to tell you how my soul is drawn by God. But I am unable for lack of suitable words. For although the soul, thus raised on high, at the time sees, understands, and knows the divine Light, the understanding is incapable of stating it in words. Nor can it grasp what exceeds its capacity… The soul abides rapt by the divine spectacle and the boundless light, and there is held fast unsupported by anything save the heavenly vision that attracts her, fixed in contemplation of the eternal Majesty… Nought besides does she experience or think, thus spellbound by the gaze she fixes on the beauty and delights of the light unbounded.

One union in particular was closer, more sublime, than any before it. Osanna, however, cannot explain the difference. For "there is no suitable likeness or comparison." This unbounded light, since, as Girolamo explains, she is not a trained theologian, she also terms the "divine

Essence" "as it shines forth in the Word" and says that in this divine essence she sees whatever events, past, present or future God wills to show her. But she cannot have been admitted to the beatific vision.

The ultimate reality then is the Godhead somehow perceived as unbounded light, much as Dante conceived or perceived it in his *Paradiso.* "All I can tell you," she wrote to Girolamo, "is that I behold a boundless radiance and in it God. God is seen and understood without word spoken in the profound humility produced by the presence of the divine majesty... I cannot say more, you must forgive me."

But Osanna also speaks of a translation of her experience into images—"*translatitia imaginatio.*" What exactly is meant? Certainly not that the visions she relates were symbols consciously invented by herself to suggest the indescribable. She saw in some way what she describes. "They are not," she says, "visions composed of sensible images. Rather the soul rapt away and united to God sees and understands things so great and sublime that no human language can express them." And she proceeds to speak of a Christmas vision of the newborn Babe which of its very nature must be imaginary, not purely intellectual. Elsewhere she says that God "shows Himself most beautiful without any sensible form, well pleased, with none of the signs whereby men show pleasure." And once more she proceeds to speak of an image, the wounds of Christ emitting rays brighter than the sun.

Her language appears contradictory. If, however, her reports are taken as a whole we may, I think, conclude that she was aware of God the background reality as somehow identical with, yet infinitely exceeding, the foreground images—the Sacred Humanity, the *Padre Eterno*—it is not always clear whether by "God" she means the former or the latter, Christ in the mysteries of His Infancy or Passion or together with angels and saints. Somehow Jesus or the *Padre Eterno* is seen in the boundless light and as one with it—somewhat as Dante saw the Human Figure of Christ inscribed in the blazing splendour of the second divine Circle. If, even so, it is impossible to conceive clearly the nature of these experiences, we must bear in mind that Osanna, like all others gifted with passive contemplation, pronounces them strictly unintelligible.

The sensible images, the humanities of these visions, since they are the product of subconscious artistry, closely resemble, as is always the case, the conscious art of the visionary's environment. As we read Osanna's accounts it is as though we were visiting a gallery of Italian *cinquecento* art.

As there, the mysteries of the Gospel are practically restricted to the cycles of the Infancy and the Passion. As we have remarked, the vision of the crucified Child combined both. Osanna's only vision of the Risen Lord is one which concludes a detailed vision of the Passion unrolled from scene to scene one Good Friday towards the close of her life. It has been an unfortunate restriction. For Catholic doctrine and the liturgy which expresses it, neither Christmas nor Good Friday is central, but Easter. Nor does Osanna possess the imagination of the creative novelist which, operating subconsciously, enabled Anne Catherine Emmerich to compose a vivid and detailed imaginary Gospel which, without contradicting any statement of the historical Gospels, expands them into a well-constructed fabric of episodes and descriptions enabling souls of the appropriate *attrait* to realise the Gospel story, as they could not otherwise.

Osanna visited or believed herself to visit in spirit the holy places in Jerusalem—doubtless an imaginative construction founded on what she had heard or read. A Franciscan, however, claimed to have seen her often in Jerusalem.

There were two other saintly Dominican tertiaries in Italy during her lifetime, like herself beatified, Blessed Colomba of Reate[7] and Blessed Magdalen Panatieri[8] of Trino in the marquisate of Montferat. That all three were secular tertiaries rather than nuns suggests a vocation made fashionable in contemporary devotion by St. Catherine of Siena, as St. Bernard made the Cistercians fashionable or in our own time St. Thérèse of Lisieux the Carmelites.

They were all alike visionaries and Blessed Magdalen's visions in particular bear a close resemblance to Osanna's.[9] She also receives in

7. Died 1501. Feast May 20.

8. Died 1503. Feast October 13—both feasts in the Dominican calendar.

her arms the Infant Jesus and visits in spirit the holy places of Palestine, "which she could describe correctly." Like Osanna, Magdalen saw and shared the Passion—displaying the sweat of blood, crown of thorns, and stigmata. "She was accustomed to pass Good Friday in ecstatic contemplation of Christ's sorrowful passion and death, which were impressed on her mind in colours so vivid, that they found external and bodily expression, not only by action and gesture, but even by a flow of blood."

The writer of this quotation has already in the seventeenth century understood the mechanism of these bodily phenomena—of the visions also, though this he did not know—that they are effects of a powerful suggestion. He also notices the dependence of the visions on the liturgy. "No festival was kept by the Church when she [Magdalen] did not see the saint in whose honour it is celebrated coming to her or behold the mystery honoured by it, with every accessory in detail, particularly during Holy Week and the Octave of Easter." This liturgical suggestion was equally present in the corresponding visions of Osanna. But in both cases the artistic suggestion, because directly visual, was far stronger than the liturgical.

Blessed Colomba of Riete died in 1501. Osanna saw her wearing two garlands or crowns (*coronae*) and accompanied by bishops in their pontificals. She is on her way to heaven. One Purification she saw Colomba with Mary Magdalen and Catherine of Siena joining with her in prayer for Mantua. She sees our Lord in her room. On one occasion He removed her heart and replaced it flaming with love. He placed his crown of thorns on her head. She tasted the blood from the wound in His side, was wounded and suffered pain in her side and finally received the stigmata, which, like St. Catherine's, were invisible. Occasionally, however, they seem to have been visible even externally.[10] We hear of occasional levitation. In the fervour of her prayer "her spirit raised her

9. These facts about Blessed Magdalen have been taken from the Latin translation of Domenico Marchesi's life printed by the Bollandists for October, *Auctarium*.

10. Father Herbert Thurston, S.J., *The Physical Phenomena of Mysticism*, p. 62.

body upwards with its own ascent." Why this instance of the power of mind over matter should be regarded as incredible or miraculous is difficult to understand.

There are also visions of Paradise, in one of which St. Dominic presents her before the throne of God. Or she sees a company of saints encircling God's throne who move towards her in pairs, another vision reminiscent of Dante.

Ill in bed she sees St. Peter sing High Mass, St. Lawrence his deacon, his subdeacon St. Clement. The choir is composed of angels. At Christ's bidding the Apostle gives her communion. She sees Christ in the Host as an Infant or Crucified—the same restriction of her visionary field as of contemporary devotion. The devil appears black and hideous, another time "like a savage dog." But he is always repulsed.

When Osanna was eighteen our Lady appeared with St. Catherine of Alexandria and St. Catherine of Siena, respectively the patroness and the visionary of the Dominicans, and told her she was to be her Son's bride. This is Silvestri's account. Osanna, however, told Girolamo that the two witnesses to the marriage were our Lady and David. Presumably all were present. She took Osanna's hand and gave it to her Son, no doubt seen as a babe on her lap, who placed a wedding ring on her finger. There it remained invisible to others, though a nun witnessed to having seen it from time to time. Here most of all the imagination of the visionary meets the imagination of the conscious artist. The National Gallery possesses a picture by Borgognone, who was painting at Milan and Pavia during Osanna's lifetime. It represents the mystical wedding precisely of these two Catherines. Standing on His Mother's lap Jesus is placing a ring on the finger of St. Catherine of Alexandria, while our Lady grasps the hand of St. Catherine of Siena that in turn she may give it to her Son.[11] It is almost a replica of Osanna's vision. This subconscious artistry, however, though it cannot prove, in no way disproves a divine operation in the soul, a spiritual union of the intimate center

11. See National Gallery Illustrations, Italian Schools (1937), p. 52, No. 298.

with God.[12]

Although Osanna and her entourage attached more value to these images and understood them more objectively than is possible today, like all mystics Osanna knew that the highest and truest experience of God is beyond images. "Often without the intervention of any likeness" (any image), "by a purely spiritual sight [*sola mentis acie*] she beheld God with indescribable delight, a delight far more intense than when she contemplated God under an image. For she now obtained in a moment greater knowledge of things human and divine than any mortal man, however acute his intellect, can obtain by most diligent study."

Osanna's prayer was frequently intercession—intercession for relatives, friends, all who asked her prayers, and in particular Italy, Mantua and her rulers, also, as we have seen, kinsmen. And the intercession is constantly followed by foreknowledge that her prayer will be granted or, if made for a departed soul, by information about its lot in the other world. It has, however, been remarked that, with but one exception, she is not shown the damnation of any individual.

The truth of Osanna's information about the state of departed souls cannot, unfortunately, be tested. We may, however, be reluctant to believe that God permitted her in all innocence to delude herself and others.

Our Lord told Osanna that her father was still in purgatory but would go to heaven in two days' time. When a wife asked her prayers she averted a domestic scandal at the cost of acute pain in her feet, freely borne to reinforce her intercession. She was promised the recovery of a dying girl. One Epiphany she was urged to pray that Mantua might be protected from the French invasion. She prayed for Marquis Francis and promised him a safe return from France, promised the Duke of

12. It appears from a note in Cardinal Schuster's *Life* of St. Benedict (English translation, p. 147, note 13) that at the sacred grove of Venus destroyed by the saint an inscription has been found recording a pagan devotee who saw the goddess in a dream and therefore restored her sanctuary. Visions *by themselves* prove nothing. It is St. Paul's subsequent life and the seal attached to it by the Church which attests the authenticity of his vision outside Damascus.

Urbino that he would be reconciled with his wife and recover his duchy, of which Caesar Borgia had deprived him. She was promised the final conversion of a sinner and meanwhile that he would not be permitted to carry out his evil designs. And so it was. Blessed Magdalen was also prophetic, foretelling, for example, a victory won by her ruler, the Marquis of Montferat.

By divine inspiration Osanna had chosen for her confessor a friar who heard her confessions for thirteen years. She held to him in spite of attempts by prudish or hostile friars to make her give him up for an older man. Her prayer prevented his election as Companion to the Vicar General, which would have involved his departure from Mantua. She foretold the slaughter of some Mantuan troops fighting the French near Parma and was assured that "few, almost none" were lost, three for their great contrition were in heaven, the remainder in purgatory. She was certain that her brother John would not recover from an illness, but as she prayed beside his bed saw Christ and Mary carry his soul up to heaven. She learned later that he had died. A sister asked why John had reached heaven before a brother who died earlier. "Because he had more sorrow for his sins." Another soul she saw rising from death to heaven, and the joyful ascent to heaven of a friar who died suddenly as the result of an accident. Another dead brother she saw in heaven. He had spent only a day and a half in purgatory. She foretold the election of the Dominican provincial Vicar and Master General. A man engaged in a lawsuit asked her to discover by prayer whether his case was just. Assured that it was not, he abandoned his suit. A woman visited her to be told with all its details "of an abominable and impure deed" she was planning. She was converted. Osanna converted a woman shamming ecstasies, saw the desire of a niece to become a nun and foretold that it would be granted. A servant wished to become a nun, but was prevented by a severe illness. Osanna foretold her recovery and entrance into religion, and later when she was a religious her recovery from another illness. She foretold the recovery of Count Borromeo's wife, also of a young girl given up by the doctors. On the other hand, she was warned of the approaching death of the Marchioness Margaret, the death and ascent to heaven of a Franciscan and the death of a man named Alduino. She promised a poverty-stricken priest that a totally unexpected resignation would make him an Archpriest, and later on that a second journey to Rome to obtain his rights would be successful.

On the other hand, Girolamo tells us, she did not know beforehand the death of a sister named Bianca.

I said that Osanna, though she sees generally souls in hell, saw no individual damnation. There is, however, an apparent exception.

Osanna was praying for the Pope, Alexander VI. Though Silvestri uses vague language, Girolamo is explicit. We will follow his more vivid account. Our Lady appeared to support Osanna's prayer for the Pope's salvation and the reform of the Church, and the Apostles united their prayer with hers. "God," however, our Lord "stood motionless with a countenance far from cheerful, but on the contrary perturbed. Nor did He answer anyone a word, neither our Lady, nor the Apostles, nor my soul." When the Pope died, his fate was revealed to Osanna—damnation, we may conclude from her grim silence.

The theology of this vision seems questionable. No saint in heaven surely can desire anything God does not will, cannot therefore pray for it. Indeed the saint's will is now God's will in him or her. Nor, when all is said, does Alexander's sin approach the infamy of a Clement V who, though respectable in his private life, as the jackal of King Philip's greed delivered the innocent Templars to torture and death? Blessed Colomba, however, delivered to Alexander in person a stern message of rebuke. Its exact content has not been divulged.

Osanna felt deeply the ecclesiastical corruption of her age. She understood the prophetic text "there is no health in them" of Christ's mystical body, "wherein there was no sound health for the multitude of sins. It was a grievous burden to her to hear God's fearful threats for the abominations and grave sins committed in the world, above all by the clergy."

Throughout her life by prayer and penance Osanna stood like Moses "in the breach" to plead for God's new Israel. Her fasts were rigorous. Often she ate nothing the day of her Communion. For prayer she cut sleep to a minimum. She used the discipline and other instruments of penance. She heard Mass daily, in her room if she were too ill to go out to church—a privilege, later granted with difficulty to Blessed Antony Grassi on his deathbed, in these laxer days readily permitted. Unlike her contemporary St. Catherine of Genoa who did not go to Confession for years—not guilty of mortal sin she was under no obligation to do so—but communicated daily, Osanna made a weekly Confession, communicated only on Sundays and great feasts. Blessed Magdalen, on the other hand, was a daily communicant. On which her biographer comments significantly: "In those times so lamentably cold in their frequentation of the Sacraments her practice appeared something marvellous" (*prodigium*).

Osanna did not confine her charity to the intercession of prayer. She was ready with comfort and advice for all who came. Her parents' death had thrown upon her shoulders the care of her brothers and sisters, and even when they died or left home she still had household duties to perform. Gladly would she have escaped the throng of visitors, have fled to contemplative solitude, become an enclosed nun or an anchoress. But her vocation was clear. She must remain in the world to help others. During a period of famine she distributed loaves in person to the needy in the streets.

In this also Blessed Magdalen was Osanna's sister. Entertaining diseased beggars at her table, she ate herself the crumbs from their bread. She visited assiduously the sick poor, converted sinners and, like Blessed Antony Grassi, reconciled enemies.

Osanna's influence at Court was so great that she was often asked to put in a word with the Marquis. A conversation with Girolamo was broken off by a messenger from the Marchioness summoning her to the bedside of her sick son. His birth had been the answer to her prayer. She attended the deathbed of the Marchioness' nurse and in a vision of our Lord, our Lady, and angels—one can see it on many a contemporary panel or canvas—was informed that she was in purgatory. Our Lord blesses the palace.

Osanna's prayer was eminently patriotic. She prayed in particular for Mantua that it might be preserved, as it was, from the assaults and devastations of the wars which began with the French invasion of Italy by Charles VIII. Blessed Magdalen in like manner protected Trino by her prayers.

In 1479 the elder Marquis, Frederick, was about to leave for an expedition against Florence. He sent for Osanna, discussed his affairs with her at length. The mystic, the ecstatic, is the reverse of impractical. He then entrusted his wife to her, asking her to take care of her and be a help to her in all things. He would let her know his news from the front. When she promised to do as he asked, he replied, "Now I can leave with my mind at rest, because I am leaving my wife and sons in your charge." "Every day letters arrived from the Marquis bringing commissions for her to fulfil. And the Marchioness followed her advice in all matters." That she should submit thus to the guidance of her husband's relative measures the ascendancy of Osanna's holiness, wisdom and personality.

Nor did Osanna lack learning. She has indeed good claim to be a patroness of Catholic women's education. As a girl she wanted to learn to read and write. Her father, however, did not approve of education for women. "He would often say that it was dangerous and unbecoming for women to be literate, for the educated woman often proved the bane and disgrace of her family." In face of his refusal, she turned to our Lady. Kneeling down before her image she said she would not get up until she had won her over to her desire.

This was by no means the only instance of such pious importunity. It is indeed strongly recommended in the Gospel. Blessed Magdalen's prayer was equally importunate and equally successful. She obtained, her biographer assures us, either wholly or in part whatever she asked. "She never asked anything of God or His most holy Mother that she did not obtain, according to the degree of her confidence, either wholly or at least in part." Nor indeed should we contrast this prayer of importunate petition with the mystic's prayer of conformity to God's will. It is as compatible with a simple union in the central depths of the spirit as stormy waves on the surface of the sea are compatible with the calm of the depths below. This is indeed suggested by the ecstasy during which

Osanna's most powerful and effective intercessions were made. She was aware that this importunate prayer was itself God's will, the Spirit praying in her, an exercise of confidence in divine Love.

As Osanna pressed her petition upon our Lady, as so often, prayer became ecstasy. When she recovered consciousness she noticed a paper on which the names of Jesus and Mary were written. She read the words easily. The paper then disappeared, perhaps blown away or mislaid. One day our Lady showed her a booklet of hymns and she could read them as easily as if she had been to school, "had for many years submitted her hand to the cane." Finally she could read even difficult Latin and could write. She certainly seems to have read widely. For she quotes Sr. Ambrose, St. Isidore, St. Gregory, St. Jerome, and St. Thomas and "the divine Denys." She was thus better educated than St. Teresa, who knew no Latin. St. Teresa, however, needed learning less than a woman whose life and work were set in a city and court of the humanist Renaissance.

When I spoke of the sources for Osanna's life I had occasion to speak of the spiritual tie between herself and the Olivetan monk Girolamo. The forty-three letters addressed to him are largely expressions of the love which united them. A boy of fifteen, Girolamo had been so deeply impressed by the sight of Osanna praying in church that he entered religion and finally persuaded her to accept him as her spiritual son. That utterances of affection are more frequent than in Blessed Jordan's letters to Blessed Diana is no doubt explained by the fact that in this case it is the woman's letters which have survived and women express their emotions more readily than men. What is expressed is in both cases the same—a love wholly spiritual without biological attraction or desire and in which only the psychological distinction between man and woman plays a part. "Spiritualized love letters" they are aptly termed by Professor Gardner.

But let the letters speak, letters which Osanna believed had been destroyed but which Girolamo secretly kept for our benefit. She did not destroy his, but assures him that she kept them safely locked in her desk. "My mother's heart rejoices as I read your letter with heartfelt tears..."

"What must be the bond of perfect charity in our dear Jesus between an only son and his unworthy mother?"

"Most dear and delightful the bond…which has linked us together so closely, unworthy mother and son in the sight of God… This morning a voice said to me, 'Unworthy mother, your dear, your beloved son will visit you today.' Not days but years seem to have passed, since last I conversed on the things of God with my dear son in Christ whom I bear engraved in my heart. Jesus is the comfort and refuge of our hearts when we are parted. When will the happy day come when we shall be united in heaven? There we shall know that nevermore can we be separated."

"When I was informed that your Reverence had arrived at your convent in Mantua, I almost fainted, so great was my delight. My sins did not deserve the good news. Had you seen your unworthy mother so changed, perhaps even in colour, you might well have said: 'What is the source of this heartfelt love? It is Christ's wounded side.' God's great goodness has made this spiritual love so strong, that I am confident, with His aid, that neither Angel nor Archangel nor devil nor any other creature will ever be able to undo it, but rather that, through divine grace, it will be made perfect in our everlasting and blessed fatherland."

"I love your soul as my own."

"May we soon be in heaven. Then we never need be parted again."

"Never have I been bound so closely to any creature in God's sight as I am bound to you."

"The receipt of your letter has given me the utmost comfort. How bitter have been my grief, tears and sighs, because I have no one I can trust to carry my letter to my dear son. Your letter proves you have received the two I wrote. Let me know as soon as you can if you receive this. Though there are no secrets in it, it will reassure me. For I do not trust the carrier. I fear you must be ill, since I have not heard from you for so long. My God, with what anxiety and longing I have waited for news."

Raised above the flesh into God, human affection—yes, the affection between a man and a woman—thus ordered and established by God is not less but vastly more than it can be on the biological and merely natural plane.

Though we hear nothing of the contemporary Carmelite Beatus John Baptist Spagnuolo, Osanna is informed in prayer of another Mantuan saint, a priest whose sanctity has not been recognized. He was Girolamo's confessor, and Girolamo attests his holiness and graces of prayer. "His prayer and ecstasies closely resemble what Blessed Osanna told me of her own. I can bear witness that their souls often saw themselves united in God's sight and that the father often told me: My mother, Sister Osanna, has risen very high. Such was their mutual knowledge that when they conversed about a vision vouchsafed by God to their souls they understood each other perfectly." Like Osanna the priest was also a prophet and foretold the downfall of Caesar Borgia. But these extraordinary graces were the recompense of suffering. For thirty years he suffered from ulcers in his feet.

Silvestri records twelve miracles worked by Osanna during her life.[13] When the boat capsized in which she was returning to Mantua from Carbonaruola, she was supported above the water. The crew and the contents of the boat were saved by a boat sent out to their rescue. A boy on a church step had given the alarm. That she hovered thus above the water recalls Christ walking on the sea of Galilee.

To feed two little boys in need of milk Osanna ordered a maid to milk a goat that had never given birth, and persisted in the order, though the maid jeered. Sufficient milk was provided.

Her prayers enabled a baker's wife to bear her child safely. It was already dead: for the doctors, to save her life, had cut off its hand, but to no purpose; until Osanna came to her aid, she could not be delivered of the dead baby.

A woman whose hand was paralyzed asked her help. If only she could spin she could earn a livelihood. Osanna placed her rosary in her hand and next day she had full use of it.

13. I relate them on Silvestri's authority, the authority of an honest man in a position to know. But there can of course be no guarantee that all these things happened as he believed and told them.

A woman was suffering from cancer. The doctors decided to cauterize it. Almost dead with fear, she begged Osanna's help. The following night the growth, she found, had disappeared. The wife of another cancer patient named Bonaventura asked Osanna's help. It was a growth between the nose and an eye. It was healed.

A matron could not eat, for she suffered from lockjaw. Osanna opened her teeth with a spoon full of food. She was cured.

A young girl, Osanna's disciple, cured acute pain in her eyes by rubbing them with tears Osanna had shed in ecstasy.

A monk of St. Justina's at Padua, suffering from fever, invoked Osanna's aid in the solitude of his cell. Though he could not communicate with her, he was confident she could hear his petition. He was healed.

A father brought his daughter to Osanna unable to stand, because her sinews were contracted. Osanna took the girl into her bedroom, to bring her out shortly, cured. She walked home.

A servant girl had swallowed poison. She sought out Osanna, who was ill. A crowd of visitors barred her way. From a distance she silently implored Osanna's assistance. No sooner had she returned home than she vomited up the poison.

Isabella, daughter of the court physician, a girl of eleven, was seriously ill with fever. Her father was also Osanna's doctor and her friend. Osanna sent Isabella her rosary. She put it round her neck and was cured. But she did not return it. She wore it constantly. Ten years later, however, she fell ill of another fever so deadly that hardly anyone who caught it lived. It was no doubt a form of the plague. Again her father appealed to Osanna. She visited the patient and her visit was the beginning of recovery. It was her last work of mercy. She returned home to meet a fatal illness, presumably the plague and presumably caught from the sick girl. If that was the case, she was literally a martyr of charity, of whom it could be said, as of her Master, she saved others, herself she could not save.

To these miracles recorded by Silvestri, Girolamo, who relates the stories of the capsized boat and the goat's milk, adds yet another, that Osanna's embrace freed a nun from diabolical possession. These divine answers to her prayer bear, like the miracles related of other saints, so striking a resemblance to those recorded in the Gospels that it is irrational prejudice to reject the former out of hand and accept the latter. The rationalist is at least more consistent than the Protestant.

Whether Osanna knew the time of her own death, Silvestri is uncertain, though he believes she did. That he records his ignorance is in his favour as a truthful witness. She had long promised to send for him on her deathbed. She now asked Marchioness Isabella to summon him from Milan. The summons reached him on a Monday—in the nick of time. Had it been delayed a day longer, it would have been too late. He arrived in time to be present when she died. The Marquis and his wife visited her on her deathbed and asked her to bless them. Her humility objected, and taking a priest's hand she moved it in blessing. But she was finally persuaded to give a blessing with her own hand. She died on June 28, 1505.

The stigmata, scarcely visible in life, appeared clearly in Osanna's corpse and were still visible more than a century and a half later when the Bollandist Father Janning visited her incorrupt body. Since a dead body cannot be the subject of suggestion by the soul that has left it, if our information is reliable, the stigmata must have appeared before death, even if perhaps there were no longer apparent signs of life.

A popular cultus sprang up immediately which was shortly confirmed by a diploma of Leo X addressed to Marchioness Isabella. The Dominicans of Mantua composed a proper office in her honour. And in 1694 a Mass and office, though from the Common of Saints, was extended to the entire order. Her feast is kept on June 20.

SAINT THOMAS OF VILLANUEVA

[1488–1555]

As St. Hugh was an ideal Bishop in twelfth-century England, so was St. Thomas of Villanueva in sixteenth-century Spain. Archbishop of Valencia for ten years, he was in the fullest sense a father in God. The great Spanish teachers of contemplative prayer, St. Teresa, St. John of the Cross, St. Peter of Alcantara and such uncanonised writers as Luis of Granada and Luis de Léon, are well known. The saint whose prayer found its primary expression in almsgiving is not as well known as he should be. It is not for lack of available information.

Shortly after Thomas' death a member of his Order, the Augustinian hermit, Munatones, Bishop of Segovia from 1556 to 1591, who knew him well, wrote a brief memoir. The evidence given for his beatification and the documents of his canonisation are at our disposal.

A full-length life was written by another Augustinian, Miguel Salon, who published it in 1588. Salon collected the evidence of surviving eye-witnesses, also making use of Munatones' memoir. He published later a fuller life. This time it was based for the most part on the evidence given in the official process for Thomas' beatification, in which he officially took part. This life, begun in 1617, was published in 1620, a year before the author's death. The Bollandists published a Latin translation from which the following life has been for the most part taken. I have also made use of letters preserved in the state archives written by Thomas to the Emperor, a royal councillor, or Prince Philip, and published in the fifth volume of a collection of documents illustrating Spanish history published in Madrid in 1844.[1]

Salon's life, though vivid, is sober and conscientious. He does not exaggerate the marvellous element in Thomas' life. He must, it is clear, often be responsible for the exact words he places in the saint's mouth. They cannot always have been the report of witnesses of accurate memory. Nor after such a lapse of time are details wholly reliable. Salon claims no personal knowledge of Thomas. Indeed he was only sixteen when he died. We can, however, have confidence in the substance of the life. Moreover, the utterances reported are both strongly individual and consistent. They can be regarded as substantially true. Like the majority of earlier hagiographers Salon neglects chronological order. The Bollandist who remarks on this has done his best to supply the defect by a chronological survey of Thomas' life before he became Archbishop. For the events of the Archiepiscopate, exact chronology is unobtainable but of little importance. Salon in fact confines his detailed information almost entirely to three periods of Thomas' life, when he was Prior at Burgos (1531–1534 and 1537–1541) and when he was Archbishop. The bulk of the life indeed is concerned with the Archiepiscopate. Apart from these periods we know very little of Thomas' life. It is not a matter for deep regret. We know more than enough to know him well. Nor was he a man whose holiness was the result of a conversion from sin or lukewarmness. As a boy he was devoted to prayer and the poor. He could but continue on the path begun with the first use of reason.

From the saint himself we have a collection of sermons on the liturgy of the Christian year and another on the Song of Songs. These I have not seen.

Thomas was born in 1488 in Don Quixote's La Mancha, at Fuenllana,[2]

1. *Colecion de documentos ineditos para la Historia de España.*
2. "*Fuen llana*"—"level spring." This is not easy to understand. Could it be the corruption or mispronunciation of an original "*fuen illena*"—"brimming spring"?

a hamlet half a mile from Villanueva de los Infantes, where he was brought up and from which he has derived his name.

His parents were Alphonso Tomas Garcia and Lucia Martinez Castellanos. They were remarkable for their charity to the poor. They supplied farmers with corn for sowing and would take no profit from the crop, merely a return of the grain lent. His mother had a private chapel and received Communion weekly. She wore a hairshirt and, when a widow, the habit of a Tertiary. She visited prisons and hospitals and would often give her own clothes to the poor—not castoffs! Her prayer was contemplative, favoured with "many heavenly consolations and delights, divine pleasures and spiritual sweetness." She survived her son, who is said to have appeared to her on her deathbed.

As a boy Thomas more than followed his mother's example. He would give the poor the lunch packed for him to eat at school. He gave away his clothes and shoes. One cold winter's day he stripped himself of everything but his shirt. Once he is said to have taken a ball of his mother's wool to give away. Nothing was found to be missing. When his mother had locked up all her store-cupboards some beggars asked an alms. Thomas gave them each a chicken taken from the hen. Though these charities show his warm compassion for the poor, one cannot but reflect that they were at his parents' cost, who must replace even the clothes he had given away. Fortunately for themselves and for him they shared his charity.

We are not surprised to hear that he fasted even on days not kept as fasts, and took the discipline.

Thomas learned Latin at home. He went to the University of Alcala just founded by Cardinal Ximenez. As it was not opened until 1508, he could not have matriculated, as Salon says, at the age of fifteen or sixteen. In any case he became Master of Arts in 1514. In 1516 his father died. He made his house a hostel for impecunious girls.

Thomas, now a Master of Theology and also probably lecturer on theology at the University of Salamanca, this same year, 1516, on September 24 joined at Salamanca the Augustinian Hermits—one of them was the following year to begin the Protestant revolt and the disruption of Western Christendom! He made his solemn profession on November 25, 1517, and was ordained priest in 1518. He said his first Mass on Christmas Day, which would always be a feast particularly dear to him. In 1519 he was chosen Prior of his Salamanca convent—surprisingly soon after his entrance into the order; "most extraordinary," Salon comments, "indeed quite unheard of."

In January 1521 Thomas presided over an election at Toledo. He was succeeded at Salamanca by Ferdinand of Toledo who, however, died or resigned a few months later, and Thomas stepped into his place. He was re-elected Prior on April 25, 1523. In 1525 he was appointed Visitor and Reformer of the province of Castile, together with Juan Gallego. In 1527 the province was divided and Thomas elected Provincial of the new province of Andalusia. He issued a diploma granting the soul of his deceased father, his mother, his brothers and their wives a share in all the Masses, prayers, and good works of the province.

His term of office expired in 1529. He probably returned to Salamanca. But we have no information about him until 1531, when he was elected Prior of the convent at Burgos, where he remained until 1534. It was probably at this time that he was appointed a censor of books for the Inquisition. On April 1, 1534, he was chosen Provincial of Castile. In April, 1537, he returned to Burgos as Prior, also now a definitor, and remained at Burgos until 1541.

As I said, Salon had access to special sources of information about these years at Burgos.

In September 1541 Thomas met the General of the Order, Seripando, at Toledo, at a gathering of provincial Priors and friars of important houses. In November Seripando presided at the provincial elections. Suspecting his intention to appoint him his Vicar throughout the Iberian peninsula, Thomas deliberately arrived late. He was appointed Prior of Valladolid.

During these years Thomas had acquired a widespread reputation as a preacher, not for his oratory, though he was a gifted orator, nor even for his learning—though he was learned—but for the fervent conviction which animated all he said. "Sometimes he would inspire fear, at others bring comfort, moving the hearts of his hearers now to sincere sorrow for their sins, even to tears, now to spiritual joy." He drew crowded audiences. In Lent he preached daily on the Gospel for the day and a special Psalm. In those days the psalms were still widely known to the laity. He converted hardened sinners, healed inveterate feuds. Under his influence many embraced the religious life. A chemist of Burgos became a friar and later followed Thomas to Valencia. Noble and wealthy girls became nuns. Nuns were led to great holiness, married layfolk persuaded to lead lives of piety.[3]

These apostolic labours, however, were fed by an interior life of intense prayer. Unlike Luther, Thomas did not permit his work to crowd out his prayer. We shall hear much more of his works of charity and for souls than we shall of his prayer. Nevertheless the latter was the soul of the former. "He was as severe upon his body as before, as intent on heavenly things, as exact in the performance of his accustomed practices of devotion." His prayer was not only contemplative, mystical. It was ecstatic. Even while preaching he would experience a rapture. "Often he would stand motionless in the pulpit, unable to utter a word, as though deprived of the use of his outer senses, so fast his soul was bound by the intensity of his affections." He did his best to conceal these divine visitations. At Burgos he said his Mass at an hour when the people had all left the church and gone home. "For he was often rapt into an ecstasy" at the altar and remained so long without moving that the friar who served him must tug at his vestment to make him recover consciousness and finish his Mass. It is said that he was seen levitated in choir. Since, however, we hear no more of levitation, this cannot be regarded as certain.

Despite his reticence Thomas occasionally let slip in a sermon something of these experiences. Salon in particular refers us to a sermon on the Transfiguration. He was speaking on St. Peter's words: "Lord, it is good for us to be here." "Though unworthy I have at times,

3. Unfortunately also to break off marriage relations. The prejudice among the devout against sexual relations of any kind was widespread and deep-rooted.

though very rarely, been permitted to climb a high mountain in company with Christ, there to see the glory of His countenance, in part at least and from afar. With what ardor, with what tears do I then cry out: My Lord, it is good for us to be here, do not permit me to go down from this mountain. Thy presence is enough for me, do not, I pray, leave me, do not go away. Here let my entire life, all my days be spent. What more could I seek? This alone I desire, this alone I ask. Suddenly, however, the presence vanishes, the glory, the peace, the delight, and I am left to mourn. Swift as a lightning flash the splendour passes away." "Very rarely" suggests that the frequency of these ecstasies has been exaggerated with the passage of time. But their occurrence is unquestionable. We hear specifically of an hour's ecstasy as he preached at Burgos and of another while he was preaching at a convent of Augustinian Canonesses he had reformed there. The latter lasted for several hours. Did his congregation disperse? If the sermon was at Mass, how did the Mass proceed? We are not told.

But the most protracted ecstasy of which we have information happened later when Thomas was Archbishop. At six in the morning he was reading None for the feast of the Ascension and had reached the Antiphon, *Videntibiis illis elevatus est*—"While they were looking on, Jesus was raised up." He fell into a trance and so remained until five in the evening (the exact hours are differently stated). Then he came to and was preparing to finish None and say Mass, when he was informed of the late hour. The Antiphon, he explained, had been taken up by a choir of angels whose music ravished him with its sweetness.

On occasion he foretold the future. Salon, one is glad to observe, points out that apart from his holy life this would not have been a proof of sanctity.

The instances Salon gives occurred partly at Burgos, partly later at Valencia. Thomas foretold the Augustinian vocation of a Fleming whose servant had been suddenly cured as he prayed for him before a crucifix venerated in Burgos Cathedral. He foretold that a young man would be cured by a particular doctor he named. He warned a rich merchant not to make a particular match for his daughter, till he had laid the matter before God in prayer and could give him advice. The merchant would not wait but pushed on with the marriage. Thomas told him that he himself would die shortly and the marriage prove unhappy. And so it was. One of his servants was delighted at the birth of a son. Thomas warned him that the child would come to an early and bad end. He was murdered as the result of a serious crime he had committed. One may, however, question the wisdom of causing the father premature and useless unhappiness. He foretold that St. Catherine's Church at Valencia would be burned. The conflagration did not happen until 1584. When he was asked why he had not set apart a burial place for a college he had founded, he replied that it would not be needed; and during the seventy years which passed before he wrote, no student, Salon tells us, died.

Some of the instances given may not, however, have involved foreknowledge. That Thomas foretold the reforming Council of Trent seems little more than a shrewd anticipation.

As we should have expected, Thomas was a model religious. Though he loved retirement and disliked conversation, he gladly heard the confessions of any who wished to make them and had recourse to him for the comfort or cure of their conscience. And he was a model religious superior—placing the religious life on the firm foundation of prayer.

He wished the friars to attach the highest value to the interior life. If it is lacking, external observance, he would say, produces not genuine religious but shams. Though affable and kind to his subjects, he maintained his authority as superior. He detested innovations for their disturbing effect. He lavished tender care on the sick, treated offenders with charity and prudence. "He found government, however, a most burdensome task, being by nature disposed to solitude and to keep the peace of his cell. Moreover, he loved to read and study the Bible and spiritual books, to meditate on the divine mysteries."

The rules he laid down for visiting convents maintain the right scale of values. "Divine worship must be given the first place. It consists, he would say, in saying Mass, reciting the Office attentively and devoutly and keeping the altars clean and suitably adorned.... This, he was convinced, was the gate through which everything good entered a religious house." Important also was the reading of Scripture and holy books. "If this is neglected the other duties of the religious life lose their savior and become tedious. Peace and charity must be maintained, idleness shunned." Sometimes Thomas behaved as if he were unaware of a friar's offence. In one such case the culprit freely confessed his sin and lived henceforward a life so holy that in two or three years Thomas made him his companion, *socius*.

Among his subjects and disciples was an eminent missionary he sent out to Mexico, Jeronimo Ximenez.[4]

It is not surprising that he won illustrious recruits for the Order, among them Alfonso de Orozco, court preacher to Charles V and his son Philip, and Alfonso de Borja of the (Borja) Borgia family, a relative therefore of St. Francis Borgia.

So universally was Thomas loved that "wherever he might be, men of every condition of life came to him to consult him about matters of conscience or the spiritual life." "Everywhere religious and seculars alike revered him as a saint…she went his way the people came out of their houses to kiss his hand or garment. Matrons of the highest rank looked out of their windows, or kneeling down begged his blessing." Even "the uncouth rustics who spare no passerby, not even a religious, their tart and rude gibes and witticisms" kept a respectful silence as Thomas passed by. At Burgos a mother had turned her daughter out of the house and shut her up in a nunnery because, when she had arranged a noble match for her, she had found her solemnly engaged to a knight, which made it unlawful to marry another. The knight begged Thomas to help him.

He succeeded in winning the mother over, also in persuading another mother to forgive the murderers of her son.

Thomas' fame as a preacher had come to the knowledge of the Emperor Charles V or, it may be, the Emperor had chanced to hear him

4. In this connection Salon tells the story of a Franciscan missionary in Mexico, who reported from the interior an opulent pagan tribe whose temple walls were covered with emeralds. More remote than these men, he reported, there were said to be camels and elephants!

preach. Anyway, sometime between 1526 and 1539 he became a court preacher. On one occasion at least he also preached before the King of Portugal. He was soon in high favour at court. But to win or keep royal favour he would not swerve an inch from the course he deemed right.

When Prior at Burgos he had preached before the Emperor at Valladolid. His sermon ended, he left the city without paying him a ceremonial visit of farewell—in his eyes an unjustifiable waste of time. On another occasion, when he was Prior at Valladolid, he was preparing to preach, when Charles called at the convent and asked for him. He sent back word that he could not interrupt the preparation of his sermon. If the Emperor wished him to preach he must leave him the necessary time to prepare. Charles was not annoyed but edified. All religious, he said, should be as free from worldly respect as he. Preaching before the Emperor, Thomas told him to his face that public offices should not be sold. These things remind us of the relations between St. Hugh and Henry II.

So great was Charles' regard for Thomas that at his intercession he spared the lives of some courtiers for whom the heads of the army and navy, the Archbishop of Toledo, and even his son Philip, had pleaded in vain.

It is not surprising that he was offered a Bishopric, the Archbishopric of Granada. He humbly refused. But the day would come when he could refuse no longer.

In 1544 the Archbishopric of Valencia became vacant. Save for a few years under the previous occupant of the see there had been no resident Archbishop since 1455, when the Archbishop became the first Borgia Pope, and the arch diocese was therefore in a most unsatisfactory condition. The Emperor intended to appoint a Hieronymite friar. It was an Order he particularly favoured and it would be to a Hieronymite convent that he would retire to prepare for death. Accordingly he ordered his secretary to make out a brief in the friar's favour. He returned with a brief made out in favour of Thomas. The astonished Emperor asked the reason. "That was not the name I gave you." "I swear to Your Majesty," replied the secretary, "I distinctly heard you name Thomas of

Villanueva. However, the mistake is easily rectified. I will write out a brief with the correct name." "You shall do nothing of the sort," replied Charles. "You wrote down the name not because anyone persuaded you or even suggested it but only because you were convinced I had said it. Your mistake therefore was the work of God. The choice is His, not mine. Dispatch the brief as you have written it."

When the document reached Valladolid, the porter was so excited by the news that he rushed with it into choir, interrupting Compline. Thomas proceeded calmly with the Office and at its conclusion reprimanded the porter severely and ordered him to be beaten.

As with St. Hugh, Thomas' humility, combined with his love for the religious life of prayer, made him refuse. He rushed off to Prince Philip, who happened to be at Valladolid, and begged his support for his refusal. Though Philip, the nobility, and the Archbishop of Toledo pressed for his acceptance, only a command from his superior the Provincial that he accept the see as a matter of religious obedience made him finally yield.

When Thomas wrote to the Prior General Seripando to inform him of the appointment, and explain that he would now be unable to carry out work on a revision of the constitutions with which he had been entrusted, Seripando replied expressing his delight that "by the instrumentality of the Emperor Charles, religion's sole defender, God has promoted you, a man of sovereign integrity and learning, to episcopal rank. We worship the design of God who chooses whom He wills and praise Caesar's faithful heart. Our holy Lord Pope will, I have no doubt, confirm with the greatest pleasure the imperial choice."[5]

A comparison between Thomas' attitude and Hugh's reveals one significant difference. Both did all they could to avoid the episcopate and

5. In a second letter written in the same strain Seripando adds: "In the sacred college there is a Cardinal, the Cardinal of England, Reginald Pole, a man of eminent virtue, sincere Christian piety and remarkable learning, whose humanity and holy life have won him the esteem of all good men. No man who does not esteem and revere him can be reckoned a good man." The last words are a prophetic condemnation of Pope Paul IV, who far from esteeming Pole wished to condemn him as a heretic.

yielded only to obedience. Hugh, however, refused outright to accept as valid even election by the Chapter, because it took place under the King's eye and subject to royal influence. Thomas makes no demur to naked choice by the crown. True, the Pope must confirm the Emperor's appointment. But even had it been unsatisfactory, in practice he would, he must do so. Clement VII had accepted even Cranmer. Immediately on his election Thomas informs a member of the royal council, Francisco de los Cobos, "I will be most obedient and carry out whatever Your Excellency may command." Though the Pope alone had authority in matters of faith and worship, the government of the Spanish church was in practice a dyarchy, divided between the Pope and the crown. Erastianism had made considerable progress since the twelfth century.[6] Thomas was consecrated at Valladolid by the Cardinal Archbishop of Toledo.[7] He then set out for his see with but one companion and two servants. And his departure was kept secret.

Having sought guidance in prayer, he abandoned his original intention of making a detour to visit his mother and travelled by the most direct route. He must be with his flock as soon as possible. We must not, however, conclude that he neglected his mother. In the sequel we are told that from time to time she visited her son's diocese when he lodged her on an episcopal domain where he could visit her easily.

This was but one instance of Thomas' constant habit to make no decision without previous prayer, fervent and prolonged, for divine guidance. "Prayer," says Salon, "was the school in which the divine Master Jesus Christ taught him what to do, reply, or say in every matter

6. In a mitigated form indeed it survives in Spain to the present day, and in France perished only when the anti-clericals tore up the Concordat.

7. Salon seems to believe that the ceremonial of the Pontifical is of apostolic origin. As ignorant of ecclesiastical history and therefore ready to defend impossible positions were most of the sixteenth-century defenders of Catholicism. In the same vein Harding will argue against Jewel that private Masses were celebrated in the primitive Church, Blosius denounce the Protestants for refusing to accept the writings of the Pseudo-Denys as the work of St. Paul's convert. It was a pity the controversy could not have been confined to the firm ground of dogmatic principles. Catholics would then not have defended many positions neither defensible nor needing defense.

that cropped up... Though the holy Bishop was endowed with signal eloquence, a judgment extremely perspicacious, extensive experience and knowledge, he put his trust not in himself but in prayer and God's providential government." Often the practice appears to result in guidance not to adopt what in itself is the best or wisest course, but simply the course most profitable to the soul of the man who seeks it. If we are to believe Salon, Thomas' prayer was more efficacious, led him to the choice objectively the right one. For example, he never took anyone into his service without previous prayer, as our Lord prayed before choosing His Apostles. But, unlike Hugh with his ungrateful steward or indeed our Lord Himself with Iscariot, Thomas never chose anyone unworthy of his choice. Can we, however, be certain that it was God's will he did not visit his mother at this time? The delay would have been only a matter of days.

Outside Valencia was an Augustinian friary, Santa Maria de Succorsu (St. Mary of Succour). As Thomas entered it a prolonged drought broke and a torrential rainfall set in. The Prior at first could not believe that the simple friar with one companion—even the servants had been dismissed—was the Archbishop he was expecting. When finally convinced, confused at his mistake, he hastily arranged the solemn procession, which conducted Thomas into the chapel. A continuous downpour detained him in the convent until New Year's Day. In such weather it was impossible to escort him ceremonially to the city and his cathedral. Meanwhile he took his share in the Offices, but refused to pontificate until he had been enthroned in the cathedral. It would give offence to his Chapter. Indeed, he was rarely present at solemn conventual Mass and Vespers, when he would be obliged to occupy a place of special honour.

No sooner had the rain ceased, than the Canons and civil authorities had the entire route between the convent and cathedral cleared of the mud it had left—no light task.

At last he could enter the city and cathedral in solemn state. Even so, he wore "a habit and cloak of black cloth extremely old and worn, with a hat so old that its colour had faded and it was threadbare." He refused to venerate a relic of the Cross on a cushion, but prostrate on the bare floor and weeping.

There was universal rejoicing throughout the city, greetings put up everywhere with verses and illuminations.

The following morning he sang his first Mass in the cathedral. It was January 1 or 2, 1545. The same day he inspected the prison for delinquent clergy. He was shocked by the dark damp dungeon—totally unfit, he said, for men dedicated to the service of God. He ordered it to be closed and filled up with earth.

The Canons offered Thomas a sum of money they had collected to furnish his palace. He asked whether he might spend it as he thought best. When they agreed, he told them he proposed to give it to the governors of the hospital, recently damaged by fire, to rebuild wards. At the same time he ordered confessors to plead the cause of the hospital with penitents in a position to assist it. For himself his new dignity made no difference to his personal poverty. His clothes were worn threadbare. A cloak presented to him he gave away to the poor. The magistrate of a township named Alcoy gave Thomas a garment of good black cloth to replace the shabby garment he was wearing. He bought three more at the same price, then gave all four to the poor, those hidden poor whose self-respect would not allow them to receive public charity.

The Chapter once sent a deputation to ask their Archbishop to dress more suitably. All they could achieve was a hat of better material.

Thomas refused to pay the price asked by a tailor for repairing two doublets and fitting sleeves to them. The tailor was disgusted by what he regarded as meanness; "the miserly skinflint," thought he. But he changed his opinion when Thomas gave his two daughters dowries of thirty libras, and twenty more to buy furniture. Another tailor, who condemned the parsimony of insisting on a doublet of cheaper material, also came to think differently when he asked a dowry for his daughters and received seventy libras. Thomas had read their thoughts and pointed out that only rigid personal economy made these gifts possible.

His old and broken shoes were resoled till they drop to pieces. A Canon surprised him mending his underwear. When he gave vent to his indignation, Thomas reminded him that, though he was an Archbishop, he was still a religious vowed to poverty. Only twice in his ten years' episcopate did he renew his Augustinian habit. It was made of cheap cloth and worn until it became so ragged that a servant would be ashamed to be seen wearing it. Finally the Canons' expostulations persuaded Thomas to buy another. But it also was made of cheap material.

Meals were frugal. Even for guests or on great festivals there was only a little meat or a bird.

Neither in his room nor elsewhere in the palace were there any costly hangings or ornaments. When his steward bought a tapestry representing our Lord taken down from the Cross, and a carpet, Thomas reprimanded him and ordered them to be placed in the cathedral. His table silver was confined to a dozen small spoons for guests and two salt cellars. The steward pointed out that a silver table service would cost less than the servants' constant breakages. "I agree," said Thomas, "but I am a religious." His bed was hard and coarsely furnished, without linen. Even so he merely pretended to sleep in it. He slept in fact on bundles of twigs with but one coverlet. He wore a hairshirt continually and kept not only the fasts of his Order but others for personal devotion. On the Wednesdays and Fridays of Advent and Lent he dined alone on bread and water.

From February until September of his first year Thomas conducted a visitation of the archdiocese. His sermons were more ardent than ever: "not human speech they seemed but flames of fire and rays flashing from heaven." The visitation bore fruit in many conversions and reconciliations, and generally an improved moral and spiritual standard. Thomas was assisted by two Visitors. He also appointed a suffragan bishop, Juan Segrian, to pontificate on solemn feasts, confirm and perform other episcopal functions he was prevented by other work from performing himself.

As we might expect from the long absence of a shepherd, the state of the archdiocese, Salon tells us, was deplorable. "Among the laity gross sin was rife, in particular divorce" (that is, permanent separation) "and many of the clergy flaunted their mistresses in public." The spectacle cost Thomas bitter nights of lamentation and penance as being responsible for his flock. He called a synod which passed many reforming decrees. The Chapter, however, refused to recognize their Archbishop's jurisdiction, claiming Papal exemption. To their indignant clamors Thomas replied with calm dignity. "God," he said, "knows the scandal your conduct is giving and the need for the enforcement of these canons. Though you may reject my jurisdiction and sentence you cannot reject God's."[8]

And in fact very shortly the Canons were obliged to invoke his intervention to defend their clerical privileges and, to obtain it, renounce their claim to exemption. A Canon, Elfo by name—he was a subdeacon—had seriously wounded an alguazil (a pursuivant). He was arrested and imprisoned by the Governor. Thomas demanded that the "criminous clerk" be given up to him. For the clergy were exempt from lay jurisdiction. The Governor stood firm. Thomas therefore laid the city under an interdict, in force from the day after the Epiphany until Holy Week. The Viceroy, who supported the Governor, asked in vain for its removal. He even threatened to confiscate the possessions of the see. Thomas was unmoved. "All you will do," he replied, "is to rob the poor." Finally, the alguazil having meantime recovered, on the day before Palm Sunday the Governor yielded and released the Canon. But he must do penance for the wrongful detention. A man of a position so exalted that he had acted for the Viceroy in his absence, he must attend the Lesser Hours and ceremonies of Palm Sunday without outer garment, cap, cloak, shoes, or girdle, in the garb of a penitent holding a wax candle. The Governor humbly performed his penance, which he had also incurred by condemning another subdeacon to be strangled for homicide. Thomas, however, told the subdeacon's father that his son had deserved his fate by bearing arms and taking a man's life.

After Easter, in a sermon, Thomas defended this clerical immunity which, he said, had existed from the beginning of the Church! But he also praised the Governor's humble submission.

8. In a letter to Prince Philip, Thomas refers to this subterfuge and the harm done by it.

For some years Thomas was troubled by a summons to attend the Council of Trent. Not only was he unwilling to abandon the diocese where his presence was so necessary—age and ill health made the journey impossible. He thanks Philip for excusing him from attendance. When, however, an order is received from the Emperor, though he pleads his state of health, he says he is ready to obey and leave the following September (1545). The Emperor gave way. But two years later he writes to Philip that his proctor at Trent, the Bishop of Huesca, has informed him "that he is being accused" at the Council "of contumacy for his non-attendance." He had been willing to go. But the Emperor had ordered him, no doubt on his representations, to stay at home. Will Philip ask his father to defend bishops who stayed away at his command? Even now if ordered he will go. Three years later still (1550) Thomas is once more obliged to plead ill health and support his plea by testimonials duly attested from Bishop Segrian, his doctor John Reyner and three other witnesses. After this solemn testimony to his infirmities he does not seem to have been troubled further.

Through his procurator, however, he submitted a number of proposals to the Council. Almost all were adopted, but not one, that only in case of great necessity shall a bishop be translated to another see, and that benefices should normally be conferred only on natives of the diocese.

Thomas' household was strictly regulated. His servants, reduced to the number absolutely indispensable, must not gad about the city but keep indoors, refrain from idle gossip, and observe a suitable rule of life. Those who could read must recite daily the Little Office of Our Lady, those whose illiteracy excluded them from this liturgical psalmody must recite the Rosary.[9] They must go to Confession and Communion at least monthly. On the other hand, he did not require from these laymen the life of a priest or religious. Only three of his servants, two who helped him to say Office and served his Mass and another charged with

9. Psalmody, we may observe, still keeps its rightful position as a form of prayer superior to the Rosary.

training the boys, were celibate. The remainder were married and with their wives and children occupied married quarters.

Any servant who was ill was visited daily by Thomas, his doctor asked about his state of health, and careful enquiry made whether he was receiving the diet and medicine prescribed. Every night Thomas made in person a round of the palace to make sure everyone had retired to his room. One night he went to the bedside of a dying muleteer to prepare him for death. When, however, the doctors arrived in the morning expecting to find him dead, he had recovered.

Thomas himself rarely left his palace—to say two Masses each week in a cathedral chapel, on Sunday to be present at Office and sermon, to visit a college he was building for higher education, and when necessary to transact business with the Viceroy—but also on a round of almsgiving.

Salon speaks of Thomas' knowledge of distant events and gives instances of it. A Franciscan convent is in need of food. As the friars are about to assemble round an empty table, provisions arrive from the Archbishop, informed at prayer of their plight. A priest imprisoned for his evil ways hangs himself. His crucifix, sweating blood, warns Thomas of the crime. The priest is cut down senseless. Thomas prays and finds him regaining consciousness.

A third instance is particularly dramatic. A man—his name of course is concealed, we may call him X—has committed what he rightly believes to be the perfect murder. No one can possibly bring it home to him, certainly not the farmer who is the dead man's brother. Lent, however, leads him to repentance and he makes his confession to a priest in the city. Little does he know that he is another brother of his victim. He is surprised by the priest's minute enquiry into the detailed circumstances of his crime, which have no obvious bearing on his guilt. However, he answers his priest's questions. The priest sends for his brother and says to him: "I have discovered beyond doubt, but do not ask me how, who killed our brother and all the circumstances of the murder. Wait a month or so and then lay information with the magistrates. They will send for the murderer and, when he finds himself confronted by a detailed reconstruction of his crime, he will become confused and contradict himself. His manner will betray his guilt and the magistrates will extract a confession by torture." The farmer does as his brother advised. Charged with his crime with all its details known, X's manner is indeed so guilty that he is put to the torture, confesses, and is sentenced to death. A priest visits him in prison to prepare him for death. But he stoutly refuses to make his confession. "But for confession," he says, "I should not be here. Confession for me has meant not life but death." This is made known to Thomas in prayer. The information verified, he requests the civil authorities to send their prisoner to him. "If," he tells them, "after investigation I find that the crime became known by any other channel, I give you my word I will return him to you to pay the penalty. If, however, I find that it became known only through a breach of the seal of confession, all theologians agree that it is your duty to ignore the offence as though you did not know it." The prisoner in his hands and sticking by his story under strict examination, Thomas sends for the farmer who laid the information and puts the fear of God into him so effectively that he makes and signs a confession that he had learned the murderer's name from his brother, the priest. It is his turn to be examined by the Archbishop. Confronted with his brother's confession, also genuinely penitent, he confesses his breach of the seal. Thomas informs the magistrates of the facts and demands X's release. He will, however, advise him to sell all his possessions and depart to a district where he is unknown, where no one will know him for a murderer, and where the sight of him will not provoke the rage of his victim's relatives. X does as Thomas asks. The priest, though repentant, is sentenced to lifelong imprisonment in the diocesan place of detention for criminal priests and forbidden ever again to hear a confession or say Mass. So far as we know, it was the heaviest sentence Thomas inflicted on any clerical offender.

In the sixteenth century nepotism was the rule rather than the exception. It was accepted as a matter of course that a Pope or, to the lesser degree of his wealth, a bishop would enrich his family. Thomas' parents were *nobiles*, a term certainly wider than our "nobility," including gentlemen entitled to bear arms. His relatives, however—the brothers of his father and his mother—were not. As the Bollandist explains, they had forfeited their position, because, to earn a living, they had taken up farming, an occupation which automatically deprived a "noble" of his status.[10] These poor relations evidently hoped their nephew's Archbishopric would mean wealth for themselves, and turned up at Valencia with expectations. Thomas was not ashamed of them, far from it. He was transacting business with two other bishops when a fanning uncle arrived "wearing tied round his neck the linen cloth worn by farmers in the villages of Castile." He was delighted to see him. "You are welcome, Uncle, take a seat." Then, having asked the bishops' leave, he began to question him about his journey, how things were going at his home town, about his (Thomas') mother and relatives, with evident signs of pleasure. Having sent his uncle away to rest, he turned to the bishops and, delighted as he was at the good fellow's visit, he told them, "This man is our uncle, our closest relative on our mother's side." Another uncle, his father's brother this time, arrived and was entertained for a month. But Thomas will not lavish upon them revenues he regards as the property of the diocesan poor. He did indeed give the last-named uncle sufficient to replace one of a yoke of oxen which had died, but explained that he did so, not because he was his uncle, but because it was a case of genuine need.

For the same reason he refused to give his mother more than a hundred escudos. A cousin gave his daughter in marriage to a person of education—*alicui viro litterato.* Thomas disapproved of a match between those of different social rank. "A farmer's daughter should not marry an educated man. You have acted unwisely." And he would give no larger dowry than he gave to the daughter of a poor man.

Two knights of Valencia became engaged to two of his nieces, thinking that an Archbishop would certainly provide a rich dowry. Thomas would give his nieces only the sixty libras given to poor girls, not the dowry he would give to a gentleman's daughter. "His cousins should

10. Later, he informs us, to encourage agriculture Philip III reversed this ruling and granted armorial bearings, therefore "noble," that is, "gentle" status, to all who farmed on any considerable scale.

not," he said, "marry gentlemen, but their own equals." This apostle of charity did not believe that Christian justice requires a classless society.

One Christmas Thomas' brother-in-law and another relative paid a visit to wish him "the compliments of the season" and in hope of a rich present. He entertained them during the festal period. But when it was over, he told them they must go. He did, however, consent to replace two mules required for field work as being genuine poor relief.

A cousin named Bonillo he entertained for a month and on his departure bought him a cart and two mules and gave him two hundred scudos. Bonillo, who had evidently been boasting of the wealth that would be his, was ashamed to return home with so little, and settled on a farm three miles from Valencia. Perhaps he was still hoping—in vain.

To other relatives Thomas gave, on the same principle, travelling expenses and oxen or mules for farm work. He would not allow his mother to visit him at Valencia but had her taken to Villar, a village belonging to the see, where she was entertained for a month and received visits from her son. His motive in this instance was to prevent his palace from being invaded by the ladies of Valencia "calling on his mother and offering to take her for walks, to see their gardens or by the sea." As the old lady had probably never seen the sea, this surely was a little hard on her.

Not even to pontificate did Thomas have vestments of his own. He used the property of his cathedral. And when visiting a parish church he was content with whatever vestments were to hand, as when, in a small village, he wore the vicar's old and torn surplice and later, when required by the liturgy, an old cope of black linen.[11]

This is an indication of the glaring inequality of ecclesiastical incomes. Certainly the Church was wealthy. But the wealth belonged to the Bishoprics and great monastic foundations. The parochial clergy were often desperately poor.

Though Valencia had been conquered as early as the fourteenth

11. Salon speaks of Thomas pontificating on "some feasts of particular solemnity." Otherwise he said Mass twice a week in a chapel of the cathedral, on the other weekdays said

century, the Moorish population, the Moriscoes, were but nominal Christians.[12] For they had been "converted" only of recent years, victims no doubt of the campaign of enforced mass conversions initiated by Cardinal Ximenes in the opening years of the century. Thomas in fact admits that they had been converted "practically speaking by force." It is not therefore surprising that they were "obstinately attached to their evil religion." "These recent converts live at their will and make bolder every day to perform in public their Moorish rites. Though baptised, they live publicly in Moorish fashion, practicing their Moorish worship." Thomas, however, was convinced that being baptised they must be compelled to live and worship as Catholic Christians. At first he had been delighted that the burden of these Moriscoes had been taken from his shoulders by the government and entrusted to the Bishop of Segovia, his fellow-student at Alcala. The Bishop, however, did little or nothing, was, indeed, called away to the Council of Trent, and finally Thomas, in his own name and that of a Canon, dispatched to Prince Philip a memorandum on the question. He has taken what action he could. A high school has been founded to educate sons of Moriscoes, house and garden purchased. There are already thirty children in charge of a rector and two assistant teachers. A hundred and forty-six parishes (*rectorias*) have been founded for the Moriscoes, each with an endowment of thirty libras, and rectors appointed. These undertakings have been financed by two thousand ducats from the revenue of the see, first-fruits and contributions from the beneficed clergy, voluntary, it would seem, only in name. Books of instruction have been printed, regulations made for the Moriscoes and alguazils appointed to enforce them, to see that they went to Mass and "lived as Christians." Special preachers have also

or heard it in his private chapel. When we compare this with St. Hugh's eagerness to take every opportunity to celebrate a solemn Mass even when travelling and in danger of hostile attack (see pp. 61, 75), we detect premonitory signs of the liturgical debacle of the nineteenth century. No longer, like St. Hugh, does Thomas regard High Mass as the norm for which Low Mass is but an unavoidable substitute. Low Mass is the norm, High Mass an additional solemnity for great festivals.

12. My authority for this aspect of Thomas' episcopate is his letters published in *Documentos ineditos*.

been chosen with authority to baptize and administer the sacraments. Collectors have been appointed to receive the confiscated revenues of former mosques and the new endowments. The high school must be completed, the new parishes visited.

In view of the religious ignorance of a population forcibly converted, the law of the Church cannot be enforced in its rigout. A brief must be issued empowering the competent authority to absolve in any fashion he thinks best, to grant plenary absolution for all apostasies or heresies incurred within the past twenty years, and to dispense marriages within prohibited degrees of relationship contracted during the same period. Authority must be given to alter existing parishes or erect new. The Moriscoes must be disarmed and not permitted to communicate with the Moors of Algiers. "They must be reformed and instructed so that they keep the Catholic faith *externally at least.*" It is regrettable that Thomas attached value to such hypocritical profession. They must no longer be able to plead ignorance of Catholic doctrine. Action must be taken against landowners who, probably for a profitable consideration "protect the Moriscoes and prevent the rectors and alguazils from forcing them to hear Mass." Philip, and this was the most important and urgent step to be taken, the key to the entire "business," must entrust the execution of these measures "to a prudent and hardworking man zealous for God's service and the salvation of these souls."

This letter was written in November 1547. But nothing or very little can have been effected. For in March 1551 Thomas informs the Emperor that the Moriscoes "are utterly lost, a flock without a shepherd and as Moorish [Muslim] as before they were baptised." No one had the necessary authority to suppress the "Moorish rites they carry out in public without fear of punishment." An apostolic delegate must be appointed with extraordinary powers, or the Inquisition set in motion, or the Ordinary (himself) given special powers to punish apostasy, but with "due moderation." In consequence presumably of this appeal to Caesar the Bishop of Segovia at last appointed a certain Gregorio de Miranda "Inquisitor and Commissary for the new converts." The number in his archdiocese Thomas estimates at sixty thousand families.

This, however, can have been no more than a gesture. For the following year Thomas is again pressing upon Philip the urgent need to appoint an ecclesiastic to take effective charge of the Moriscoes, who had not even been disarmed and might make common cause with a Turkish fleet off Mallorca. Evidently the evil results of compulsory conversion rendered even the sanctity of Thomas unavailing. As he realised bitterly, with the new Moorish Christians he had failed. It could hardly have been otherwise.

Thomas was also continuously distressed by the corrupt administration of justice in Valencia, "the lack of justice here." Family ties were more powerful than justice in the courts. The officers of justice failed to perform their duty.

Though to the utmost of his power maintaining strict discipline, Thomas showed great kindliness and humility in his dealings with his clergy. He had occasion to reprimand a rural dean and a parish priest for preaching an apocryphal indulgence. When they proved to him that they had been deceived by a skillful forgery of his signature he at once begged their pardon.

A Canon he had publicly rebuked lost his temper and insulted him in public. Not only would Thomas not permit the treasurer to lay hands upon him, he rescued him from the Inquisition by putting the blame on his own severity and brought him back to breakfast.

All Thomas' tact, charity, and firmness won but a partial success in his campaign against the clerical concubinage which was widespread, had become open, even generally accepted by public opinion. Salon's account is revealing. Vehement sermons, he tells us, converted some offenders, "but they were only a few." Consequently, after public threats in a sermon, Thomas prepared and even had printed a decree inflicting severe censures and penalties on all priests who kept a concubine. No sooner was this known than "the entire city was in an uproar, so many were guilty of the sin and among them clergy of the first rank." So strong was the opposition that Thomas thought it prudent to compromise. If some reform and the remainder will at least keep their concubinage private, he will not publish the decree. He must have secured that measure of reform. For he did not publish it. When a theologian found fault with this laxity, Thomas defended himself by the teaching of St. Augustine that when a particular sin is widespread and has infected the larger and more considerable portion of the community, the safer course is to be content with fervent prayer and preaching rather than provoke a disturbance by censures and anathemas.

Thomas did not, however, refrain from doing all he could with prudence to secure observance of the law. On occasion, when a priest's life was particularly scandalous, he adopted severe measures, at others he trusted to gentler methods; sometimes he appears to have tried both methods upon the same offender. And Salon has reported many successes. Having in vain reprimanded a particular Canon both privately and in public for his vicious life, he changed his tactics and showered upon him marks of special friendship. At the end of two years, when he judged the time ripe, he asked the Canon if he would go for him on a confidential and delicate mission to the Holy See. When the Canon said he would very gladly do so, he told him to go home, make his will, and settle his affairs before a journey so long and dangerous. When he had done this, Thomas kept him six months hidden in the palace, only one trusty servant aware of his presence, while he persuaded him to a complete reformation. At the end of the time he sent him home, everyone believing he had returned from Rome. It must have involved many untrue answers on his part to enquiries about his journey, and the idolaters of veracity may blame Thomas for staging an elaborate deception. Reasonable people, however, will judge that he was right to safeguard the Canon's honour and dignity.

It was not a priest, however, but a lay offender who experienced another instance of Thomas' charity. A storm threatened a village. The villagers determined to seek help from our Lord in His sacramental presence. But the priest was away from home. An aged layman took the Host from the tabernacle, bore it to the church door and there gave a blessing with it. The storm passed away from the village. When the story reached his ears, Thomas sent for the old man, praised his zeal and faith but rebuked his presumption and breach of the Church's rule. For penance he must provide two tall wax candles to burn on Sundays from the beginning of the Canon to the priest's Communion.

Thomas also showed mercy to a repentant priest who one Good Friday, because the choir had omitted something to be sung—nowadays much is always omitted—lost his temper and swore abominably.

He persuaded a cleric, probably a priest, to break off relations with the mother of his three children. But he arranged a marriage for her, educated the children, and provided a dowry for the daughter.

He converted another profligate cleric arrested in a brawl. Two others were persuaded to renounce their mistresses. They were extremely poor and had supplemented their inadequate stipends by support from the women. Thomas made provision for their livelihood, also arranging marriages for the women and assisting them with a dowry. He converted the priest of an important parish so thoroughly that, not content with patiently enduring a few days' imprisonment ordered by the Archbishop, he insisted on spending two months in a dark prison living on bread and raw herbs, until he was finally ordered to return to his parish.

A priest who after promise of reform had lapsed into his old life was finally converted by Thomas' tears and burning words; others converted by witnessing the merciless scourging he inflicted on himself to expiate their sins. One priest in particular was converted, after holding out through eight days' imprisonment, by the sight of the wounds inflicted by Thomas' discipline, and broke off the liaison. His mistress was a rich woman and he too had been supported by her. Such situations are eloquent of the clerical poverty of which I have spoken. Thomas arranged for him to say Mass daily in a particular church, for which he would receive a monthly stipend of thirty reals.[13] Another priest holding a high place in the cathedral Chapter had seduced a novice in a convent and kept her in his house as his mistress. He too was converted by Thomas' words, tears, and discipline. The Archbishop arranged a marriage for the girl.

One of the most attractive views of Thomas' character, however, is to my mind the following episode.

A priest of good repute complained to him of the immoral life led by another priest, giving rein to his righteous indignation and denouncing the culprit unsparingly. When he had brought his tirade to an end, "For the love of God calm yourself," said Thomas. "If you have not yourself fallen into the same sin of human weakness, it is God's mercy, not your virtue. Of yourself you are every bit as weak and wretched as he, and so are we all. Moreover, even if you are not guilty of this particular sin, do you imagine you are free from other sins? Can't you understand that the anger which brought you here to accuse him, though you had never rebuked him in private, as the Gospel bids you, is itself a sin and a mortal sin at that?" Having dismissed the accuser with a flea in his ear Thomas sent for the accused and brought him to repentance. But once again he provided for the priest's former mistress and her family, and clothes for the priest himself.

Salon reckons the income of the see of Valencia at twenty-five thousand ducats at most, no doubt a wealthy endowment. But he estimates the amount spent by Thomas on alms at some seventy thousand or even eighty thousand ducats.[14] As we read of his charities, we are indeed left with the impression that he possessed Fortunatus' purse, never failing when the needs of the poor must be met. And we shall in fact hear authenticated stories of funds or food unaccountably multiplied. We must indeed allow for even gross exaggeration in this estimate of Thomas' charitable expenditure, and he may well have received assistance from other charitable donors. In one instance we know this was the case. Even so, it seems certain that the expenditure was far more

13. Salon observes that in Thomas' day one real and a half purchased more than four reals when he wrote this second life about 1617, inflation comparable to that from which we are suffering.

14. Elsewhere, however, Salon says that of the entire twenty-five thousand ducats all but five thousand required to meet indispensable charges were given in alms. He must surely mean that twenty thousand ducats were officially spent from the income of the see, but that somehow the twenty thousand proved elastic and provided seventy thousand or eighty thousand.

than the receipts. "Pray, trust, give" was the principle of Thomas' action. It was certainly successful.

For the poor, in particular the aged and infirm poor, the palace was a haven of refuge where they were certain of a kind welcome and assistance. Thomas listened to their stories with patience and sympathy, giving even the most filthy beggar a seat near his own. He would leave his breakfast to attend upon a poor man, as once to confirm the invalid son of a pauper. He gave strict orders that no poor person must be sent away and that, however he was occupied, he must be informed at once if any poor man asked to see him. "However many came to see him and at whatever time of day he never seemed put out. No time was inconvenient, no need left unrelieved."

To beggars at his gate Thomas gave a loaf, a dish of pottage, a draught of wine and a piece of money; if sick or infirm, a portion of mutton and two coins. The number of beggars ranged from four to five hundred or more. Nor were alms refused even to the dishonest paupers who asked twice over hoping to pass unrecognized. (Do we think he ought to have refused the beggars and set up a Charity Organisation Society? I hope not.)

These avowed paupers, however, were not the only destitute. There were large numbers of those whose self-respect made them conceal their poverty. They cannot be called precisely poor gentlefolk. For they included unsuccessful artisans. But there were among them a considerable number of *nobiles*, gentlemen, and even members of the nobility. For the impoverished gentleman or nobleman was another widespread social evil. Many preferred to live in semi-starvation rather than lose caste by an occupation incompatible with their social rank. Thomas was at pains to seek out these unfortunates and relieve their want. He also assisted the incapacitated, for instance a farmer who had lost the use of his right hand. When his almoner stopped the monthly payment made him of seven reals, Thomas reprimanded him and paid up the arrears. He provided material for the domestic crafts of those pre-industrial days, weaving, for example, or the baiting a poor widow could practice. In this way he put many of these hidden poor in a position to earn a livelihood.

It is not enough, he would say, merely to give an alms. The poor must so far as possible be delivered from their poverty. He gave assistance to a weaver of silk that he might not be obliged to sell below the just price. In every parish he instituted guardians of the poor to discover and relieve the destitute—very different from the "guardians" of the nineteenth-century poor law. He was lavish in relieving the clerical poverty of which we have had so much evidence. Priests in the city parishes, in extreme poverty because they had nothing to live on but Mass stipends or, if beneficed, their benefice was worth very little—some moreover with a mother or sisters to support—were assisted by regular monthly payments and when necessary sick relief given to their dependents.

A complaint was made against a priest who to support his mother and sister wove silk even on Sundays and feasts. Thomas sent for him and expressed his approval of what he had done. It was lawful, he said, even on Sundays and feasts to provide for his and their needs. Nevertheless to avoid giving scandal it was advisable to abstain from work on those days. In lieu of the lost earnings Thomas will give him twenty reals a month.

A cathedral cantor asked leave to visit his sick mother at Guadalajara. Thomas enquired into his finances. "You will want to give your mother some delicacies." He gave him forty libras and a mule.

An impoverished nobleman was in receipt of his alms. His almoner complained that his house was much better furnished and with richer ornaments than the palace. He surely was no fit subject for charity. But Thomas replied that the nobleman was right not to sell ornaments and furniture necessary to keep up his position. He gave him a hundred and fifty libras a year.

For all his superabundant charity Thomas did not believe in social or economic equality. St. John Chrysostom was an advocate of a Christian communism on the model of the apostolic Church at Jerusalem. Catholics evidently are free to adopt the view of either saint. For my own part I prefer Thomas of Villanueva's.

To an impoverished nobleman of high rank from Aragon he let land below its market value, no doubt to be re-let by the nobleman at a profit. To a poor gentleman who had asked for a hundred reals he gave four hundred. There were alms too for matrons reduced to poverty.

As we must have noticed already, one of Thomas' favourite charities was the provision of dowries. For a dowry was indispensable. If a parent could not provide a suitable dowry, he could not make a match for his daughter. "Throughout his tenure of the see," Salon tells us, "no poor girls were married without receiving from Thomas some financial assistance." A girl, for example, is engaged to a carpenter. Thomas gives an additional thirty libras above her dowry to purchase the tools of her husband's trade. As we have seen, he graduated the dowries in accordance with the bride's social position.

It was a practice all too common to expose unwanted children at church doors. To provide for these unfortunates was another charity Thomas had much at heart. Consequently the gate of his palace became the place where many infants were abandoned. All were taken in. At times Thomas was supporting fifty or sixty, even seventy or eighty, of these children. But no number was too great for his charity. One night when a baby was left outside the palace, the servants caught sight of a man hurrying off. They could have caught him but hesitated to do so, fearing their master might not approve. They judged rightly. "Had you caught the parents," he said, "what could we have done about it? Their penury is suffering enough for them."

Thomas rented two houses near the palace, placing a nurse in charge of each, that babies might be brought to them at any hour. And there were other orphanages for them in charge of nurses.

On the first day of every month[15] all the nurses and their charges were summoned to the palace and inspected by Thomas. If a child was clean, well kept, and well cared for, he gave the nurse a bonus; if not, he reprimanded her and withheld the gratuity. He made provision for their clothing—"for they were as dear to him as if they had been his own children." "If the King," he told the nurses, "entrusted his children to your

15. Elsewhere Salon says it was only on great feasts. A regular monthly inspection is perhaps more likely.

charge, what good care you would take of them. The King of Heaven has entrusted His children to me and I on His behalf to you."

To encourage the destitute to leave their babies at his palace Thomas ordered the outer gate to be left ajar till nine o'clock in the evening in summer, seven o'clock in winter, and the approach to the palace kept dimly lit, with a bell to pull when the door was shut. Once a mother came one morning to nurse the baby she had left the evening before. When this was discovered, Thomas insisted that she should notwithstanding be paid her nurse's wage. For the medical service of the poor Thomas had opened a pharmacy and for a considerable salary had hired the services of two physicians and a skillful surgeon named Alator, one of the new Christians, that is to say Christian Moors. Once he declared he could do nothing for a baby girl born with feet twisted the wrong way. Thomas bade him apply the usual ointments to her sinews and joints and bind them up. "Trust in God." Without any pain the deformity was corrected—a miracle, maybe, or perhaps divine use of manipulative surgery.

Thomas also received poor orphans and brought them up. Among them were the children of a tailor, the eldest four or five years old. They grew up to trust and love him as a father. In due course he had each apprenticed to a trade. And he made himself responsible for three boys, sons of a widow with a very large family, and took charge of them. We have found the same love and care of children in St. Hugh. It would seem that an ideal father in God must be a man of strong paternal instinct sublimated to embrace not only his diocesans, children in God, but often these adopted children. Thus the renunciation, for Christ's sake of physical fatherhood is compensated and rewarded by a far larger family of spiritual sons.

To sew clothes and bedding for his orphans Thomas employed a staff of seamstresses. They informed him that they were unable to keep pace with the demand. "Say no more, my daughters," he answered, "you are working for the poor. Our Lord will supply the necessary strength. How gladly you would have sewn grave-clothes had our Lady asked for them to wrap her Son's body. And that precisely is the work you are doing when you sew for the poor." When he knew his death was at hand he paid the nurses' wages and the costs of maintenance for two years ahead.[16]

One evening there was nothing left for a crowd of poor folk. Thomas retired to his chapel to pray. A merchant arrived with a basket containing a thousand ducats. One day in midwinter Thomas, like St. Martin, gave a half-naked beggar his winter cloak.

He had ordered a room to be built above the porch where he could say Office quietly, and the cost proved greater than he had expected. One is surprised he had not insisted on an estimate. He was found walking in the room saying his rosary and weeping. When a Canon asked the reason of his grief, he feared, he said, God would call him to account for thus spending the money of the poor. The builder, hearing of these regrets, assembled his workmen and went with them to the Archbishop. "For heaven's sake, Your Grace," he said, "do not complain about the cost of this job. You are giving alms to all these poor men who depend on their wages to support themselves and their families. If Your Grace were not building this room, since it is winter, they would almost all be out of work." Thomas saw the sense of this, ceased to grieve, and enquired who of the men were married and what children they had. Where the need was great he gave alms in increase of wages. It was the classical procedure of the Speenhamland magistrates condemned by the political economists. But saints care little for "the dismal science." He also when necessary supplied clothes and bedding.

Another work of which Thomas repented was building a college for the Augustinian students at his University of Alcala. For he became convinced that he had no right to spend outside his diocese money which belonged to his diocesans. It was for them, on the other hand, that he founded a college at Valencia for poor students. Even so he endowed it insufficiently from a scruple that he might defraud other poor persons. An increase in the endowment he intended to make was prevented by his death.

16. What happened to these orphanages after that? Salon is silent; his silence is disquieting.

Among his crowd of paupers Thomas noticed a cripple staring up at him. He sent for him and said, "What do you want, brother? Are not my alms sufficient?" "For myself they are, but I have a wife and two children to feed." "Do you know any trade?" "Yes, I am a tailor. But crippled as I am in hands, feet, and legs, I can no longer work." Making the sign of the cross over him Thomas said, as St. Peter to that other cripple at the temple gate, "In the name of Jesus of Nazareth the crucified lay aside your crutches and go back sound to your home and employment." He too was cured immediately. Sick persons given up by doctors were cured when Thomas had visited them, read the Gospels, and made the sign of the cross over them.

Reluctant though he was to leave his palace, Thomas and his confessor went out to make personal visits to the poor. Sometimes they were returning only when the cathedral bell rang for midnight Matins. "Let us go in," Thomas would say, "and help the Canons with their Office."

After his weekday Masses in the cathedral Thomas took a seat near the High Altar and women, head and face veiled, laid before him their spiritual or temporal needs under a pledge of secrecy, as if told in confession. Where necessary he would order their confessors to give assistance with equal secrecy.[17]

A flood had put the mills of Valencia out of action and corn had to be sent away to be ground. More numerous than ever were the poor clamoring for food. There was not sufficient flour in the Archbishop's stores. But he would not allow them to be sent away unrelieved. "Rather will my servants and myself go hungry. But I put my trust in God. There will be enough." The flour lasted until the mills were once more working.

At a time of famine, by special arrangement with his farmers, Thomas obtained an additional supply of corn and stored it in his new room above the porch. One evening three widows arrived, impoverished gentlewomen, one with many small children. Thomas told his steward

17. Speaking in this connection of the Archbishop's carefully guarded and perfect purity, Salon tells us that he would not allow his servants to see him with bare feet. One must regret this prudery. But what a trifle it is seen in the light of his heroic charity.

to give them corn. "There is none left," he replied. "The granary is empty and was swept out only this morning." "Kindly go and see if there is not something left for these women." Finally they went together to the granary and found it full of corn. A woman named Mariana de Sotomayor who lived in the palace—no doubt the wife of a servant—deposed that no one could have brought in any corn without her knowledge.

There are other reports of resources multiplied. It was sometimes found that more clothing and bedclothes had been distributed than had been supplied.

On one occasion Thomas' servant discovered that since he left Valencia he had spent more in alms than he had brought away with him.

From time to time the suffragan Bishop, Segrian, and the other diocesan Visitor, Master Porta, visited the parishes of the diocese bestowing alms wherever they went. They were supplied with money for expenses and alms and clothing to distribute, but were forbidden to accept any presents other than a little fruit, a flask of wine, or other trifling token of welcome which it would be churlish to refuse. Nor must they confine their alms to the old Christians but on the contrary must give the Christian Moors a priority.

If anything necessary for divine service was found to be wanting and the parishioners were not obliged or not accustomed to supply it, Thomas must be informed and would make due provision.

Once the alms purse was lost and diligent search failed to find it. After prayer at Mass it was discovered inside the other purse and full of money, though much had already been spent. On another occasion it was stolen. Porta was obliged to draw for alms on the expenses purse. After a sleepless night he once more had recourse to prayer and Mass. A man entered the sacristy, as he was unvesting, returned the purse and confessed his theft. He explained that, as he was making off with the stolen purse, his way was barred by the figure of a bishop clothed in the garb of a religious. He thought it a phantasm, the creation of his own fear—these sixteenth-century Spaniards were not indiscriminately credulous—and tried another road. Once more the apparition met him. Convinced and penitent, he had come to make restitution. When the visitors returned to Valencia, Thomas spoke to Porta of his sleepless night, "but" he added, "the Lord cured your anxiety." How he knew he would not tell.

Charles V was fortifying the Balearic island, Ivica, as a naval base against the Turks and Moors. He asked Thomas for a loan of twenty thousand[18] ducats towards the cost. At first he was for refusing outright to deprive his poor of the money. But on second thoughts, because the fortification was needed for the defense of the country, he lent half the sum asked. Already, indeed, in 1546 in a letter to the Viceroy, he had agreed that it was the duty of prelates to assist the Emperor in his defense of the Church. Accordingly, "in spite of the impoverishment of my revenues by the cost of the Bulls" confirming his appointment—for which, he wrote in another letter, he was heavily in debt—and of setting up his household, expenses exceeding eleven thousand ducats, nevertheless to assist His Majesty in such great need he is ready to give the greater part of the six thousand ducats asked.

In this connection we may remember that, although St. Hugh refused to finance Richard's wars on the Continent, he was prepared to meet the feudal obligation of his see to contribute to home defense.

How exposed in fact the coast of Spain was even at this height of Spanish power was shown when on St. Barnabas' Day (June 11) 1552 a notorious pirate, Araix, raided the coastal town of Cullera in the Valencian archdiocese, inflicted great slaughter and carried off a rich prize of captives and loot. Thomas dispatched a certain Father Verdoley, later a Carthusian, his almoner, and two attendants, to distribute relief to the sufferers. He sent eight hundred ducats. All the captives were ransomed, the peasants furnished with funds to purchase corn, wine, and oil and where needed to replace mules or oxen; and provision made for the widows of the slain. When this had been done, it was found that the amount distributed in relief was twice the amount entrusted to the Archbishop's delegates. It must, however, be said that a citizen of

18. The entire sum could hardly have been expected from the normal revenue of the see. A special levy was, I suppose, intended.

Valencia, Gaspar Escolano, had contributed to the relief fund administered by the Archbishop six thousand libras. So his grandson informs us. Salon should not have suppressed the fact. Thomas' lavish charity was not diminished by the generosity of another.

Though he had accomplished so much, Thomas, like St. John Vianney at Ars, was never happy in his office. Both craved for a life in which their thirst for uninterrupted communion with God could be satisfied. Though mistaken, they cannot be charged with a selfish piety. For they were convinced that they were unequal to their responsibility for the souls of others and that prayer could be more fruitfully apostolic than active apostolic labours. Thomas therefore from time to time implored the Emperor for leave to resign, but was quite rightly refused.

He had indeed suffered for many years from serious illness. The testimonials sent to the Emperor in 1550–1551 to excuse him from attendance at Trent—from bishop Segrian, his doctor, a body servant and two others—give us detailed information. Since 1549 he had suffered from hernia, a rupture so extensive that it required a special surgical instrument. In particular a severe attack one Christmas Eve had made it impossible to attend Matins or sing the principal Mass of the feast. It had necessitated hours of treatment. Another attack had occurred when he was riding over a bridge on his way to visit the Viceroy, and he had been obliged to return home. When ordered by his doctor to visit for his health a village named Buriasol, "little more than half a league" from the city, he dared not go lest riding might produce another outbreak of his rupture. In addition he suffered from stomach trouble. A mouthful of cider had caused two days' pain. And he could eat only food for invalids. Nor was this all. He also suffered from quinsy, particularly in January, and from gout.

This complex of maladies can hardly have improved during the years following and must have contributed to the sense of insufficiency which weighed on Thomas and his longing for release from the burden of office and a life of unfettered prayer.

In 1554 when Thomas renewed his insistence, Charles returned an evasive answer. He is coming to Spain the following year, will visit

Valencia and there take such measures as will promote the service of God and give satisfaction both to the city and Thomas himself. Noncommittal as it was, when Charles arrived at Barcelona the following February (1555) Thomas sent Porta to remind him of his promise. Still evasive or undecided, Charles replied that he could not visit Valencia until he had completed a journey through Aragon. Thomas was disappointed, but comforted when at prayer he heard a voice from his crucifix: "Be not disturbed. On My Mother's birthday you shall come to Me and rest."

He understood and prepared for death.

In consequence of a dearth, he had spent an exceptional amount in alms during Lent. Nevertheless at Easter four thousand escudos remained. He ordered alms to be doubled till the sum had been exhausted.

On August 28 Thomas said Mass in honour of his Order's patron, St. Augustine. The following day, August 29, he fell ill with angina pectoris. He heard but could not say Mass and made a general confession.

September 2, Monday. He received Communion from Bishop Segrian. He addressed the Canons present, bidding them be scrupulously obedient to the holy Roman Church and her teaching and show pity and compassion to the poor.

September 3, Tuesday. His illness caused universal mourning. Mass was solemnly sung, public prayers offered. "The clergy led the way with sorrowful countenance, most of them barefooted, reciting the litany in a low tone to obtain God's mercy. The laity followed, the majority, the women in particular, barefooted, all weeping and sighing but in deep silence. Nothing could be seen but tears, nothing heard but groans."

September 4, Wednesday. The doctors pronounced Thomas better. The city rejoiced. But he believed the words from the crucifix and awaits death. Death was in fact very often preceded, one might almost say announced, by a sudden improvement in health, the final effort of animal life[19] against its extinction. He had an account taken of all his money. The amount is uncertain. In the same chapter Salon speaks of five thousand libras and of three thousand ducats—unless indeed one of these two figures is a misprint or a mistranslation—and other accounts mention other sums.

September 5, Thursday. Thomas sent for Bishop Segrian, a Canon, and a Dominican friar, and bade them collect the guardians of the poor throughout the city and through them distribute the entire sum in alms, with a careful regard to the honour of the poor ashamed to make known their poverty. All that day and the next the distribution continued. It included the provision of dowries for poor girls. Some received as much as sixty ducats, no one less than four libras. These libras were enclosed in packets. A poor armorer had been obliged to pawn his possessions to pay the next half-year's rent. He was given a packet containing four libras. When he opened it, he found the coins were all half-reals amounting in all to about thirty libras—and all contained in a packet intended to hold four. He was now able to pay off his rent and purchase material to forge swords. He became one of the wealthiest armorers in the city. Salon, however, adds that this was the only attested case of multiplication during this distribution—which increases our confidence in him.

September 6, Friday. At None Thomas was informed that some thousand libras remain over. He urged the three to press on with the distribution, that he may not die with so much as a penny in his possession.

September 7, Saturday. He was delighted to be told that all the money has been spent. But his pleasure was diminished by the information that a further sum has just been received. He ordered it to be given to his servants, also the furniture of his palace. The gaoler, however, was absent and received nothing. Thomas sent for him, and in due form, in the presence of witnesses, gave him the bed on which he was lying. "But of your charity let me lie in it till I die." The doctors gave up hope. Thomas extorted their verdict from Segrian and Porta, then turning to the crucifix repeated many times the Psalm verse, "I was glad when they said unto me: we will go into the house of the Lord." In spite of his sufferings "his mind was as lucid, his use of his faculties as complete, as though he felt nothing. He received every visitor with a welcome and

19. In man this animal life is a mortal function of his immortal spirit, as it is the soul, the life of the corporeal organism.

a joyful countenance as though he had been in good health." At ten o'clock that night he was anointed. He chose for his place of burial the Augustinian convent, Santa Maria de Succorsu. "If God's divine goodness," he said, "having regard not to my sins but to His infinite pity and mercy and the merit of His precious blood, shall take me into His glory, I will never forget this church and city. It will be no less dear to me when I am dead, than when I lived here and sought its good to the utmost of my power." He insisted on being allowed to pass his last night alone.

September 8, Sunday, Our Lady's Birthday. At four in the morning Thomas rang for his confessor and made his last confession. His throat was blocked so tightly that he could not receive Communion. Later on Bishop Segrian, the almoner, and others came in. St. John's Passion was read until seven o'clock. Mass was said at an altar in the bedroom, "not only because it is so great a festival but that I may not die without seeing my Creator and Redeemer."[20]

The Mass began some time after seven. At the elevation Thomas adored the Host with tears. He then recited slowly Psalm 30: "In Thee, O Lord, I have put my trust." As the celebrant received Communion he had reached the verse: "Into Thy hands, O Lord, I commend my spirit." They were his last words. He died about eight in the morning.

The body lay some hours in state in the palace hall. Masses were said beside the bier. Later the doors were opened to the public. An enormous crowd pressed in, mourning and lamenting. Salon reckons the number as about two thousand. About two o'clock the body was taken to the cathedral amid a crowd of mourners. "Have mercy on us, Father. What shall we do who have lost our father?"

Still later in the day it was taken to the convent of Santa Maria. Tears and sobs choked the chanting of the clergy. As the procession made its way through the crowd, a child of nine or ten fell from a high story into a patio. The mother invoked Thomas' help and the child landed safely on his feet.

---

20. We must regret the emphasis of a period for which the Mass was not primarily the Eucharistic sacrifice but the sight of our Lord in the Host.

September 9, Monday. Religious came from all the mendicant Orders and sang Lauds of the Dead, followed by Mass and the Absolution. At eight, Lauds of the Dead were sung a second time and Bishop Segrian sang Mass. The people were then turned out and with them the parochial clergy. The cathedral Chapter, the magistrates and Governor, some noblemen and the Augustinian friars remain. The body was buried.

On the ninth day a solemn Requiem was sung in the cathedral by Bishop Segrian in the presence of the Viceroy. It was followed after a further interval of nine days by a solemn Mass at Santa Maria.

A marble effigy, carved at Genoa, was placed on the tomb, which became a center of cures and other favours. Thomas was beatified in 1618, canonised in 1658. On September 22 his feast is kept by the Universal Church.

For his Office there are two special antiphons:

Dispersit, dedit pauperibus: justitia ejus manet in saeculum saeculi.
["He distributed and gave to the poor. His righteousness abides forever."]

Eleemosynas illius enarrabit omnis ecclesia sanctorum.
["Every church of the saints shall tell of his almsdeeds."]

BLESSED ANTONY GRASSI

[1592–1671]

THE ATTRACTION OF St. Philip's charm is worldwide. The charm of his disciple Blessed Antony Grassi is almost unknown except to his brethren of the Oratory. It is a pity. For the charm of the founder revived in the disciple. I was sensible of it when some years ago I made Blessed Antony's acquaintance in the Attwater-Thurston edition of Butler's *Lives.* With his talent for conveying, whenever his material admits of it, the distinctive personality of a saint within the narrow compass of such compression, Attwater made me desire to know more of Antony. Soon afterwards I was able to obtain a copy of the only full-length biography in English, written by Lady Amabel Kerr immediately after his beatification, and published in 1901.

Though written in accordance with the hagiographical convention of its time, it is free from exuberant sentimentality and, if not of outstanding merit, is a competent and informative work. She is certainly a narrator who can tell a story. She must have taken her material from a life by the saint's companion and disciple, Father Cristoforo Antici, supplemented perhaps by depositions made in view of a beatification expected over two centuries before it was achieved. I have felt no misgivings in making it my authority.

Antony was born in the city where he spent his long life, Fermo. It is a town, then in the Papal States, on a hill about four miles from the

Adriatic and twenty from Loretto. His birthday was November 13, 1592. His father Vincenzo, we are told, away from home was roused from sleep by a voice informing him that a son had been born to him who must be called Antony and would be a great servant of God. There were four more children. As Antony did not believe that Oratorian detachment should cultivate family ties, we hear little of them. His timely action, however, saved the property of his brother Domenico from destruction by rioters. His sister Eleonora, the only one of three whose name we know, trusted her brother so implicitly that in the full assurance of subsequent approval he spent money she had left in his charge to relieve the starving poor. And he attended a nephew's deathbed.

When still a boy Antony lost his father and was brought up by a devout mother. From childhood he was outstandingly pious. Daily Mass, attendance at sermons, a little altar at home where he preached, severe mortifications—this precocious piety in itself need mean little, might have been largely a mimicry, the product of upbringing in a pious family. But when, as in this case, it is continued into a life of heroic sanctity, it is the expression of an authentic love of God, of a soul from its first unfolding open to God. The center of the boy's religious life was the Fermo Oratory, and his director a member of the Roman congregation, formerly a companion of St. Philip, Father Flaminio Ricci, who to recover his health had returned to his birthplace. From childhood Antony thus drank the authentic spirit of St. Philip from one who had known him so well.

That Antony's vocation should be Oratorian[1] and that he should seek admission to the Fermo congregation was under these circumstances almost a foregone conclusion. His mother, rather surprisingly, opposed it. She could hardly have thought her son indispensable as the family breadwinner. For the Grassi were well-to-do landowners well furnished with rents. Lady Amabel Kerr thinks it was a matter of family

1. The Oratorians are not a religious order, but congregations of secular priests. Though they have a rule of common life, they take no vows. And although the congregation possesses funds for its use each priest retains his private property. Every congregation is an independent unit. There is no central government.

prestige. Antony held firm—convinced moreover of the danger to religion which might arise from family ties—and entered the Oratory on October 11, 1609, in his seventeenth year.

His life henceforward, with two exceptions—a Jubilee visit to Rome and the lightning stroke that nearly cost his life—is uneventful. Chosen superior of the Oratory in February 1635 he was re-elected twelve times in succession and held the office when he died. Dates in his life are very few. For dates mark events and Antony's life is not outwardly eventful.

Only one such stands out like a rock rising up from a plain—the stroke of lightning to which I have just alluded.

Though the legend of the Holy House of Loretto cannot be traced back before the opening years of the fifteenth century, and in the sixteenth a Catholic traveler to the Holy Land had remarked the impossibility of the alleged translation of the Holy House from Nazareth, it was universally believed.[2] Antony certainly never entertained the least doubt—how could he?—that the sanctuary of Loretto was indeed the house where the Archangel visited Mary and the Word was made flesh. The belief gave rise to a corresponding devotion. Year by year till the eve of his death he made his pilgrimage to the shrine, where he passed long hours absorbed in prayer. Nor in this connection is the authenticity of the shrine relevant. It is a sensible expression of the central truth of Christianity, the Incarnation, and therefore all devotion paid there is devotion to that mystery. Moreover, the prayer of so many devout pilgrims over the centuries has impregnated the atmosphere of the sanctuary, bestowed upon it a holiness independent of its historical origins. Though the Holy House is not the scene of the historical Incarnation, it is holy ground nevertheless, where the Incarnation has been continued down the centuries as the Word has become Incarnate in Christ's members, when He has been born in souls at prayer. It is one of those garments, of which the Platonist Smith speaks, which Truth assumes, the better to communicate with simple and unlearned, in his contemporary

2. For a full discussion of the legend see *Dictionaire d'Archéologie Chrétienne*, Article "Lorette."

language, "idiotical,"[3] men. It was in 1621 on one of these pilgrimages that Antony had an escape from death so narrow that he was convinced it was due to our Lady's intervention. And in that connection he departed from his usual reticence and has left us a detailed account of the occurrence, from which I quote, as Lady Kerr has translated it.

It was on September 4. Antony was kneeling on the steps beneath the dome. He had just made his confession and his heart was filled with a compunction and a loving aspiration to God such as even he had not experienced before. Suddenly a storm burst and a flash of lightning struck him. "I felt shaken and as if I were outside myself; and it seemed to me that my soul was separated from my body and I was in a swoon." "I seemed to be standing in a room of fire and I wondered to myself whether the faces of angels or of devils would appear to me. But neither appeared. Aroused by a great crash, as though of thunder, I opened my eyes and perceived that I had fallen down the steps head foremost. I saw on the pavement some pieces of stone and the air thick with a smoke so dense that it seemed like powder… I perceived that a piece of skin had been torn from a finger." It reminded him of a priest killed by lightning with no mark on his body except the peeling of a piece of skin. "When I looked at my finger, I felt sure that I too should die. A burning heat seemed to consume the interior of my body and when I tried to move my legs I had no sensation in them. I feared that the scorching heat in my inside would reach my heart and then I should die." He lay there powerless, comforted by the thought that, if he must die, he would die in our Lady's home. A passerby spoke to him, called for help and a chair was brought. "When I was placed in the chair I had another fainting fit" but "this time I was conscious that my head, arms and legs were hanging down useless, and though both sight and speech failed me, my hearing was acute and I heard someone suggesting the holy names of Jesus and Mary. A little wine was given to me and my speech returned

3. Though Blessed Antony was very far from unlearned, his theological learning did not embrace archaeology or historical criticism. In these respects most scholars in the seventeenth century were "idiotical."

and I asked for Extreme Unction." This, however, was not administered until he had been taken to his lodging, put to bed, and by the doctor's order given "oil of sweet almonds." "After this there was some abatement of the scorching heat within me. It was nevertheless so intense and made my breath so burning, that when my companion bent over me and caught it, it burned his throat." Next morning he was able to go to church and receive Communion, and the following day returned to Fermo. Traces of scorching were found on his underclothes which were sent to Loretto as a thanks-offering. It was then that he made a vow of annual pilgrimage.

Fancy cannot but play with the bare possibility that on one of these pilgrimages to Loretto, in 1649, Antony may have met or at least seen a foreign priest who had just arrived to die as a Canon of the chapter, the poet Crashaw. One could indeed have wished that he might have attended the poet on his deathbed, the saint of ecstatic devotion and joyous love helping their singer in his last need. This unfortunately cannot have been the case. Antony, however, must surely have been told of this English Canon and his untimely death and have prayed for his soul.

Antony fashioned his Oratorian life and ruled the Oratory on the principle of a strict, even a literal, observance of St. Philip's government of the Roman Oratory and of detailed conformity with his rule of life. He wished not only to be himself a copy of his spiritual father but to make the Fermo Oratory a copy of the Roman, as it had been under St. Philip's rule. And he had been prepared for this by St. Philip's friend and successor Father Ricci. Between master and disciple, however, there was a significant difference. "When in Rome," writes Lady Kerr, "he had picked up a saying of Father Alessandro Fideli's to the effect that, though St. Philip *was singular in nothing,* he did everything in a singular spirit; and it was precisely in this absence of singularity that Blessed Antony believed the essence of his vocation to consist." "St. Philip singular in nothing"—truly an amazing remark of Fr. Fideli's. For he pushed singularity to the point of eccentricity. His biographers Ponelle and Bordet speak of his extravagances, "strange exploits," "the number and enormity of the follies he could commit in public." To dress with clothes inside out, to walk the streets smelling a bunch of broom or admiring a marten fur he wore for a month, to "perform ridiculous dances" before an audience of Cardinals and prelates, to wear strange clothes in choir, deliberately garble the Latin of his Mass, even have his hair cut in church while Mass was being sung—if these things are not singular, who in the name of heaven is singularity?[4]

In this, however, Blessed Antony did *not* copy St. Philip. No such singularities are recorded of him. And far from permitting himself St. Philip's liberties in church, he was such a stickler for reverence, that he suppressed conversation with a severity we should expect from a nineteenth-century Englishman rather than a seventeenth-century Italian. He discarded, that is to say, from his imitation of St. Philip what expressed the temperamental genius, to retain what belonged to the saint. He thus reproduced the spirit of St. Philip freed from externals inimitable and in both senses peculiar which he could have but mimicked and burlesqued. He thus presented the substance of Philip's sanctity, as it is communicable, separated from incommunicable accidents. And this surely was no slight service to what we may call St. Philip's posthumous life in his Oratorian family and to those whose spirituality has been molded or influenced by the Oratory.

What then were the two predominant features of Antony's spiritual life and teaching: the two, no doubt rightly, chosen by Lady Kerr—both fruits of the spirit—peace and joy.

In his omnibus requiem quaesivi: "In all these things I have sought rest." The text came frequently to Antony's lips, as is signified by its choice to adorn the engraved portrait made after his death. "In all things"—yes, nothing made him lose perfect equanimity, complete peace of spirit. Though ready to converse when occasion required, he loved silence. "He spoke habitually in a low voice, and loud talking jarred on the silence his soul kept in the presence of God. If anyone raised his voice unduly," he "winced and protested with his gentle gaiety

4. For all this see Ponelle and Bordet, *Life of St. Philip Neri*, ch. 3, English translation, pp. 140ff.

of manner." "Father," he pleaded, "only a few inches of voice, I pray you." It was in this spirit of peace that he ruled his congregation. His correction was often no more than a look of reproach. His commands took the form of requests. And when one of the fathers, quite exceptionally, lost his temper and abused his superior before the community, his answer was to repeat his favourite text. When some of the fathers complained that his methods were too easygoing and urged more severity he replied, "I do not think I shall know how." Then he sat down in a chair, and "arranging his collar and putting on a look of pompous dignity," he asked whether that was the correct procedure. His critics smiled and admitted their mistake.[5]

No wonder so tranquil a spirit was an active peacemaker. "Blessed are the peacemakers" was Antony's beatitude. The people of Fermo were not only hot-tempered but vindictive. It was a city of feuds and vendettas. But Antony could reconcile foes who would listen to no one else. He was too tactful to irritate enemies he wished to reconcile by suggesting to either that he might possibly be in the wrong. He assumed that each man's account of the quarrel was correct and used arguments of a higher order. "It is very likely," he would say, "that your enemy is not at all deserving of your forgiveness, but Jesus Christ who gave His life for him and you deserves it." "God loved us, though there was nothing worthy of love in us and even though we were His enemies. Thus, even if we are unable to see anything in our neighbour which could make us love him but rather the contrary, regard for God should make us try to love him." Or with the common sense which recommends charity, one defect should never be considered in anyone, "but the whole of his actions should be considered, in which, as a rule, more good than evil is to be found."

Among the many enemies thus reconciled was a mother who had vowed vengeance against her son's murderer. For in dreams her dead

5. How unlike saints can be! Blessed Antony's unruffled serenity—the rest he sought and found in all things is in striking contrast with the impetuosity, even violence of word and gesture which to the end of his days Blessed John of Montmirail, though assisted by the silence and discipline of his monastic rule, never overcame.

son bade her obey Father Antony's behest. When he himself forgave the threats, slanders, and violent abuse of his brother-in-law, the figure of our Lord on his crucifix bent nearer to embrace him—as the result of a splinter in the wooden crosspiece. Antony on his deathbed told the story of the crucifix to his Archbishop, and one of the fathers fitted it to his pardon of his brother-in-law. The similar story told of St. John Gualbert—the merciful knight—is uncertain. In the case of Antony we have better evidence. A gentleman swore an implacable feud against the Fermo Oratory. Antony persisted in greeting him when they met in the street. When the gentleman, infuriated, asked him how he dared to do so, he replied "It was not you I saluted but your guardian angel."

The Cardinal Governor and Archbishop of Fermo conceived the happy thought of appointing the Angel of Peace, as his fellow citizens termed him, "public peacemaker," to be as such at the disposition of anyone who desired to settle a quarrel.[6] From his deathbed Antony made peace between two brothers whom the Archbishop had tried in vain to reconcile.

With peace, joy. "Joy," wrote Keats, "whose hand is ever at his lips bidding adieu." There is a joy which does not bid adieu, because it is *adieu*, directed towards God. This is the joy of the saint, the joy of Antony. "Be joyous," he would say, "because St. Philip likes to see joy in his houses." "It is a mistake to think that, if we give ourselves to a spiritual life, we must be gloomy. God does not like sadness or melancholy in His service. He wishes us to be joyous. The value of joy to a soul is beyond all calculation." At this point he makes contact with the Puritan and Platonist Sterry who, widely severed as he was from the Church, was truly *anima naturaliter Catholica*, and, had the course of history run otherwise, might well have been not the chaplain of a Protestant dictator but the saint of an English Oratory. "Holiness and happiness are one thing in God and the soul." "Joy is love flaming. Spiritual joy is the laughter of divine Love in our spirits." "Joy is love flaming." In Antony

6. Evidence surely of a paternal rather than a tyrannical government in the states of the Church.

it flamed even to outward vision as the aureole he was seen by several persons to wear, while he said Mass.

The peace and the joy were fruits and expressions of the fundamental holiness which is conformity to the will of God. "To do the will of God is our food." "If we do everything because it is His will, the merest trifles become full of merit. No prayer is more pleasing to God than that which His Son taught us: Thy will be done." "The secret of contentment and of remaining unmoved is to fix your eyes on eternity. If we pay attention to what is going on around us, we are sure to be perturbed. The saints were never moved because they always looked at God and received everything from His hands." "The way to find peace is to repose in the Will of God without paying any attention to what we want ourselves…he who has done this has begun to taste the joys of heaven." This, it may be said, is a commonplace of Christian teaching. No doubt. But contemporary spirituality had fixed upon it for peculiar emphasis as the compendium of holiness, a short cut to sanctity. Antony may even have read in the Italian translation the treatise widely influential for many years in which the English Capuchin—the Fermo Oratory entertained relations of close friendship with the Capuchins—Father Benedict Canfield offered a "Rule of Perfection containing a Brief and Perspicuous Abridgement of all the whole spiritual life, reduced to the only point of the Will of God." For it was not until many years after Antony's death that the book fell victim to the anti-Quietist scare and, though free from Quietism, was placed on the Index.[7]

A will united to the will of God is the substance of prayer. What then of Antony's? Was he a mystic? If by mysticism we understand intimate union with God, every saint is as such a mystic. If, however, we understand by it consciousness of this close supernatural union, mysticism is not indispensable to sanctity. For, as I have pointed out already, the man or woman of transparent temper, that is to say whose nature is such that the central life of the spirit comes more or less readily to the

7. For Canfield and his "*Règie de Perfection*," see *Benoît de Canfield, Sa Vie, sa doctrine et son influence,* by Optat de Veghel, O.F.M. Cap. (Rome, 1949).

conscious surface, becomes aware of this union when a person of more opaque temper is unconscious of it or becomes aware of it only when its intimacy is far greater than it is when the person of transparent temper becomes aware of it. There can, however, be little doubt that Antony was a mystic in the strict sense. Though we do not hear of such accidental concomitants of the mystical intuition as visions or voices, the long hours he passed absorbed in prayer are sufficiently eloquent. At Loretto he would spend six hours in silent devotion, and when questioned about his prayer replied simply, "*somme dolcezze*"—supreme delight. He gave evidence of the psychological dualism which is a characteristic of the highest state of unitive prayer, the central spirit occupied with God and conscious of His presence, the more superficial consciousness engaged with earthly business. Moreover he possessed faith, which, as the mystics tell us, is the medium of even the most sublime union and contemplation, in the supreme degree. "With him faith amounted to something as near self-evidence as can be, and he affirmed that no revelation from heaven could make it surer." This is undoubtedly the evidence of God's revelation possessed by St. Teresa and given to Fr. Augustine Baker in his first experience of passive contemplation. And we are told of brief ecstasies when he elevated the Host at Mass. The most perfect form of prayer in his view is to rejoice in God's glory, for it is a foretaste of our eternal prayer.[8] Antony thus presents the substance of unitive prayer and the intuition of it with very few of the accidental concomitants which have too often been permitted to obscure its essence. Pure prayer, in short, and the pure Oratorian spirituality without any distracting accidents, however striking or even valuable in themselves, molded the spirit of Antony, and he was their personal embodiment.

With these dispositions it is not surprising that he delighted to embellish the church and celebrate with the best he could give of

8. Fr. Baker, in the *Secretum*, speaks less highly of this prayer of congratulation, presumably, because it may employ images and concepts and does not necessarily involve aspirations of the will to union. It can, however, dispense with the former and include the latter, which we may suppose to have been the case with the prayer praised by Antony.

ornament and music the great feasts of the Church's year.[9] He would press his friends to keep these feasts at the Oratory and thus share his joy. The Oratory indeed has been and still is more liturgical than other post-Tridentine foundations.

That such love of God issued in a corresponding love of his neighbour we could take for granted. But we cannot pass over unmentioned Antony's lavish charity to the poor. No sooner had he received his rents than he laid in a store of coins which he distributed lavishly in the streets, as he judged the necessity of the recipient. The remainder he gave away through others. In connection with this almsgiving we hear of a miracle attested on oath by a Father of the Congregation, named Falcone. At his request Antony gave him a few coppers for a beggar at the door. "Before I had time to go on my errand, I perceived that the coins had changed to silver. 'Father,' said I, 'look; you have given me silver pieces.' 'God sent it you,' he replied." Nevertheless time, perhaps a long time, had elapsed and memory is liable to illusions. Possibly the copper coins were removed and replaced by silver. Suspense of judgment is perhaps indicated.

It is, however, quite impossible to explain by an illusion of the subject the "miraculous" gift of a medal. The recipient was a nun of Fermo, Anna Gertrude Frontini, who gave evidence at the canonical process. She was suffering from an inflammation of a finger of her right hand pierced by a thorn or splinter and intolerably painful. After office she remained in choir crying with pain and asking her Guardian Angel to suggest to Father Antony to cure her. For Antony had a particular devotion to the Guardian Angels and with simple faith used to employ them as heavenly postmen. "All at once I felt a medal which fell from above my head, enter the breast of my habit. I took it out and saw that on one side it bore the effigy of St. Thomas of Villanueva, but I did not know who the saint was on the other side. There was no cornice or gallery

9. The altarpiece by Rubens discovered by Professor Longhi in the Church of the Fermo Oratory—it represents the Adoration of the Shepherds—was commissioned before Antony was elected Superior. If it was painted at Fermo, the youthful Antony may have watched the artist at work. It is reported in the *Daily Telegraph for* November 7, 1953.

over the place where I knelt from which it could have fallen, and I know it fell from above, for I saw it pass my face." Convinced it had been sent to cure her, she bound it to the injured finger. By the following morning the finger had been completely cured, no trace of the injury left. Certain that the medal was Father Antony's gift the nun put it to the proof by sending to enquire from him the name of the saint on the reverse of the medal, "without saying a word" of the way she had received it. The saint replied without hesitation that the saint was St. Nicholas.[10]

A country gentleman went in terror of a gang of brigands and their leader who levied blackmail upon him, threatening his life if he refused to pay. Antony told him to say every day the prayer to our Lady *Sub tuum presidium* and fear nothing. As he continued the devotion he took courage and declined to pay the sums demanded by the brigand. Shortly afterwards the robber was killed in a brawl with his own band. The gentleman could live in peace.

We hear of a posthumous miracle closely akin to several recorded above of St. Thomas. Antony had been the constant benefactor of an orphanage known as the Conservatorio. Shortly after his death the institution was reduced to such poverty that the Matron could not provide wine for some workmen engaged on repairs. Application was made to the Oratory and refused on the ground that there was not enough wine to meet the needs of the house. The undermatron indignantly exclaimed that Father Antony would not have refused and she was convinced could help them from heaven. She then went to the empty cask in the cellar to find it full to overflowing with wine. What are we to say of such miracles? Father Thurston, having carefully sifted the evidence, concluded that several cases of alleged multiplication of food or wine are sufficiently proved. And this particular miracle was in fact one of the two officially approved for Antony's beatification. Nor is it reasonable to accept the miracle of Cana and of the multiplied

10. Was he St. Nicholas of Myra or the Augustinian St. Nicholas of Tolentino (September 10), remarkable for his miracles and moreover a saint of northern Italy? He was almost certainly the latter, as St. Thomas of Villanueva was also an Augustinian friar, and St. Nicholas of Myra would surely have been recognized.

loaves and fishes and deny *a priori* its repetition by members of Christ's mystical body.

Telepathy and prevision are constant phenomena of Antony's life. Again and again he had knowledge of an unconfessed sin, even when the penitent had himself forgotten it, though the knowledge remained in his subconscious. And more accurately than the doctor in attendance he knew and foretold that a patient would or would not recover. An apparently slight illness he might pronounce fatal, foretell the recovery of someone at death's door. A doctor at Fermo, Guerriero Guerrieri, witnessed on oath to Antony's successful prediction of recovery or death. Often when he had pronounced an adverse verdict, Antony had said, "He will not die," and when he had regarded the illness as slight, had foretold death by saying "*Paradiso*, *Paradiso*." In every instance the result had justified the pronouncement not of the doctor but of the saint. Finally Guerrieri would not venture an opinion about a case until he had consulted Antony.

Antony often claimed knowledge of the state of a soul after death, that it was in purgatory or in heaven. These latter pronouncements, being unverifiable, cannot claim more than possible, or at most probable, truth. But the former were repeatedly verified. A penitent, for example, named Giuseppe Marcelli had promised Antony to remain at Fermo for St. Philip's feast. A message reached him that his wife was seriously, even dangerously, ill. He asked Antony to release him from his promise that he might return home immediately. After silent prayer Antony, with joy written on his countenance, told his friend that he might go home if he wished, but would find his wife better and out of danger. He must be back at Fermo in time for the feast. On his return home that evening Marcelli found his wife, as Antony had predicted, out of danger, and without waiting to hear the doctor's report hastened back to Fermo to thank him for the prayer which had saved her life.

Though Antony's deliberate mortification closed his eyes to the architectural and artistic features of Rome when he made his Jubilee pilgrimage, he was far from being insensible to natural beauty. It was his custom every Saturday to say Mass in a sanctuary of our Lady on the coast, Sancta Maria a Mare. On one such occasion a friend who possessed a country house close by provided for him a picnic meal in a vineyard. "Oh," he exclaimed, "this is beautiful! There is only one thing wanting to make it perfect"—that "a nightingale would perch on this tree over our heads and sing to us." At that moment a nightingale flew onto a bough close by and broke into song. We are reminded of the bird who, a world away, accompanied the praises of his contemporary St. Rose of Lima. For like her he loved the song of birds and liked to walk in lanes where they were abundant. And he did all he could to dissuade anyone he could influence from shooting the birds and thus putting an end to their song of praise. (One could wish that he had been more successful in this and by his prayer and recorded example had prevented the massacre of birds which has made Italy so painfully silent.)

The military governor of the Marches, the Count of St. Angelo, had given up the practice of his religion. Having occasion to visit Fermo, from a motive not of piety but of curiosity, he called on Antony and the porter took him up to his room. Unaccountably to himself, he hesitated to knock on the door and was standing outside when he heard Antony say: "Go and open the door. The Count of St. Angelo is standing in the passage." The words filled him not simply with surprise but with compunction for his sins, and he had hardly spoken to Antony when he asked him to hear his confession. The saint told him first to go down to the church, hear a Mass and pray for the grace to make a good confession. As he obeyed, his contrition grew more powerful and he made his confession in the best dispositions. He left the Oratory a changed man, filled with consolation and prepared to endure with patience a painful affliction in penance for his sins.

So the years passed, uneventful, but filled by the one supreme Event of human history, the accomplishment in yet another member of Christ of the mystery of God's human Incarnation. From the Fermo Oratory the peace and the joy of holiness shone upon all who came within its sphere of influence. And a powerful, though unobtrusive, ministry of reconciliation was exercised, of men with God and with one another for His sake.

Old age came on with its suffering and, what was harder to bear, its progressive weakness. The year of his death Antony paid his last visit to Loretto with the full knowledge that it was his last, and reluctantly wrenched himself from the beloved shrine. The saint like his Master ends his life on the cross. First Antony must abandon his sermons, inaudible for lack of teeth. Then he must leave the church and keep to his room. Finally a fall downstairs forced upon him the close guardianship of a lay brother. He could no longer answer sick calls, though, when strictly forbidden to leave the house, he visited—perhaps by miraculous aid—the deathbed of a dying sinner, a man given to murderous feuds, Palmieri by name, who would confess to no other priest. Having heard his confession he foretold and began a cure. Finally he is confined to his bed, though for little more than the last fortnight of his life. It was November 27, 1671. Every morning from December 1 Archbishop Gualtieri said Mass in the sick man's room, as he put it himself, became his chaplain. And he passed most of the day there. "You have only to command me," he said, "for I am your chaplain as long as your illness lasts. My duty, therefore, is to carry out your wishes in everything." Those disposed to charge prelates of the *ancien régime* too indiscriminatively with pride of office, luxury, and display might do well to recall an Archbishop's humility before holiness.

From his deathbed a few whispered words reconciled two brothers who had obstinately resisted the Archbishop's pleading, and restored the sight of one of his brethren, Father Remigio Leti, who for the past nine years had been too blind to say Mass. For he told him to do so, and attempting to obey, Father Leti found that he could see sufficiently well.

But the agony of his own cross was unremitted. In reply to the Archbishop's question, "I feel," he said, "intense pain from the the soles of my feet to the crown of my head." But he suffered "very willingly"—*oblatus quia ipse voluit*—and "turning his eyes towards his crucifix he added, 'I am most content.'" Only when Mass was being said in honour of our Lady did he experience a respite from his pain. To the tortures of nature seventeenth-century medicine added its own, inflicting upon him an operation he knew to be useless to remove a growth from his side. On the evening of December 11 he took his solemn farewell of the community. For he knew the end was at hand. First to his old friend and future biographer Father Cristoforo Antici, then to the assembled fathers, he confided: "I have no fear of death, for St. Philip has obtained for me the grace of confirmation in faith, hope and charity… Oh, what a beautiful thing it is to die a son of St. Philip." On the evening of Sunday, December 13, his passion ended, and while the Archbishop was reciting the Loretto litany, at the words *Regina Sanctorum omnium* he passed away.

Popular veneration and miracles followed. And a canonical process was begun with a view to his beatification. The cause, however, was not introduced until 1748, to be soon interrupted, and was not revived until 1874. Antony was not in fact beatified until the Jubilee Year 1900. His feast is kept in the Oratory on December 13.

This is his Collect, kindly sent me by my old friend Fr. Vincent Reede of the Edgbaston Oratory:

> *Excita, Domine, in Ecclesia tua spiritum, quo Beatus Sacerdos tuus Antonius animorum concordiam ac decorem domus tuae indesinenter promovit.*
> ["Stir up, O Lord, in Thy Church the spirit which inspired the untiring labour of Thy blessed priest Antony to plant concord in men's hearts and adorn Thy house."]

But the Fermo oratory exists no longer.

POSTSCRIPT

ANY ATTEMPT TO make saints live for modern readers is confronted by a formidable obstacle. The lives which in most cases are our sole or principal source of information, even when their writers are honest and well informed, are written in accordance with a convention of hagiographical literature. It varies somewhat at different periods. But the pattern is substantially the same throughout. It is determined by three dominant themes. The saint is a wonder-worker, is an ascetic, is a flawless example of all the Christian virtues.[1]

Today the general attitude towards the miraculous is more or less skeptical. So skeptical indeed are we, that even Catholics are sometimes disposed to shirk an aspect of sanctity about which they are, subconsciously at least, uncomfortable. This, however, does not alter the fact that our ancestors were excessively, at times even grossly, credulous, on the lookout for miracles. More important, however, is a recent change in our view of natural law. We can no longer be so certain as our fathers were, how far the competence of natural forces extends, what therefore divine power may effect by employing, not superseding, natural agencies. We can indeed be certain that a particular event is beyond the capacity of natural forces to produce without the intervention of a spiritual agent. Such events in fact are the operations and works of man. We cannot, however, decide with similar certainty whether an event is beyond the capacity of natural forces used as the instrument of spirit—we have no reason to think we have developed all the powers of controlling matter latent in the human spirit. Recent experiments in telepathy and clairvoyance, including precognition, suggest a vast field of natural energy whose exploration has barely begun. Precognition, I believe, is the emergence to consciousness of the central self's abiding present, present throughout to the entire succession of superficial experiences from birth till death. Telekinesis is the movement of an object without perceptible physical agency or contact. A particular form of telekinesis, in spiritist parlance called an apport, is the appearance of an object visible only as it approaches, where no physical force has brought it and often when it must have passed through a solid object, a wall for example, or locked cupboard door. Since we now know that solid objects are in fact fields of electronic energies far more empty than filled, it is not perhaps so difficult to conceive that an object can be dematerialized, resolved into its electrons, and rematerialized by the rearrangement of its electrons in the original pattern when an obstacle has been penetrated. Telekinesis and apports are in fact normal accompaniments of the poltergeist phenomena well attested by honest and hard-headed witnesses from many periods and countries and everywhere presenting the same features. The instances in Father Thurston's recently published *Ghosts and Poltergeists* should sufficiently support his conclusion that, whatever the explanation, the facts cannot reasonably be denied. Moreover the evidence suggests that the cause of these poltergeist manifestations may be the subconscious energy of a child or adolescent medium.

Similar phenomena are found in the lives of saints. Knowledge of things not normally knowable is found in the lives of Blessed Jordan of Saxony, Blessed Osanna, Blessed Antony Grassi, St. Thomas of Villanueva. Precognition is shown by Blessed Antony Grassi, Blessed Osanna, St. Thomas of Villanueva, and, less certainly by St. Hugh. One could

1. This of course is true only of lives of saints written as such. It is inapplicable to the biography, for example, of Blessed Charlemagne, when the biographer does not envisage his subject as a saint.

add that it was of frequent occurrence in the life of St. John of the Cross. Examples of objects moved without perceptible agency are the medal which descended upon the nun who had asked the aid of Blessed Antony and cured her, the paper received by Blessed Osanna on which the names of Jesus and Mary were written, and the corn which filled St. Thomas of Villanueva's empty granary.

But when these phenomena occur in the lives of saints they possess a religious significance and value lacking elsewhere. Nor is that the only difference. Knowledge of what is in the minds of others and of events still in the future is far more frequent and, what is more important, far more certain than elsewhere. The proportion of successes to failures is far less outside the religious sphere than in the case of saints. Unlike the clairvoyant, the saint sees far more often than he fails to see and is never, or hardly ever, mistaken. And prophecies have been made by saints which have been fulfilled only after their death—for example, St. Thomas' prophecy that a church would be burned. These, at any rate, seem to fall outside any of the suggested natural explanations.

Stigmatization we have met only in the case of Blessed Osanna of Mantua, and even then not before her death. For a well-documented and judicious study of the subject I would refer my readers to the compilation from the writings of Father Thurston, entitled *The Physical Phenomena of Mysticism.* He shows that the stigmata have by no means been confined to authentic saints. In one recent instance they were experimentally produced by suggestion. In my opinion it is not easy to refuse assent to his conclusion that the mechanism operative in producing stigmata is suggestion. This, however, does not preclude the possibility, in the case of St. Francis at any rate a moral certainty, that the suggestion was itself a divine operation in the soul of the subject, though its bodily result was the natural product of that divine suggestion. But I do not ask any reader to agree with me until he has studied the evidence for himself in Father Thurston's book, and the arguments of that cautious and critical scholar.

Moreover, though the cures effected by saints, alive or after death, can be paralleled by the achievements of faith healing without sanctity, they display an assurance, a power, a degree of success not attained by healers who lack their holiness. I do not of course question that divine interventions, answers to prayers, works of God, occur frequently in the lives of devout Christians who, however, could not be regarded as saints. But they are seldom if ever so striking, so spectacular, as in the case of saints, nor do they so plainly bend the laws of nature to their purpose. The conclusion surely emerges that, even if in many cases the mechanism of these abnormal phenomena and performances is the same, whether they are found in the lives of saints or in the lives of ordinary persons, and even apart from religious belief, in the former case it is set in motion by an extraordinary operation of the grace, the power, of God at work in the saint, which renders its employment far more successful than it could be in the course of nature. Not, however, invariably successful. If God withholds His action, a saint may in good faith use his merely human power, and fail or find himself ignorant or powerless. A paranormal phenomenon, that is to say, which elsewhere is produced solely by the natural energy of the human spirit, is in the saint the product of divine power working in and through that natural energy and its operation.

The world, such as we know it to be, is a texture of energies corporeal and spiritual, a universal interplay of energies. It is natural therefore that weaker energies yield to more powerful, corporeal to spiritual. Why, then, should we be surprised if corporeal energies are employed by spiritual, in other ways than by our normal volition, to produce effects determined by the latter? May not the energies which compose material objects be indefinitely malleable by spiritual energies? God, however, is perfect energy, absolute spirit. Is it not therefore supremely natural that a created energy should be pliable to the divine? How then can we distinguish between a work of God employing the forces of nature, enabled by His employment to do what otherwise would have been impossible to them, as a lump of metal, for example, when employed by man can become or act as it otherwise could not; and a work of God thrusting them aside, a miracle in the strictest sense?

When all is said I cannot see that it matters very much whether an occurrence is or is not in the strict sense a miracle, if it can be recognized as an intervention of God in answer to prayer. If, for example, a miracle accepted for a canonisation is a work of God performed at the saint's intercession, why need we concern ourselves with His *modus operandi,* whether He has used or overthrown the operation of natural forces? If God's hand is seen, it is of no religious significance whether it is bare or wears the glove of natural cause and effect.

Therefore while refusing to accord to miracles—after all no indispensable feature or by themselves sufficient proof of sanctity—the importance devoted to them by the hagiography of the past, we must not shamefacedly ignore them. Whether they are or are not miracles in the strict sense, they are works of God displaying His divine power and providing corroborative testimony to His servants' holiness.

A difficulty felt by many today, even Catholics, is the merciless, seemingly inhuman, asceticism practiced by so many saints. How, we ask, is this unsparing warfare against the body, the refusal of its most innocent pleasures, often even of what are normally regarded as necessaries, this fakir-like self-torture, consistent with the Incarnation and its consequences, the resurrection of the body, the veneration of relics, the use made by the Church in her worship of art and sensible ritual? Undoubtedly, throughout the history of the Church, Catholic thought and conduct display in respect of the human body what at first sight appears to be a contradiction. The Church seems at once to honour the body and despise it, to accept and refuse its demands. The contradiction, however, is merely apparent. It is a matter not of contradiction but of complement. For the body has two aspects, a twofold relation to the human spirit. In one aspect it is a biological organism, like the body of an animal, a body of which the spirit is the life, in technical language the form, that is the formative principle, the soul. In this aspect the spirit ensouls the body. And in this aspect the body most certainly should be despised and kept in subjection. It is, in truth, what the Platonists termed it, the prison of the spirit, the slaves' prison, *ergastulum,* as it is called in the collect for St. Benedict's feast.[2] What more intolerable

2. In the Benedictine supplement.

bondage for an immortal spirit than the stark fact that by far the greater part of man's time, labour, and resources must be devoted to the biological, the animal needs of the body? That disease can paralyze the spirit's action, a blow deprive a man of the use of reason, brainwashing techniques make him deny his convictions? And—what no doubt weighed most with the saints—that the body, unsubdued, can cause man to sin? It is not surprising that St. Paul called the body in this aspect of it the "body of our humiliation."

There is, however, another and a higher aspect and function of the body. It can and does even now in the condition of this mortal life serve the spirit in its own proper life above the biological level. For scientific research, philosophical speculation, aesthetic appreciation, and artistic creation the body is the instrument of the spirit in its distinctive work, the knowledge and service of truth and beauty. The soul's supreme activity, the prayer which unites it with God, and the fact that the body's sufferings can be united with the redemptive suffering of Christ—in these things sanctity is served by the body and could not operate without its service. In the higher aspect in which it is not "ensouled" but "inspirited," the body is altogether honourable. Nor will this aspect and function of the body, its "inspiritation" as contrasted with its "ensoulment," perish finally, like its ensouled and biological aspect, at death. It will be the exclusive aspect and function of the risen body, inspirited but no longer ensouled.[3]

Though the principle of bodily asceticism is thus justified, we may and must admit excesses in its practice by many saints. Limitations of human vision and necessities of his conflict with the ensouled body made it difficult, if not impossible, for a particular ascetic to do equal justice to both aspects of his body, to honour sufficiently its inspirited functions and make sufficient provision for them. A saint's bodily penance has at times been excessive, in some cases we may suspect alloyed

3. *Possibly* this inspiritation without ensoulment should be called "superformation" of the body rather than its "information." But the exact nature of the relationship is beyond our knowledge.

with unconscious masochism, his view of the body unbalanced as between its lower and higher aspects. On other hand we must recognize extraordinary vocations, as in the case of the Stylite saints,[4] that a penance itself extravagant may be justified by its appeal and impressiveness in a particular climate of opinion. The Stylite St. Simeon drew crowds and exercised far and wide a most salutary moral and spiritual influence.

It is, however, the stereotyped pattern of Christian virtues which has done most to render the saint a lay figure, a lifeless dummy. For faultlessness and life are incompatible. No living man can be flawless.[5] Since the Church restricted the honours of sanctity to those officially beatified or canonised—the earliest known instance is the canonisation of St. Ulrich in the last decade of the tenth century—a saint must have displayed an heroic love of God and his neighbour for God's sake. At an earlier period the tribute of a public cultus was often accorded on easier terms.

This heroic love excludes deliberate formal sin, the willful cherishing of a thought, utterance of words, performance of an act known or believed to be displeasing to God, contrary to His will. And these things are indeed absent from the lives of saints, if they have always been saints or after they have become so. But the conditions of our mortal flesh do not admit perfect knowledge of what is morally right, what God in fact wills. The beliefs, ideas, and practice of a saint's environment, the results of his education, must often obscure or distort his moral vision as, for example, when a St. Pius V or a Blessed Ruysbroeck approve judicial torture. Aldous Huxley has rightly condemned St. Francis' approval recorded in the *Fioretti* of Brother Juniper's action, when, to provide a dainty for a sick friar, he cut off the trotter of a *living* pig. Since it is impossible to determine how much truth has survived in this late compilation, we may hope the story is untrue. But to be sure it is untrue would be wishful thinking. If it is, as it may be, true, it is inconsistent with the love

4. Ascetics who lived on the top of a pillar.

5. Our Lord and His Mother belong to an exceptional category not considered here.

of animals normally displayed by the saint who preached to birds, saved a lamb from the butcher, and concluded a treaty with Brother Wolf.[6] In any case his authentic testament ordained that an obstinately heretical friar should be handed over to the Inquisition with all it might imply, torture and the stake. Nor does the Catholic conscience, certainly not the conscience of English-speaking Catholics, endorse the Curé d'Ars' indiscriminate condemnation of dancing,[7] or of the theatre by the saints of the primitive Church and the majority even of later saints. Limitations moreover of personal vision, defects of understanding, the results of individual temperament, prejudice, or passion, prevent knowledge of what in a given concrete situation is morally right or make it impossible to advert to what might otherwise have been known. In consequence a saint without the least intentional opposition to God's will may commit even a grave fault. Many years ago a priest told me from his personal knowledge of what was, as he told it, uncharitable conduct on the part of a nun, generally regarded as saintly and who may well be raised to the altars. When he told it, I thought: Either he has misrepresented the facts or the nun in question is not after all the saint she is reputed to be. With more knowledge today I know that the facts *may* have been such as the priest represented them, but the nun nevertheless a genuine saint. For some invincible limitation of knowledge or a temperamental interference may have made her act uncharitably in ignorance of doing so.

St. Bernard, as his letters reveal him, was too ready to put the worst interpretation upon the conduct of those whom he regarded as enemies of God's cause, to believe the reports of their opponents. Such for example was his view of Abelard. On one man in particular he pours out the vials of his invective—"This unrighteous man." "Our common bane." "The barren fig tree." "This vile and infamous person." "A man publicly infamous." "He is rotten from the soles of his feet to the crown of his

6. The story of the Wolf of Gubbio, also from the *Fioretti*, has been confirmed by the discovery of a wolf's skeleton buried in the outer wall of the church at Gubbio.

7. As is proved among other things by the frequent notices of parochial dances, some even made from the pulpit.

head." "Religious men cannot bring themselves to receive with a sound conscience even the sacraments from this man's leprous hands." "Let a saint write of a saint" was the supposed comment of St. Thomas when informed that St. Bonaventure was writing a life of St. Francis. Here a saint is in fact writing of a saint, St. Bernard of St. William of York. Even though the latter was not yet as holy as he finally became and Yorkshire resentment of foreign interference may have contributed to the popular cultus which finally led to his canonisation by Honorius III, he could not have deserved such abuse. But there can be no doubt of St. Bernard's intentions, when he penned these rash and uncharitable judgments. He was convinced that he was fighting for God against the powers of darkness. There was fault but not willful sin. And this Bernard of flesh and blood with his human defects and faults but aflame with love for God and His Church is more vital, more credible, less remote, a more persuasive apostle of holiness than the faultless plaster of Paris Catholic repository saint which a conventional devotion would set in his place.

In this connection we may profitably remember Meredith's words:

> Beauty that makes holy
> Earth and air, may have faults from head to feet.[8]

Also a profound saying which goes to the heart of the matter: "In His world," a world of inevitable limitation and ignorance, "God does not ask a perfect work but infinite desire."[9] The saint is the man whose desire is infinite, being a soul-devouring desire of God.[10]

The more serious then is the misfortune that, where no surviving correspondence or other writing allows a saint to speak for himself, the lives on which we must depend for information have so often been written and the facts bowdlerized to make their subject as "faultlessly

8. "Love in the Valley."
9. Alec Robertson, *Contrasts: The Arts and Religion*, p. 12.
10. Where finally it is God's own love of Himself received by the soul, it is in the strict sense infinite.

null" as a saint was expected to be. Happily his personality is often too powerful for his biographer, and in at least a few recorded acts or sayings breaks out of the sanctimonious prison erected for his literary shrine. And the simple honesty of a biographer, his delight in retailing reminiscences of the man or woman so dearly loved, may be too much for the demands of pious convention. It is for the modern biographer therefore to take, if he can, these significant hints, to make the most of this material for a genuine and lifelike picture. When this can be successfully accomplished and an authentic and therefore uniquely individual portrait painted, it will be seen that, although mediocre goodness, whatever its merits, is not news, holiness is far more interesting than wickedness. For it is more, immeasurably more real, immeasurably more living.

The biographer of a saint, that is to say, must not go about, censer in hand, censing his image. To the extent of his skill and the material at his disposal he must present a living human being, such as we might have known ourselves, wholly credible and attractive for the very limitations and blind spots which prove him, though one of the holiest, also one of ourselves. Sanctity, that is to say, not standardized and must not be treated as though it were.

Its essence, heroic love of God and of our neighbour in and for Him, is indeed always the same. In consequence saints of the most diverse periods and places are fundamentally akin. In all alike we are aware of the same presence of God, see the same countenance of the Risen Lord. But the psychological surface differs widely and is never even, never wholly of a piece. A saint speaks for himself, is not the mere mouthpiece of a patterned holiness. And he speaks for himself as he stands at a particular place and at a particular moment.

Holiness is conformity to reality, being communion with it, sin conformity to what is comparatively unreal, sinking down into its comparative nonentity. This conformity, this union with reality, must perforce realise the possibilities of the subject. He, she, must be more real than other men and women, must therefore achieve his, her personality as no others can. And the saint must be more alive than other men. For he is in vital contact with life, receives it as his own. The sinner, however vital in the order of natural energies, is in the inmost depths of him dead. For he has cut himself off from life. To be sure, since the divine life given to the saint is beyond every image and concept, unimaginable and inconceivable, neither itself nor his contact with it can be described. What is most holy in a saint cannot be conveyed to others as intellectual or artistic genius can, vital energy or human achievement. The saint's best part must escape the most skillful biographer. This also weights the scales against those who attempt to make sanctity visibly persuasive, to depict a saint. And it is a standing temptation to fall back upon the clichés of conventional hagiography. Nevertheless by judicious selection or presentation of the evidence, not to support a thesis or to fit a preconceived notion of holiness but simply to portray the saint as he or she was and was seen to be by those who knew him, who knew her, it is possible to hint what cannot be said, to display glimpses of what cannot be made clearly visible. Even this limited measure of success will show God in His saints, the saints as transparencies of His inaccessible light, agents of His inscrutable will. They will be seen as fully human, yet by God's gift of Himself divine, countenances wholly individual, as individual as men's bodily faces, yet bright with God's glory.

Whether the present writer has succeeded in such an undertaking he cannot tell. But that at any rate has been his aim. And, since a saint is after all revealed in his unique personality, not by what a biographer says about him, but by his own words and actions, when they are truly significant, he may hope that the words and actions he has related will have told their story. It is an exciting story, as exciting as any ever told, the story of adventurous spirits, explorers of infinity: in the words of Léon Bloy, pilgrims of the Absolute.

CLUNY MEDIA

Designed by Fiona Cecile Clarke, the Cluny Media *logo depicts a monk at work in the scriptorium, with a cat sitting at his feet.*

The monk represents our mission to emulate the invaluable contributions of the monks of Cluny in preserving the libraries of the West, our strivings to know and love the truth.

The cat at the monk's feet is Pangur Bán, from the eponymous Irish poem of the 9th century. The anonymous poet compares his scholarly pursuit of truth with the cat's happy hunting of mice. The depiction of Pangur Bán is an homage to the work of the monks of Irish monasteries and a sign of the joy we at Cluny take in our trade.

"Messe ocus Pangur Bán,
cechtar nathar fria saindan:
bíth a menmasam fri seilgg,
mu memna céin im saincheirdd."

Made in United States
North Haven, CT
04 June 2024

53304328R00128